RETRIEVAL &

Ressourc

IN CATHOLIC THOUGHT

MW00788297

The middle years of the twentieth century marked a particularly intense time of crisis and change in European society. During this period (1930-1950), a broad intellectual and spiritual movement arose within the European Catholic community, largely in response to the secularism that lay at the core of the crisis. The movement drew inspiration from earlier theologians and philosophers such as Möhler, Newman, Gardeil, Rousselot, and Blondel, as well as from men of letters like Charles Péguy and Paul Claudel.

The group of academic theologians included in the movement extended into Belgium and Germany, in the work of men like Emile Mersch, Dom Odo Casel, Romano Guardini, and Karl Adam. But above all the theological activity during this period centered in France. Led principally by the Jesuits at Fourvière and the Dominicans at Le Saulchoir, the French revival included many of the greatest names in twentieth-century Catholic thought: Henri de Lubac, Jean Daniélou, Yves Congar, Marie-Dominique Chenu, Louis Bouyer, and, in association, Hans Urs von Balthasar.

It is not true — as subsequent folklore has it — that those theologians represented any sort of self-conscious "school": indeed, the differences among them, for example, between Fourvière and Saulchoir, were important. At the same time, most of them were united in the double conviction that theology had to speak to the present situation, and that the condition for doing so faithfully lay in a recovery of the Church's past. In other words, they saw clearly that the first step in what later came to be known as *aggiornamento* had to be *ressourcement* — a rediscovery of the riches of the whole of the Church's two-thousand-year tradition. According to de Lubac, for example, all of his own works as well as the entire *Sources chrétiennes* collection are based on the presupposition that "the renewal of Christian vitality is linked at least partially to a renewed exploration of the periods and of the works where the Christian tradition is expressed with particular intensity."

In sum, for the *ressourcement* theologians theology involved a "return to the sources" of Christian faith, for the purpose of drawing out the meaning and significance of these sources for the critical questions of our time. What these theologians sought was a spiritual and intellectual communion with Christianity in its most vital moments as transmitted to us in its classic texts, a communion that would nourish, invigorate, and rejuvenate twentieth-century Catholicism.

The *ressourcement* movement bore great fruit in the documents of the Second Vatican Council and deeply influenced the work of Pope John Paul II.

The present series is rooted in this renewal of theology. The series thus understands *ressourcement* as revitalization: a return to the sources, for the purpose of developing a theology that will truly meet the challenges of our time. Some of the features of the series, then, are a return to classical (patristic-medieval) sources and a dialogue with contemporary Western culture, particularly in terms of problems associated with the Enlightenment, modernity, and liberalism.

The series publishes out-of-print or as yet untranslated studies by earlier authors associated with the *ressourcement* movement. The series also publishes works by contemporary authors sharing in the aim and spirit of this earlier movement. This will include any works in theology, philosophy, history, literature, and the arts that give renewed expression to Catholic sensibility.

The editor of the Ressourcement series, David L. Schindler, is Gagnon Professor of Fundamental Theology and dean at the John Paul II Institute in Washington, D.C., and editor of the North American edition of *Communio: International Catholic Review*, a federation of journals in thirteen countries founded in Europe in 1972 by Hans Urs von Balthasar, Jean Daniélou, Henri de Lubac, Joseph Ratzinger, and others.

RETRIEVAL & RENEWAL
Ressourcement
IN CATHOLIC THOUGHT

Medieval Exegesis, volumes 1-3:
The Four Senses of Scripture
Henri de Lubac

Letters from Lake Como:
Explorations in Technology and the Human Race
Romano Guardini

Divine Likeness: Toward a Trinitarian Anthropology of the Family
Marc Cardinal Ouellet

The Portal of the Mystery of Hope
Charles Péguy

In the Beginning:
A Catholic Understanding of the Story of Creation and the Fall
Joseph Cardinal Ratzinger

In the Fire of the Burning Bush:
An Initiation to the Spiritual Life
Marko Ivan Rupnik

Love Alone Is Credible:
Hans Urs von Balthasar as Interpreter
of the Catholic Tradition, volume 1
David L. Schindler, ed.

Hans Urs von Balthasar: A Theological Style
Angelo Scola

The Nuptial Mystery
Angelo Scola

Joseph Ratzinger in *Communio*

VOLUME I

THE UNITY OF
THE CHURCH

Pope Benedict XVI

Introduction by
David L. Schindler

William B. Eerdmans Publishing Company
Grand Rapids, Michigan / Cambridge, U.K.

© 2010 Wm. B. Eerdmans Publishing Co.

Published 2010 by
Wm. B. Eerdmans Publishing Co.
2140 Oak Industrial Drive N.E., Grand Rapids, Michigan 49505 /
P.O. Box 163, Cambridge CB3 9PU U.K.

Printed in the United States of America

15 14 13 12 11 10   7 6 5 4 3 2 1

Library of Congress Cataloging-in-Publication Data

Benedict XVI, Pope, 1927-
Joseph Ratzinger in communio: Volume 1 — The unity of the church /
Pope Benedict XVI; introduction by David L. Schindler.
        p.   cm.   — (Ressourcement)
ISBN 978-0-8028-6416-1 (pbk. : alk. paper)
1. Catholic Church — Doctrines. 2. Theology.
I. Title.
BX1751.3.B453   2010
230'.2 — dc22
                    2009043676

www.eerdmans.com

Contents

CONTENTS

Introduction

The Unity of the Church is the first volume of *Joseph Ratzinger in* Communio, which will bring together in three volumes the articles by Cardinal Joseph Ratzinger published in the North American edition of *Communio* since its inception in 1974. The articles are grouped very roughly into three themes: Church, anthropology, and theological renewal. The lines between the themes are of course not clean. Cardinal Ratzinger — Pope Benedict XVI — rarely writes on any churchly matter that does not manifest its implications for man and culture, and vice versa. Indeed, this indissoluble linking is one of the main distinguishing features of his theology. Grouping the articles into three volumes as we have done nevertheless provides a larger unity of theme that may be helpful for readers.

As is well known, Ratzinger, along with Hans Urs von Balthasar, Henri de Lubac, and others, was one of the founders of the international Catholic journal *Communio,* which began in Germany (and Italy) in 1972. Most of the articles published in this and the subsequent two volumes, however, especially those written after Ratzinger left his professorship at Regensburg to become archbishop of Munich-Freising in 1977, were not written expressly for the journal. The articles consist rather of papers, book reviews, interviews, lectures, and the like completed for various occasions and made available to the national editions of *Communio.*

We are grateful to Emily Rielley and Agata Rottkamp of the American *Communio* for their work in editing the volumes, and to Nicholas Healy for his help in arranging the themes.

8 December 2008   DAVID L. SCHINDLER
Feast of the Immaculate Conception

What Unites and Divides Denominations?
Ecumenical Reflections

Do the denominations have anything in common? This was the question put to the speakers at an ecumenical discussion held at the Catholic Theological Faculty of the University of Regensburg.[1] At first glance it seems a meaningless question, because no one seriously doubts that they do. One is more inclined to wonder whether what should really have been asked was whether there actually is still anything to keep the denominations apart? For many people that question could be expanded more or less along these lines: Aren't the divisions only kept in being by the inertia of habit, especially by the dead weight of institutions which just as a matter of fact exist and are not willing to retire of their own accord? Before the late Council, Patriarch Athenagoras and Pope John are reported to have said jokingly that only the hairsplitting and obstinacy of theologians maintains the division between the Churches — the learned will not agree among themselves, and project their dispute over the whole of Christendom, though they cannot make any sense of it anymore. In the meantime, theologians — I recall names such as Lengsfeld,[2] Schuster,

---

1. 19 January 1972. The two other speakers were Franz Mußner (New Testament) and Traugott Koch (Systematic Theology, Lutheran).

2. P. Lengsfeld, "Sind heute die traditionellen Konfessionsdifferenzen noch von Bedeutung?" *Una Sancta* 26 (1971): 27-36, 32: "The main obstacle that really prevents the

This article first appeared as "Was eint und trennt die Konfessionen? Eine ökumenische Besinnung," in *Internationale katholische Zeitschrift: Communio* 2 (1972): 172ff. English publication in *Communio: International Catholic Review* 1, no. 2 (March-April 1972): 115-119.

I

Ohlig[3] — have addressed the same reproach in all seriousness to holders of office. Only the Church authorities, they say, have an interest in division, which is only kept in existence by them for the sake of their own survival. This is a remarkable change in the situation — have the theologians reached agreement in the meanwhile? Have they seen through their controversies as mere shadow-boxing? A certain suspicion that there must be something wrong can scarcely be avoided at the sight of such a rapid change. One wonders what change of mind suddenly made something possible that for centuries never came to anything. In the laborious search for truth, sheer new insights hardly come so suddenly and decisively.

This remarkable phenomenon needs closer examination if the real weight of such assertions is to be rightly judged and correct conclusions drawn. Without denying the complexity of the matter, I should nevertheless like to venture the following diagnosis. On the whole, the swing of thought evidenced by such assertions is to be explained more in terms of the sociology of knowledge than by strictly theological considerations. The first reason is the new self-confidence gained by Catholic theologians as a result of their position at the Second Vatican Council. Hans Küng has emphasized on several occasions since then that the succession of teachers (i.e., professors of theology) stands

---

denominational Churches from coming together no longer lies in the sphere of belief and doctrine but in the obstinate tendency to self-preservation of ecclesiastical apparatus or organizations." Lengsfeld, it is true, himself speaks (34f.) against "hasty reunion at the present time": "A merger of the various ecclesiastical organizations would produce such an agglomeration of power that the reforming forces would scarcely have any chance left. . . . An institutional reunification carried through quickly without prior reforms would be like an amalgamation of two nursing homes" (34).

3. K. H. Ohlig and H. Schuster, *Blockiert das katholische Dogma die Einheit der Kirchen?* (1971). On the cover of the book we read: "Whilst the Church authorities still cling to rigid but theologically extremely questionable positions, the differences between the denominations have been long since rendered obsolete by the vital interests which Christians have in common." The statement in the book which comes nearest to this thesis is less clear-cut: "The . . . situation of dialogue between Christians is therefore completely misunderstood or distorted if people think they must first wait for the outcome of the talks between the official Churches, or even think that these official Churches must first wait for identity of views among the various theologies." One is surprised by the almost juvenile optimism with which the two authors of this small and in itself pleasant book undertake to solve in a hundred pages all the problems still pending between the denominations. If we only set about it correctly, they seem to be saying, there is an answer ready to every question.

equal and independent, side by side with what previously was exclusively known as the apostolic succession, i.e., the sequence of bishops and their office.[4] This thesis is only a particularly bold expression of the new and increasingly widespread claim of theology and theologians generally.[5] This indicates the second step in this development. The theologians' new self-assurance in conjunction with the social situation as a whole created a certain feeling of solidarity in the face of the Church authorities. For if the latter in virtue of their prescribed role are charged with maintaining what already exists, theology found itself by the very nature of the case, as it were, to be the advocate of change (which also corresponds to the role of the intellectual in society).

A further factor was the tardy and, consequently, all the more overpowering penetration of the modern mentality into theology, which previously had to a certain extent moved in a world of its own. This has brought theology almost abruptly to a resignation before the question of truth which since Kant has increasingly characterized modern thought. The outcome, on the one hand, has been a retreat into purely factual studies, and a sociological interpretation of the concept of truth, on the other. The truth which previously they had argued about so bravely and with all too much assurance, suddenly appears unattainable anyway. What remains as the function of the human and moral sciences, and therefore of theology as well, is the rational construction of the praxis of human social life. When the question of truth ceases to be raised, the division of Christians into different denominations does in fact lose all meaning; the only thing then is to try to replace it as soon and as thoroughly as possible by more rational forms of human association.

If the main features of this analysis are correct, it immediately clarifies our initial thesis. The new mentality which is the main reason for the new position of theologians will be based on the increasingly sociological character attributed to the question of truth. What can be said

---

4. Cf. H. Küng, *The Church* (1967), 434-436; idem, *Infallible?* (1971), 151, 189f., etc.; one is struck by the remarkable way teachers, professors, and prophets are treated as completely identical.

5. As an example we may once again refer to K. H. Ohlig and H. Schuster: "The functions of the Church's magisterium and that of theology are neither opposed to one another, nor can they be entirely separated; there is not even a primacy of the first over the second" (*Blockiert das katholische Dogma die Einheit der Kirchen?* 34).

here? First of all, I think, we must most certainly admit that the new outlook has shown up some merely apparent truth for what it is, and in many matters has certainly resulted in a more sober and realistic judgment than theological controversy succeeded in achieving. Many divisive factors were, in fact, sociological, not theological in origin, not determined by truth itself. This being admitted, we must quite plainly add that all in all such a shift certainly does not bring us to the kernel of the New Testament, that is, to what alone justifies the very existence of Christendom: faith in truth disclosing itself. In this respect, we might note in passing, there could be a task of the highest importance for the Church hierarchy in the new situation, that of keeping open the question of truth, of insisting on its acceptance, as opposed to the retreat into positivism and sociology.

We must, however, return to our question of what the various denominations have in common and what separates them. Another assertion which one hears springs more and more frequently from the same trend of thought. Experience shows, we hear, that a German Protestant and a German Catholic stand closer to one another, understand one another better, than a German and an Italian Catholic, a German and an Indian Catholic, etc. Such statements are all the more persuasive because they correspond to most people's personal experience. It is easy then, on account of their optimistic aspect, to lose sight of their fatal corollary. In fact, the hope that beckons here is very dubious; at all events one must thoroughly examine just what it amounts to before building on it. Has a new unity really come about, making the old divisions illusory, making it meaningless to maintain the old demarcations and unities? To affirm this would mean attributing such absolute preponderance to sociological, cultural, and national factors that scarcely anything would be left of the universality of the Christian faith, of the universal communication in the truth across cultural frontiers. In that case, all that would still count would be culture, civilization; the profound identity which faith strives to create despite the most radical difference of civilizations and cultures would no longer exist. The growing unity that people are conscious of would open up new divisions. Furthermore, the specifically unifying power of faith would be destroyed, because it would once again be confined within the limits of existing sociological bodies. Faith seeks to create unity in distinction, the People of God of the peoples of this world; but that is precisely what is refused it by such considerations. The sociological reduction not only unites, it also separates. And the search for manifest truth not only separates, it also unites, and does so more radically, that is, in a way that goes to the root of the matter.

If, after these reflections, we take another look at the Regensburg discussion's remarkable question about what is common to the denominations, it is clear enough, I think, that the question is still worth asking. There is, of course, no doubt at all that something in common does exist (and to that extent the question is rhetorical). But where the really unifying element with a real future lies, and where the merely superficially common is in evidence, is something that calls for careful examination. Before going on, then, we may summarize our conclusions as follows. Having examined certain statements about the Christian world as a whole, we hold that it would be true to say that theological dogmatism and the self-perpetuating tendency of institutions have developed and are still producing divisive factors which do not concern the real question of faith. These must be vigilantly tracked down, and here both the self-criticism of the various groups and their mutual criticism is called for. But we must add that it would be an oversimplification to solve the division on purely sociological terms by tracing it back to the part played by institutions or by renouncing universal understanding of the truth as such. Perhaps the division is in fact largely the result of "roles" obtruding themselves and hiding the truth, for it does not come from truth or faith itself. But, precisely if that is so, too superficial and sociological a settlement (or even a straight verdict of guilty against the "other" role) will not do.

An incidental remark here. So far, only two factors have been mentioned, each blaming the other for the split: the Church authorities and the theologians. In justice to the facts, however, a third element should be included, and even given greater prominence: the communities themselves. One small incident by way of example. After a lecture which I was permitted to give in a Lutheran course on pastoral care, some of the ministers asked me whether I knew of any means of making the views I had expressed intelligible to the members of their congregations. They said that from their pastoral experience they could only say that the real supports of their congregations, the members who believed and acted upon their faith with the most vigor, were also those least accessible to ecumenical contacts. That may have altered to some extent, but is still largely correct on both sides. Those who have accepted the Church and its faith, those who are rooted in it and have found a home in it, affirm it in the form it has assumed in the course of history and thereby affirm the exclusion of the other. They cannot lay aside as unimportant today what they have been taught to be decisive. Their assent to faith and their churchmanship are so closely connected that there is a risk of destroying the first if any attempt is made to disturb the second. Here, too, there are certainly merely human divisive factors determined by social roles. But it is no good merely discrediting the conservatism of pious people; here again, and here above all, questions of great gravity are involved.

The way should now be finally clear for a positive treatment of the problem. What do the denominations have in common? First of all, the crisis of faith vis-à-vis the problems of modern life; the kernel of belief in Jesus Christ, Son of God and Redeemer of mankind. Common to all, despite their divisions, is the linking of belief with Church and divine worship on the one hand, and to the universal precept of love on the other.

First the crisis. It is still an extremely ambiguous factor. For it means first that all Churches have the same human beings, the same problems, the same opportunities, but also the same decomposition of belief. The Lutheran theologian Karl Hammer has recently described the not very glorious chapter of German theology of war from 1870-1918. Because of the differing sociological starting points, very different judgments were passed on the 1870 victory and on the new German Empire by Catholics and Protestants, but the common situation they all occupied in the World War brought about a terrible uniformity in forgetfulness of the second article of faith and the paganization of the first.[6] The rapprochement brought about in this way could serve as a classic example of a merely sociological community which creates no real Church unity in the line of faith. But that is only one side. We also know that a common struggle in the distress of the age for a living contemporary faith was and is a powerful help to slough off a purely hu-

6. K. Hammer, *Deutsche Kriegstheologie 1870-1918* (1971). At the same time it should be said that while the compensating factors that are certainly present are not passed over in Hammer, they are not given their full force. He probably does not take sufficient account, either, of the problems created by the situation.

man past and its egotism and to find the center of faith which unites us. The most effective stimulus to ecumenism has come in this way. The distressing situation of missions opposed to one another was largely the starting point of the worldwide ecumenical movement. When Christians do not look at one another in order to dispute but go together from the Lord toward men and the world, they do in fact find their way to one another. For theology and Church, a decisive ecumenical opportunity lies at the point where they enter critically and openly into present-day matters on the basis of faith. In the committee at the 1971 autumn session of the Faith and Order Commission of the World Council of Churches, which was to examine the question of whether a common formulation of faith is possible in the world of today, in our discussion we came more and more clearly to the point that common formulations are difficult when we start from within our particular theologies; we noted on the other hand the remarkable fact that in sermons and in the prayers that we try to compose, practically no difference is perceptible. What hope there is in this observation that where it is a question of announcing the faith, we find ourselves largely in agreement despite the unsolved problems!

This brings us to the two other points already mentioned. The possession of the Bible, of the Old and New Testaments, gives Christendom very much more than a book in common. Even the latter would be no small matter, for despite all problems of interpretation this book, to an astonishing extent, makes statements so clear that they are not to be obscured, whether by the magisterium or the cavils of theologians. And the Bible is more than a collection of statements worthy of consideration. Those who accept the very varied literature composed over a period of roughly a thousand years which is contained within the covers of the Bible as *one* book, as *the* book, those, that is, who accept the Bible, in principle accept the decision, in faith, of the ancient Church which brought together and recognized this literature as the Word of God. Quite logically, the Reformation of the sixteenth century read the Bible within this conception of faith, in intrinsic conjunction with the baptismal creed of the ancient Church, the western form of which we know as the Apostles' Creed. If this fundamental decision is once again clearly recognized with the real claim it involves, it should not be too long before all sides can distinguish between essential and non-essential and so find the way to a diversified, pluriform unity.

I do not want to pursue this here, but simply to add a final remark. Commonly, the Church as a reality is regarded as what really divides, and in many respects this is so. But it must not be forgotten that not only the Roman Catholic Church and the various Eastern Churches claim and desire to be the Catholic Church, in the sense of the Church of the first centuries, but that the Reformation churches too, especially those of the Confession of Augsburg, sought and seek the genuine, original catholicity.[7] The consequence is that despite the differences of theological interpretations and of historical starting points within the various denominations, a surprisingly similar life persists, both positively and negatively. Against all divisions, the essential Christian content has again and again asserted itself with surprising uniformity, just as the humanity of men expresses itself in a very similar way in different contexts. I should like to draw two conclusions from this.

1. The true chance for ecumenism does not lie in revolt against the Church as it is, in a Christianity as free of the Church as possible, but in a deepening of the reality which is the Church. What continually surprises me in all contacts with the work of the World Council of Churches is the correlation between faith and Church which is taken for granted; precisely in this, too, Christians with every kind of background recognize one another as unexpectedly close.

2. In practice, this means that one cannot live ecumenism against one's own Church, but only by trying to deepen it in relation to what is essential and central. This means that one must seek the center in one's own Church, and this, after all, for all Christians and Churches is truly only one. Conversely it means, as J. J. von Allmen rightly notes, that at any event one may not seek the center in traditions that are *purely* one's own, which are not found in the *whole* of the rest of the oecumene.[8]

---

7. For the period between 1530 and 1535, this is vividly shown with a wealth of material in V. Pfnür, *Einig in der Rechtfertigungslehre?* (1970). For the present day, we may refer above all to the works of P. Brunner and E. Schlink.

8. J. J. von Allmen, *Essai sur le repas du Seigneur,* quoted from the German translation, *Ökumene im Herrenmahl* (1968), 99f. At the same time it is clear that Church cannot be identified quantitatively with Church and Tradition. In other words, the whole principle cannot be applied without spiritual discretion. I should like to refer quite generally to von Allmen's book as a classic work of truly ecumenical theology. I have no hesitation in saying that I know I am far closer to him than to much that has been published recently by Catholic theologians.

All this, however, can never be done by merely rational calculation. It presupposes spiritual experience, penance, and conversion. And again, it begins quite concretely by overcoming mutual mistrust, the sociologically rooted defensive attitude against what is strange, belonging to another, and that we constantly take the Lord, whom after all we are seeking, more seriously than we take ourselves. He is our unity, what we have in common — no, who is the one who is common to and in all denominations.

Translated by W. J. O'Hara

Eschatology and Utopia

The phrase "eschatology and utopia" combines two concepts which are quite far apart in content and in origin. They seem to have nothing in common but the reference to a possible better world in the future and the consequent stimulus to hope. The task of comparing the two concepts, which I undertake in this article, demands that I first of all clarify the exact content of the two words. In this effort I shall rely largely on the analyses of Wilhelm Kamlah, who has already investigated their import in his study of utopia, eschatology, and the teleology of history.[1]

According to Kamlah, utopia, as a literary and philosophical genre, originated in the humanistic philosophy of the Renaissance, with Thomas More as its first classic author. Utopia became a form of political philosophy, one which might be more exactly described as Platonism with Christian elements. Thus it can be asserted that utopia takes up again that task to which Plato first set himself with his plan for the ideal state. This shows us clearly the presuppositions and goals of the classic utopia. Utopia in this restricted sense is not tied to a philosophy of history: it does not assume that there is a forward-moving dynamic in history or that its own role is to sketch out future goals and thereby

---

1. Wilhelm Kamlah, *Utopie, Eschatologie, Geschichtsteleologie: Kritische Untersuchungen zum Ursprung und zum futurischem Denken der Neuzeit* (Mannheim: Bibliographisches Institut, 1969).

This article first appeared as "Eschatologie und Utopie," in *Internationale katholische Zeitschrift: Communio* 6, no. 2 (March-April 1977): 97-110. English publication in *Communio: International Catholic Review* 5, no. 3 (Fall 1978): 211-227.

help to bring about their realization. Ernst Bloch's understanding of utopia as the revolutionary goal that inexorably prods the historical process onward is thus seen to be conceptually inexact. As our reflections proceed, we shall see how his model can be better integrated into the history of thought. Utopia, we repeat, does not grow out of a dynamic philosophy of history but out of Platonic ontology.[2]

Kamlah defines the basic idea of the classic utopia as "the rational model of the optimal happiness-enabling institutions of a community," which "are proposed as a critique of existing abuses."[3] This definition leaves out an important factor. More speaks of *instituta et mores*. In other words, he does not treat institutions as self-subsistent regulatory mechanisms; rather he views them only in closest association with the custom on which they are based, that is, with a tradition of human responsibility. The significance of this is clearly brought out by de Tocqueville's portrayal of democracy in America. But this connection is not for the moment the object of our inquiry.

In clarifying the concept of utopia, it is important first of all not to take it as a future reality. Instead we must relate it to the concrete existing civil society approximately as we relate the pure mathematical forms to their empirical realization. And thus the design of utopia will have approximately the same significance for the concrete civil society as the meaning of mathematical operations has for the understanding of reality: here is where the ideal norm of the law, namely justice, is thought out and formulated as purely as possible — a theoretical experiment that provides norms by which to measure political reality. The aim is not to bring about utopia in the future but to measure present politics against the highest norms and thus to achieve the optimal approximation of civil society to the norm of justice. Accord-

2. In history, of course, the borderline cannot be drawn exactly. It would probably be hard to make Campanella's *City of the Sun* fit the above distinction (cf. Kamlah, *UEG*, 32); in the eighteenth century it becomes well-nigh impossible, as in the case of Pietism (cf. Kamlah, *UEG*, 19 and 32f.). Strictly conceptual distinctions, such as we try to make in this article following Kamlah, remain therefore problematic. Not least in importance is the custom, already very deep-rooted, of using the word with quite a different thrust from that of the definition we have here tried to derive from the word's origin. For this reason "utopia" always from this point on appears in quotation marks, whenever I use it in the technical sense defined above and contrary to modern usage.

3. Kamlah, *UEG*, 23. Cf. 18.

ingly we can sum up by saying that utopia is political philosophy in the sense of the activity of practical reason within the framework of ontological thought.

Eschatology, by contrast, is a statement of faith. Based on the confession of the resurrection of Jesus Christ, it announces the resurrection of the dead, eternal life, and the Kingdom of God. I myself would not identify, as Kamlah does, eschatology with the *proclamation* of this statement of faith.[4] It would be much better to call eschatology a product of the fusion of Christian faith and the Greek searching for the Logos, that is, for the "reason of things" that holds them together. It means the effort of thinking through the inner logic of the Christian dogmas about eternal life, probing this logic from the inner unity of the whole of the Christian message about God, world, and man, and thus bringing its content to bear on human thinking in a meaningful way. This quest for a logic of faith allowed the Church Fathers to call the faith a philosophy, in the sense of a meaningful overview of reality.[5] Such a quest certainly takes the bite out of the radical opposition of eschatology to utopia which is found in Kamlah's portrayal of the latter as the rational model of institutions and the former as the proclamation of the end of all distress.[6]

Still, there is a difference which is so great as to make it seem hardly possible to connect the two concepts in a meaningful way. For utopia is an appeal to human action guided by the practical reason, while eschatology addresses itself to the receptive patience of faith. The difference would be in fact unbridgeable, if faith and reason, receiving and acting, were mutually impenetrable. Hence the decisive question for our inquiry is: Can the eschatological message, which directs men primarily into the passivity of a receiver of gifts, become also a practical statement, one that is oriented to action? And can it engage the practi-

---

4. Kamlah, *UEG*, 26: "Eschatological proclamation is not just an expression of hope but a call to hope. . . . The proclamation of the end . . . — that is eschatology."

5. See among others J. Leclercq, "Pour l'histoire de l'expression 'Philosophie chrétienne,'" *Mélanges de science religieuse* 9 (1952): 221-226; Hans Urs von Balthasar, "Philosophie, Christentum, Mönchtum," *Sponsa verbi*: Skizzen zur Theologie, Band II (Einsiedeln: Johannes Verlag, 1961), 349-387. Instructive is also E. R. Curtius, "Zur Geschichte des Wortes Philosophie im Mittelalter," *Romanische Forschungen, Zeitschrift für romanische Sprachen und Literatur* 57 (1943): 290-309.

6. Kamlah, *UEG*, 26.

cal reason? Since a statement that would relegate a human being to the strictest passivity would leave its receiver without any concrete content, it would thereby become meaningless in fact and could not be maintained for long. For this reason, if for no other, from the beginning the search was on for a practical meaning of the eschatological proclamation. This means that eschatology of its very nature demanded to be coupled with something else, as it is in the title of this article. This synthesis of eschatology with models of action appears, it seems to me, in four basic forms, each of which stands in a different relationship to "eschatology and utopia."

1. The Chiliastic Model

The most striking attempt to synthesize eschatology with action is the experiment which history labels chiliasm. The name is derived from Revelation, Chapter 20, where it is announced that Christ and the saints will reign on earth for a thousand years before the end of the world. The term refers to a conception which is indeed based in eschatology, that is, in the expectation of a new world of God's making, but is not satisfied with the *eschaton* beyond time and beyond the end of the world. Instead, it virtually duplicates eschatology by expecting God to achieve his purpose with man and history in this world as well as in the next, so that even within history there must be an end-time in which everything will be as it should have been all along. This entails a confusion of the intra-historical and the meta-historical categories. Chiliasts are waiting for something in history, but in forms which per se do not belong to historical thought; the meta-historical becomes miraculous by being expected in an historical form.

Such a schizoid expectation has its roots in the plurality of meanings and the plurality of forms taken by the Old Testament and Jewish hope of salvation. In the coronation oracle of Psalm 2, as in the whole line of the Davidic tradition (first clearly formulated in Nathan's prophecy), it appears as a preview of a second David and Solomon,[7] as

---

7. On Psalm 2: Hans-Joachim Kraus, *Psalmen,* I. Teilband (Neukirchen: Erziehungsverein, 1960), 11-22. On Nathan's prophecy: Hans Wilhelm Hertzberg, *I & II Samuel: A Commentary* (Philadelphia: Westminster Press, 1964), 281-288. On messianic hope in gen-

THE UNITY OF THE CHURCH

what Martin Buber called a theopolitical statement. It is to be a political entity, a kingdom of David and Israel, but with the power, security, and success that presuppose the unmediated political activity of God himself. In the realm of the apocalyptic, this theopolitical blueprint fades out and is transferred to the transcendent realm; in addition, the apocalyptic realm developed a philosophy of history that made the end somehow datable and said that it would follow by a logic of historical evolution.[8] Thus the apocalyptic brought about the intensification of the theopolitical thrust which we call apocalyptic or chiliastic politics. Both are clearly exemplified in the Bible.

Jeremiah finds himself faced with a theopolitical attitude which he would like to replace with a rational policy based on theological responsibility. His opponents are theopolitical: they are convinced of an absolute divine guarantee that neither the Temple nor Jerusalem nor the House of David will fall, and they treat this guarantee as a politico-military entity, although their feeling of security finds no basis in rational political thought. In opposition to this thinking, Jeremiah demands a rational policy, which would deal with Babylon according to what the actual distribution of power will allow; this is what he regards as an expression of faith in God and of responsibility toward him. We have here two clearly different conceptions of the relation between faith and reason, between faith and realism — and ultimately two different conceptions of God. The partisans of one cannot but charge those of the other with unbelief and misbelief. The course followed by the prophet's opponents confused two different realities and thus abandoned rationality. This led to the fall of Jerusalem and the temporary loss of Jewish independence. It was clearly theopolitical, but not quite chiliastic; for, while it was based on the certitude of the Davidic oracle as well as of the Temple prophecies, it was not tied to a determinate historical design.[9]

---

eral: Walther Eichrodt, *Theology of the Old Testament,* vol. 1 (Philadelphia: Westminster Press, 1961), 472-511; Friedrich Dingermann, "Israels Hoffnung auf Gott und sein Reich: Zur Entstehung und Entwicklung der alttestamentlichen Eschatologie," in *Wort und Botschaft,* ed. Josef Schreiner (Würzburg: Echter Verlag, 1967), 308-318; Martin Buber, *Kingship of God* (New York: Harper & Row, 1967).

8. A bibliography and a good summary of the recent state of research into the history and significance of the apocalyptic are found in Ulrich Duchrow, *Christenheit und Weltverantwortung* (Stuttgart: Ernst Klett, 1970), 17-55.

9. On Jeremiah, see especially Arthur Weiser, *Das Buch Jeremia,* 5th ed. (Göttingen:

In contrast to this, the Qumran War Scroll contains an unabashedly chiliastic political doctrine. On the one hand, the forty-year war between the Sons of Light and the Sons of Darkness is described with a love of military detail that suggests that the author used a Hellenistic military manual;[10] on the other hand, this is all woven into the apocalyptic design for history, in which God the warlord, with his troops led by Michael, establishes the indestructible kingdom. The figure of Jesus must be viewed against this background. His position is that of Jeremiah, predicting the final destruction of Jerusalem for such a confusion of faith with politics. His failure, historically speaking, corresponds exactly to that of the prophet. To this extent the synthesis of eschatology and politics, which is formulated in chiliasm, is eliminated from the options open to those who decide to follow Christ; in individual historical situations, of course, it was not so easy to draw the line. If today a disguised chiliasm presents itself as the basic pattern for Christian behavior, this is not the first, but only the most logical attempt to receive the old idea and with it to make Christianity into a practical power in the struggle for the present and the future.

To summarize the pertinent features of the chiliastic program, we can say that the decisive thing about it is the expectation of an historical golden age, which in itself surpasses the possibilities of political action but is to be established by political means. Its possibility is guaranteed by the logic of history, which adds something to political means, so that it seems right to employ political means according to a metapolitical logic and to hope that this will produce something which political means by themselves cannot produce. If you want historical examples, take Marxism — this is where it belongs, not in the realm of "utopia." The two schemata in Marx, as presented by Daniel

---

Vandenhoeck & Ruprecht, 1966); Josef Scharbert, *Die Propheten Israels um 600 v. Chr.* (Cologne: J. P. Bachem, 1967), 61-295, 459-478; Curt Kuhl, *The Prophets of Israel* (Edinburgh: Oliver & Boyd, 1960), 104-120. On the kinship between Jeremiah's attitude and the positions taken by Isaiah and his successors, see Otto Kaiser's instructive explanations of Is 22:1-14 in his *Isaiah 13–39: A Commentary* (Philadelphia: Westminster Press, 1974), 136-147. Jesus' prophecies about Jerusalem (Lk 19:41-44, Mt 23:37-39 with parallel passages, and Mk 13:14-19) must be understood as continuations of Jeremiah and Isaiah.

10. Martin Hengel, *Victory Over Violence: Jesus and the Revolutionists* (Philadelphia: Fortress Press, 1973), 14. This little book and Hengel's related study, *Was Jesus a Revolutionist?* (Philadelphia: Fortress Press, 1971), are basic to the questions we are studying.

Bell,[11] are astonishingly close to the methodical mixing of the Essene War Scroll. Marx gives the most exact economic analysis, but connects it with a prophecy to which the analysis itself gives no support whatever. The only difference is that in place of God and Michael he puts the logic of history.

2. The Model of the Great Church: Synthesis of Eschatology and "Utopia"

Both the historical evolution of the motive forces and the flow of the images make it tempting to try to turn eschatology into a practical and even partly rational statement by means of chiliasm. Thus the suggestive power which the chiliastic model has gained today, especially in the form of theologies of liberation, becomes somewhat understandable. Nevertheless, what we have here is no synthesis between the hope of faith and the rationality of political action, but only a combination in which both ingredients get spoiled. It is astounding how the mixture of an almost abstruse military exactitude with wild-eyed theological expectations, which we encountered in the Qumran War Scroll, is to be found in the literature of liberation theology. Anyone who considers the matter soberly must concede that theology's only contribution here has been to connect goals and grounds with political reasoning in such a way as to give rise to a course of political action which is carefully planned in detail but as a whole is profoundly irrational. There is no real connection between the promise and the approaches to it; particular projects are meaningful, but the scheme as a whole must be branded a delusion.[12]

The church and true believers could never find a solution in militant chiliasm: the political situation in which the movement originated made that impossible. Jesus had taken up Jeremiah's doctrine and had

11. Daniel Bell, *The Coming of Post-industrial Society* (New York: Basic Books, 1973), 54-63.

12. The most important survey of "liberation theology" is Roger Vekemans's *Teología de la liberación y cristianos por el socialismo* (Bogotá, 1976). I have tried to say something about what it presupposes in church history and the history of ideas in the article "Der Weltdienst der Kirche," which I contributed to *Zehn Jahre Vaticanum II*, ed. A. Bauch, A. Glässer, and M. Seybold (Regensburg: Pustet, 1976), 36-53.

suffered the same fate. The execution of James, the brother of the Lord and the first bishop of Jerusalem, perhaps belongs in this context: exactness in fulfilling the Law could not have been a source of conflict; the question of the political commitments of the faith was. For example, the Christian community stayed out of the Jewish war; they claimed that Jesus himself had advised them to leave Jerusalem (Mk 13:14). The notion of a kingdom of Christ on earth as a preliminary to the final kingdom of the Father is found in the Apocalypse and in Irenaeus, as well as in other orthodox Fathers. In neither case does the idea have any political bite. For Irenaeus it is really only a postulate of his Christology and concept of God.[13] Controversy in the early Church made it more and more clear that this kind of chiliasm, while as such it does not violate the basic Christian design and to this extent is not heterodox, yet has no further relevant statement to make and to this extent is worthless as a temporal model. That finished chiliasm's career as an attempt at synthesis in the realm of church doctrine.

Mainline orthodox thought has always found its key interlocutor not in apocalyptic literature and its philosophy of history but in Plato and his ontology. This means that Christians turned from the militant realization of eschatology through chiliastic politics to the relations between eschatology and "utopia." What form did this take? What reasons were adduced for it? If we look closely, we will see first of all that Plato's political philosophy is not so alien to the thought-patterns of eschatology as it might at first seem. In the stereotypes of Plato which are common in philosophical and theological treatises, one finds two completely different and generally irreconcilable impressions. On the one hand we have the dualistic Plato, the teacher of other-worldliness;

---

13. On Irenaeus see Hans Urs von Balthasar, *Herrlichkeit*, 2. Band (Einsiedeln: Johannes Verlag, 1962), 92ff. (Eng., *The Glory of the Lord: A Theological Aesthetics*, vol. 2: *Studies in Theological Styles* [San Francisco: Ignatius Press, 1984]): "The reign of the just on earth for a thousand years . . . is [Irenaeus's] way of taking seriously the Old Testament promises of finally and irrevocably possessing the land . . . Irenaeus is the advocate of the . . . new earth. . . ." Incontestable historical interpretations of the martyrdom of the Lord's brother (reported in Josephus, *Antiquities*, Book 20, Section 200; Loeb Classical Library edition of Josephus, vol. 9, ed. Louis A. Feldman [Cambridge, Mass.: Harvard University Press, 1965], 494-497) are of course not possible, but the James type of Christianity on the one hand and the contemporary political milieu on the other allow us to make a meaningful diagnosis of the kind attempted above.

on the other hand we have Plato the politician, with his theoretical and practical attempts at the reconstruction of the critically ill Greek *polis*. Now, sketching Plato's thought has its limits because we can only guess at his "secret doctrine," and that found in his writings only takes the form of different kinds of parables and adumbrations, which cannot ultimately be systematized.[14] Still, we can be fairly sure of two things: one, that Plato's philosophizing pivots around the philosophical martyrdom of Socrates, and, two, that this philosophizing, ever mindful of the death of the just man in conflict with the laws of the State, is constantly in search of the rightful, righteous State.[15] And this is precisely where we find the connection between "eschatology" and "utopia" as furnished by Plato: the individual and the community can continue to exist only if there is an overarching just order of being from which they can derive their standards and before which they stand responsible. "Reality" can be structured meaningfully only if ideas are real; the reality of the ideal is a postulate of experienced reality, which thereby shows itself to be a second-class reality. Plato's otherworldliness and his theory of ideas, while not invented for mere political purposes, are definitely parts of a political philosophy: they represent the standards which are presupposed by every effort to organize the political community. In this connection Helmut Kuhn has spoken of the Socratic difference between goods and the Good;[16] this difference uncovers both the core of Plato's doctrine of ideas and the core of his political philosophy, and thereby reveals the relationship of one to the other. Starting from this difference, Plato worked out his "utopia" as regulative of the political reason. Whereas chiliastic politics mixes faith and reason in a way injurious to both, Platonic thought succeeds in making a real synthesis: politics remains an affair of the practical reason, the polis re-

14. The limitations of every interpretation of Plato have recently been emphasized by Heinrich Dörrie, *Von Plato zum Platonismus* (Opladen, 1976); see especially the dialogue with Josef Pieper, 60ff. On the "secret doctrine" see among others Konrad Gaiser, *Platons ungeschriebene Lehre* (Stuttgart: Ernst Klett, 1963), and Hans Joachim Krämer, *Arete bei Platon und Aristoteles* (Heidelberg: C. Winter, 1959).

15. With this attempt at interpreting Plato compare Duchrow, *Christenheit und Weltverantwortung*, 61-80. Something can also be found in my *Eschatologie, Tod und ewiges Leben*, vol. 9, in the *Kleine Katholische Dogmatik* edited by Johann Auer and myself (Regensburg: Pustet, 1977).

16. Helmut Kuhn, *Der Staat* (Munich: Kösel, 1967), 25.

mains polis. But reason gets more room to operate by being given a glimpse of what is truly just, namely Justice itself: the Good has not less but more reality than particular goods have.

Wilhelm Kamlah has come to the conclusion that "utopia" is not a medieval (nor an early Christian) but rather a "modern undertaking of human thinking, speaking, and writing."[17] He is correct in the sense that the formal genre named utopia is a creation of Renaissance humanism. It undoubtedly constituted a step forward in political self-critique and in the quest for a rational structuring of political action. But it is no reason to deny that the medieval political treatises, such as, for example, the pertinent passages in Thomas Aquinas's *Summa* and Commentaries on Aristotle, remain substantially faithful to the theme of the Platonic utopia, filling out and remodeling its basic idea with material from the political philosophy of Aristotle and from Christian tradition.[18] This is not the place to analyze the historical progress of this Greek-Christian synthesis. Instead I would like to attempt a brief sketch of its essential elements as I see them. It seems to me that three viewpoints are decisive here.

(a) The idea of history's being brought to its consummation within history forms no part of the eschatological expectation; rather, quite the opposite: eschatology expresses the impossibility of perfecting the world within history. The various items in the depiction of the end of the world actually express a renunciation of the expectation of salvation within history. Besides, this denial that history can contain its own consummation seems rationally intelligible to me insofar as such an expectation is irreconcilable with the perpetual openness and the perpetually peccable freedom of man. Nevertheless, chiliasm conceals an even more profound error. In chiliastic planning, the salvation of the world is to be awaited, not from the moral dignity of man, not in the depths of his moral personality, but from mechanisms that can be planned — which inverts the values which support the world. The implementation of a-rational hopes with rational strategy, which we met before, probably proceeds from this deeper inversion of values.

(b) The negative message of eschatology, that is, the renunciation

17. Kamlah, *UEG*, 16.

18. On Thomas's political philosophy, see U. Matz, "Thomas von Aquin," *Klassiker des Politischen Denkens,* 3rd ed., ed. H. Meier, H. Rausch, and H. Denzer (Munich, 1963), vol. I, 114-146; on the sources see Marie-Dominique Chenu, *Toward Understanding Saint Thomas* (Chicago: Regnery, 1964), 336f.

of the intrinsic perfectibility of history, does not need to be proved to us nowadays. If that were all eschatology had to say, the only conclusion one could draw would be complete resignation and naked pragmatism. But we need to pay attention to the positive message too: eschatology asserts together with the intrinsic imperfectibility of history its perfectibility — outside history. But this completion outside itself is, in spite of that, really a completion of history. What is outside it is still *its* perfection. From the logic of this idea it follows that the rejection of the chiliastic attempt and the adoption of eschatology as eschatology is the only way to maintain the meaningfulness of history. For, while history cries out for a meaning, it cannot contain within itself its meaning for good and all. Thus, either it is meaningless, or it is consummated as itself outside itself and then has meaning in transcending itself. This leads to the insight that eschatology, precisely because it is not a political goal, functions as guarantor of meaning in history and makes "utopia" possible — "utopia," a model of the maximization of justice, an ideal for political reason to aim at.

(c) Accordingly, eschatology is not necessarily bound to any philosophy of history but only to ontology. Since it does not put its own logic of history into execution, it can be allied with a philosophy of decadence as well as with one of progress.[19] Its pivotal point is not a scenario for the rest of history but a concept of God that becomes concrete in Christology. The absorption of eschatology into Christology, which occurred in principle with the decision to believe in Christ, means that it was also absorbed into the concept of God and that the apocalyptic pattern of the theology of history retreated into the background. This new location of eschatology within the theological system is surely the central reason why its thrust could be combined with the tradition of Platonic thought.

3. The Utopian City of the Monks

Kamlah's thesis that utopia is a modern undertaking stands in need of yet another restriction: Christian monasticism is nothing else than the

---

19. The profound difference between Augustine's pessimism and the medieval idea of progress is beautifully presented by Alois Dempf in *Sacrum Imperium* (Munich: Oldenbourg, 1929, reprinted 1962), 116-398.

attempt to find utopia in the faith and to transfer it to this world. The expression *bios angelikos,* which monasticism used to describe itself, expresses this purpose very accurately — to live the life of paradise now and thus to discover Nowhere in the Now/here.[20] This is why monasticism takes its beginning from the utopian saying of Jesus, "Sell what you have, give it to the poor . . . and follow me" (Mt 19:21).[21] The monk knows that Jesus' own life, which he proposes to imitate, was quite literally a u-topian life: "The foxes have their dens and the birds of the sky their nests, but the Son of Man has *no place* to lay his head" (Mt 8:20). The practical effect is that the monks withdraw from the inhabited world to go into the un-world, the desert. This existential turn-around, which is what *fuga saeculi* amounts to, has been beautifully formulated by Cyril of Scythopolis when he says that the monks made the desert into a *civitas,* the non-world into a world.[22] Here we have a pneumatic revolution, which shows itself in the earthly self-expropriation of the convert, chiefly by providing him with a new standard of living, disclosing to him in the face of the old world and its *civitates* a new *civitas.* This struck people of the Roman Empire most forcibly when they saw the ineradicable class differences of their world automatically fade away as one crossed the threshold into the monks' world: the difference between slave and free, which perdures in the "world," is here, in accordance with Galatians 3:28, abolished.[23]

---

20. On the question of the "life like that of the angels," see especially Suso Frank, *Angelikos Bios* (Münster: Aschendorff, 1964); on early monasticism in general see H. Jedin's *Handbuch der Kirchengeschichte* (Freiburg: Herder), Band II/I, *Die Kirche von Nikaia bis Chalkedon,* by Karl Baus (1973), 347-409; Louis Bouyer, *The Spirituality of the New Testament and the Fathers* (New York: Desclée, 1964); and Uta Ranke-Heinemann, *Das frühe Mönchtum* (Essen: Driewer, 1964).

21. Cf. Athanasius, *Vita sancti Antonii,* cc. 2-4 (PG 26: 824-846); *The Life of St. Antony,* trans. Robert T. Meyer, Ancient Christian Writers, vol. 10 (Westminster, Md.: Newman, 1950), 19-22. Cf. the parallel action in the life of St. Francis: *I Celano* 22; *Legenda trium sociorum,* 25; Bonaventure, *Vita S. Francisci* III, 1; and the comments of Omer Englebert, *St. Francis of Assisi, A Biography,* 2nd ed. (Chicago: Franciscan Herald Press, 1966), 64ff.

22. Cyril of Scythopolis, *Vita Sabae,* c. 15, ed. Eduard Schwartz (Texte und Untersuchungen zur Geschichte der altchristlichen Literatur 49, 2), 98, lines 2f. Cf. Chr. von Schönborn, *Sophrone de Jérusalem: vie monastique et confession dogmatique* (Paris, 1972), 25ff.

23. *Regula S. Benedicti* 2, 16ff. (ed. Basilius Steidle, Beuron, revised 1975, p. 64): "Non ab eo persona in monasterio discernatur. . . . Non convertenti ex servitio praeponatur ingenuus, nisi alia rationabilis causa existat."

This new form of utopia differs from the Platonic form, first, by considering utopia partly realizable in the power of faith, and second, by not looking to the world as such or to its political bodies for realization, but rather looking to the charismatic non-world, which is engendered in the *voluntary* turning away from the world. On the other hand, some relation to the world was inevitable, and in Western monasticism, which followed Benedict and his rule more than any other, it soon became evident. The monastic community showed people how to live together and offered them islands of survival in a stormy age. Paradoxically, the result was that the monks' existence gradually became very "topian," a part of the world which everyone took for granted, an established institution instead of an alternative to life in the world. Anton Rotzetter paints a compelling picture of how, in reaction to this, St. Francis's idea for his order was wholly shaped by the passion for utopia, and how in its manifold expressions it was held together precisely by the idea of the realized utopia.[24] Surprisingly, the question of relations with the world, with established human communities, now becomes more clearly defined, chiefly by the fact that now it is the cities that constitute the "desert" into which the monks move in order to change them from deserts into the real City. More important, it seems to me, for the way in which we put our question, is the idea of the Third Order, which contains the attempt to transfer the utopian life-model of the monks to the worldly life in the normal vocations. The Third Order means the attempt, you might say, to move the whole City of Man some distance along the road toward utopia and thereby to make a comprehensive reform of the real by the utopian ideal. It must be admitted that this was attempted essentially by appealing to individuals, or at most by forming people into associations: the movement did not have a properly political ethos.

In this context one must remember the figure of Joachim of Fiore, who made the fateful connection between monastic utopia and chiliasm. Originally they had nothing to do with each other. Joachim reversed the pattern found in Irenaeus of Lyons and made the trinitar-

---

24. Anton Rotzetter, "Der utopische Entwurf der franziskanischen Gemeinschaft," *Wissenschaft und Weisheit* 37 (1974): 159-169. On the concrete difficulties of the Franciscan project, see K. S. Frank, "Utopie — Pragmatismus: Bonaventura und das Erbe des hlg. Franziskus v. Assisi," ibid., 139-159.

ian God himself the principle of progress in history. The old notion that to be a monk was to anticipate the world of the spirit now takes on a chronological meaning: to be a monk means to anticipate the next phase of history. In this manner, utopia is historicized and made into a historical goal to be striven for actively.[25] Medieval and monkish as Joachim's statements are when taken individually, structurally they open the way to Hegel and Marx: history is a forward-thrusting process, in which man actively works at his salvation, which cannot be known through the bare logic of the present but is guaranteed by the logic of history.

4. The Evolutionist Design of Teilhard de Chardin

Teilhard de Chardin's contribution was his attempt to connect Christian eschatology with the scientific theory of evolution by defining Christ as the Omega point of evolution. Natural history and human history are for him stages of one and the same process, whose characteristic he sees in its movement forward from the simplest elements of matter to ever more complex units in the direction of the Ultracomplex, that is, of the amalgamation of man and the cosmos in an all-embracing unity. The image of the body of Christ and of Christ as the head of the cosmos, as it is sketched out in the epistles to the Ephesians and the Colossians, allows Teilhard to identify this vision with the confession of Christ and Christian eschatological hope. Although there are certain parallels between this scheme and Marxist thought-patterns, it must be noted that Teilhard has neither a real philosophy of history nor a concrete political program. For this reason, he can hardly be classified as a chiliast. His idea is rather that technical progress, in spite of the statistically inevitable quota of breakdowns which it shares with evolution as a whole, continues the purposeful activity of evolution, in which its part is to build the Noosphere over the Biosphere as the next-to-last stage of complexity. If evolution is going in the direction of technical progress, then the most suitable form of poli-

---

25. On Joachim, see especially Dempf, *Sacrum Imperium*, 269-284, and compare my *Theology of History According to St. Bonaventure* (Chicago: Franciscan Herald Press, 1971), 95-118.

tics would seem to be one directed by technocrats. Thus science builds utopia in virtue of its immanent progress, though not without relapses. Here, faith in science takes on mythical traits; if we think of things this way, we are always on the verge of plunging into resignation, which restricts itself to the feasible.

This brings us to the problematic of the present, which consists in having to choose between chiliasm with its irrationality and positivism with its rationality and its hopelessness. Faced with this dilemma, it could be the function of the Platonic-Christian-humanist "utopia" to insist that the concept of reason be broadened and that not only the demand for what can be empirically verified, but also the demand for the values by which the empirical is set in order, be seen as one of the tasks of reason — which therefore must always be schooling itself in the great religious traditions of mankind. Thus I hope that I have made clear what the function of eschatology is in this context. Clearly it should not be viewed as a kind of theological supplement to the penal code, as was frequently the case in the authoritarian states of modern times, when the pastor was the policeman who had to apply to human conduct the otherworldly sanctions decreed by the church in alliance with the state. That would be a negative utopia of fear and egoism. The task is rather to perceive a wider spectrum of reality. Empirical reality and the rationality which confines itself to this empirical reality can only end up demanding the withdrawal of man, who not only de facto in the present state of our knowledge but in principle transcends the merely empirical. The issue is this: Will not only usefulness but also values be recognized as realities, so that reasoned humane conduct becomes possible?

Meanwhile, it is beyond question that the traditional humanist-Christian utopia is deficient in many respects. Its designers knew that reality touches on justice only asymptotically, but they were not sufficiently aware that knowledge too keeps approaching its goal without ever reaching it. The result was that they took their models too statically and finally, as we see in the case of Catholic natural law doctrine, which is a classic form of "utopian" thought. When we become aware of this, we see that in this area knowledge can arise only out of a perpetual alternation of theory and practice. When we start to apply "utopia," we immediately see how little we understand of it; we are forced to make new designs, which in turn make new practices possible, and so on. The static element in Platonic thought is thereby changed in favor

24

of realistic historical thinking, which absorbs the correct insights of the philosophy of history without allowing them to become the foundation of an autonomous logic of history.

A second problem seems to me to lie in the right ordering of *instituta* and *mores* to each other. The tradition of the Christian doctrine of the state, in contrast to Plato's search for the best state, has done little to develop the critique of institutions and the creative search for better institutions. At present, however, the threat comes from exactly the opposite direction — from a complete oblivion of the second basic ingredient of political life, the *mores*. We are talking not about *morality* but about *custom* or lifestyle, that is, a complex of basic convictions which express themselves in ways of living which give shape to the consensus about the basic values of human life. Alexis de Tocqueville has impressively demonstrated that democracy depends much more on *mores* than on *instituta*. Where no common persuasion exists, institutions find nothing to lay hold of, and coercion becomes a necessity. Freedom presupposes conviction; conviction, education and moral awareness. Wherever "utopia" becomes a mere treatise on institutions, it forgets the decisive truth that the management of the forces of the soul determines the fate of a community more than the management of economic means. A complete design for "utopia" must try to answer not only the question, Which institutions will be best? but also the question, How shall the forces of the soul be managed? How can we make sure that basic values can be realized in common? The stronger the underpinning of *mores,* the fewer *instituta* will be needed. The question of education, that is, of opening up reason to the whole of reality above and beyond the merely empirical, is not less important for "utopia" than the question of the proper distribution and control of power. The neglect of *mores* does not enlarge freedom; it prepares the way for tyranny: this prognosis of de Tocqueville has been confirmed only too exactly by the developments of the last hundred years. Perhaps we should look for the eschatological dimension of "utopias" in the acceptance of values as realities rather than in the sanction. In the *mores* politics, which "utopia" is meant to serve, points beyond itself; but without the *mores* the "utopia" that describes only *instituta* becomes a design for a prison instead of a search for true freedom.

Translated by James M. Quigley, S.J.

Liturgy and Sacred Music

Liturgy and music have been closely related to one another from their earliest beginnings. Wherever man praises God, the word alone does not suffice. Conversation with God transcends the boundaries of human speech, and in all places, it has by its very nature called music to its aid, singing and the voices of creation in the harmony of instruments. More than man alone belongs to the praise of God, and liturgy means joining in that which all things bespeak.

But if liturgy and music are closely connected with one another by their very natures, their relation to one another has also been strained, especially at the turning points of history and culture. Therefore, it is no surprise that the question concerning the proper form of music in the liturgy has become controversial again. In the disputes of the Council and immediately thereafter, it seemed to be merely a question of the difference between pastoral practitioners, on the one hand, and Church musicians, on the other. Church musicians did not wish to be subject to mere pastoral expediency but attempted to emphasize the inner dignity of music as a pastoral and liturgical norm in its own right.[1] Thus, the controversy seemed to move essentially on the level of application only. In the meantime, however, the rift has grown deeper. The

---

1. Compare Joseph Cardinal Ratzinger, *Das Fest des Glaubens* (Einsiedeln: Johannes Verlag, 1981), 86-111. Eng., *The Feast of Faith* (San Francisco: Ignatius Press, 1986).

This article first appeared as "Liturgie und Kirchenmusik," in *Internationale katholische Zeitschrift: Communio* 15, no. 3 (May 1986): 243-256. English publication in *Communio: International Catholic Review* 13, no. 4 (Winter 1986): 377-391.

second wave of liturgical reform advances these questions to their very foundations. It has become a question of the essence of liturgical action as such, of its anthropological and theological foundations. The controversy about Church music is becoming symptomatic for the deeper question about what the liturgy is.

1. Surpassing the Council? A New Conception of Liturgy

The new phase of the will to liturgical reform no longer sees its foundation explicitly in the words of the Second Vatican Council but in its "spirit." As a symptomatic text, I shall use here the learned and clearly drafted article on song and music in the Church in the *Nuovo Dizionario di Liturgia.* The high artistic rank of Gregorian Chant or of classical polyphony is in no way contested here. It is not even a question of playing off congregational activity against elitist art. Nor is the rejection of a historicist rigidification, which only copies the past and remains without a present and a future, the real point at issue. It is rather a question of a basically new understanding of liturgy which one wishes to use in order to surpass the Council whose *Constitution on the Sacred Liturgy* bears two souls within itself.[2]

Let us briefly attempt to familiarize ourselves with this conception in its fundamental characteristics. The liturgy takes its point of departure — we are told — from the gathering of two or three who have come together in the name of Christ.[3] This reference to the Lord's words of promise in Mt 18:20 sounds harmless and traditional at first hearing. But it receives a revolutionary turn when this one biblical text is isolated and contrasted with the whole liturgical tradition. For the two or three are now placed in opposition to an institution with its institutional roles, and to every "codified program." Thus this definition comes to mean: it is not the Church that precedes the group but the group that precedes the Church. It is not the Church as an integral entity that carries the liturgy of the individual group or community; rather the group

2. See 211a: "The documents of Vatican II reveal the existence of two souls"; and 212a: "This series of hints, derived more from the spirit than from the letter of Vatican II" (Rainoldi and E. Costa Jr., "Canto e musica," in *Nuovo Dizionario di Liturgia,* ed. Domenico Sartore and Achille M. Triacca [Rome: Ed. Paoline, 1984]).

3. Ibid., 199a.

is itself the specific place of the origin for the liturgy. Thus the liturgy does not grow out of a common given, a "rite" (which as a "codified program" now becomes a negative image of bondage); it arises on the spot from the creativity of those who are gathered. In such a sociological language, the sacrament of orders presents itself as an institutional role that has created a monopoly for itself and dissolved the original unity and solidarity by means of the institution (= the Church).[4] Under these circumstances, we are told, music then became a language of the initiates just like Latin, "the language of the other Church, namely, of the institution and its clergy."[5]

The isolation of Mt 18:20 from the entire biblical and ecclesiastical tradition of the common prayer of the Church has far-reaching consequences here. The Lord's promise to prayers of all places becomes dogmatization of the autonomous group. The solidarity of prayer has escalated into an egalitarianism for which the unfolding of the ecclesiastical office means the emergence of another Church. In such a view, every given coming from the whole is a fetter one must resist for the sake of the freshness and freedom of the liturgical celebration. It is not obedience to the whole but the creativity of the moment that becomes the determining form.

It is obvious that with the adoption of a sociological language there comes an adoption of evaluations. The value structure that the sociological language has formed constructs a new view of history and the present, the one negative, the other positive. Thus, traditional (and also conciliar!) concepts such as "the treasury of *musica sacra*," the "organ as queen of the instruments," and the "universality of Gregorian chant" now appear as "mystifications" for the purpose of "preserving a certain form of power."[6] A certain administration of power, we are told, feels

---

4. Ibid., 206b.

5. Ibid., 204a: "The celebration assumes the form of a splendid 'opus' for whose attendance and protagonists mysterious powers are recognized: the cultural difference thus begins to become a 'sacral' difference. . . . Music is on the way to becoming, like Latin, a learned language: the language of another Church, which is the institution and clergy."

6. "Think . . . of the repetition of thought forms and prefabricated judgments; of the fabling and concealment of facts in order to sustain a certain form of power and ideological vision. Think of common mystifying expressions such as 'the great patrimony of sacred music,' 'the Church's thought on chant,' 'the organ, queen of the instruments,' 'the universality of Gregorian chant' . . ." (200a). Cf. 210b and 206b.

threatened by processes of cultural transformation and reacts by mask-
ing its striving for self-preservation as love for the tradition. Gregorian
chant and Palestrina are tutelary gods of a mythicized, ancient reper-
toire,[7] elements of a Catholic counterculture that is based on remyth-
icized and supersacralized archetypes,[8] just as in the historical liturgy of
the Church it has been more a question of a cultic bureaucracy than of
the singing activity of the people.[9] The content of Pius X's *Motu Proprio*
on sacred music is finally designated as a "culturally shortsighted and
theologically empty ideology of sacred music."[10] Here, of course, it is not
only sociologism that is at work but a total separation of the New Testament from the history of the Church, and this in turn is linked with a
theory of decline, such as is characteristic for many Enlightenment situations: purity lies only in the original beginnings with Jesus. The entire
further history appears as a "musical adventure with disoriented and
abortive experiences," which one "must now bring to an end" in order
finally to begin again with what is right.[11]

But what does the new and better look like? The leading concepts
have already been indicated in previous allusions. We must now pay attention to their closer concretization. Two basic values are clearly formulated.
The "primary value" of a renewed liturgy, we are told, is "the full and authentic action of all persons."[12] Accordingly, Church music means first
and foremost that the "people of God" represents its identity in song. The
second value decision operative here is likewise already addressed: music
shows itself as the power that effects the coherence of the group. The familiar songs are, as it were, the identifying marks of a community.[13] From
this perspective, the main categories of the musical formation of the liturgy arise: the project, the program, the animation, the direction. The
how, we are told, is more important than the *what*.[14] The ability to celebrate is above all the "ability to do." Music must above all be "done."[15] In

---

7. Ibid., 210b.
8. Ibid., 208a.
9. Ibid., 206a.
10. Ibid., 211a.
11. Ibid., 212a.
12. Ibid., 211b.
13. Ibid., 217b.
14. Ibid., 217b.
15. "The members of the believing assembly, and above all the animators of the rite

order to be fair, I must add that understanding for different cultural situations is shown throughout and an open space for the adoption of historical material also remains. And above all, the paschal character of the Christian liturgy is underscored. Singing is not only meant to represent the identity of the people of God, but also to give an account of our hope and to proclaim the Father of Jesus Christ to all.[16]

Thus, elements of continuity do exist in this wide breach. These elements enable dialogue and give hope that unity in the fundamental understanding of the liturgy can be found again, which unity, however, threatens to disappear through the derivation of the liturgy from the group instead of from the Church — and not only theoretically, but also in concrete liturgical practice. I should not speak in such detail of all this, if I thought that such ideas were to be ascribed only to isolated theoreticians. Although it is incontestable that they cannot be based on the text of the Second Vatican Council, the opinion that the spirit of the Council points in this direction won acceptance in so many liturgical offices and their agents. In what has just been described, an all-too-widespread opinion today holds that so-called creativity, the action of all present, and the relationship of group members who know and address one another are the genuine categories of the conciliar understanding of the liturgy. Not only chaplains, but sometimes even bishops, have the feeling that they have not remained true to the Council when they pray everything as it is written in the missal; at least one "creative" formula must be inserted, however banal it may be. And the civil greeting of those present, with friendly wishes at the dismissal, has already become an obligatory ingredient of the sacred action which one would hardly dare to omit.

2. The Philosophical Ground of the Program and Its Questionable Points

With all this, however, the core of the change in values has not yet been touched. All that has been said until now follows from placing the group before the Church. But why do this? The reason lies in the fact that the Church is classified under the general concept of "institution"

... will know how to acquire that fundamental capacity that is a 'knowing how to celebrate,' in other words a knowing how to do . . ." (218b).

16. Ibid., 212a.

and that institution bears a negative quality in the type of sociology adopted here. It embodies power, and power is considered an antithesis to freedom. Since faith (the "imitation of Christ") is perceived as a positive value, it must stand on the side of freedom and thus also be anti-institutional in its essence. Accordingly, the liturgy may not be a support or ingredient of an institution either, but must form a counter-force that helps to cast down the mighty from their thrones. The Easter hope to which the liturgy is to bear witness can become quite earthly with such a point of departure. It becomes a hope for the overcoming of institutions, and it becomes itself a means in the struggle against power. Whoever reads only the texts of the *"Missa Nicaraguensis"* might gain the impression of this displacement of hope and of the new realism that liturgy becomes the instrument of a militant promise. One might also see the importance that does, in fact, accrue to music in the new conception. The stirring force of revolutionary songs communicates an enthusiasm and a conviction that cannot come from a merely spoken liturgy. Here there is no longer any opposition to liturgical music. It has received an irreplaceable role in awakening irrational forces and common energies, at which the whole is aimed. It is, however, at the same time a formation of consciousness, since what is sung is little by little communicated to the spirit much more effectively than what is only spoken and thought. Moreover, the boundary of the locally gathered community is then passed with full intention by means of the group liturgy. Through the liturgical form and its music, a new solidarity is formed through which a new people is to arise which calls itself the "people of God." But by "God" is meant only itself and the historical energies realized in it.

Let us return once again to the analysis of the values that have become decisive in the new liturgical consciousness. In the first place, there is the negative quality of the concept "institution" and of the consideration of the Church exclusively under this sociological aspect, and furthermore, not only under the aspect of an empirical sociology but from a point of view that we owe to the so-called masters of suspicion. One sees that they have done their work thoroughly and attained a form of consciousness that is still effective as far as one is ignorant of its origin. But suspicion could not have such an incendiary power if it were not accompanied by a promise whose fascination is inescapable: the idea of freedom as the authentic claim of human dignity. In this respect, the question about the correct concept of freedom must represent the core of the discussion. The controversy about the liturgy is thereby brought back from all superficial questions of artistic direction to its core, for in the liturgy it is in fact a question of the presence of redemption, of the access to true freedom. The positive element in this new dispute lies without a doubt in this disclosure of the core.

At the same time, that from which Catholic Christianity suffers today becomes visible. If the Church appears only as an institution, as a bearer of power and thus an opponent of freedom, or as a hindrance to redemption, faith is living in self-contradiction. For, on the one hand, faith cannot do without the Church; on the other hand, it is thoroughly against it. Therein lies also the truly tragic paradox of this trend of liturgical reform. For liturgy without the Church is a self-contradiction. Where all act so that they themselves may become the subject, the One who truly acts in the liturgy also disappears with the collective subject "Church." For it is forgotten that the liturgy is to be the *opus Dei* in which God himself acts first and we are redeemed precisely through the fact that he acts. The group celebrates itself and in doing so celebrates nothing at all. For it is no cause for celebration. That is why the general activity becomes boredom. Nothing happens when he whom the whole world awaits is absent. The transition to more concrete objectives, as reflected in the *Missa Nicaraguensis,* is thus only logical.

The proponents of this way of thinking must be asked directly: Is the Church really only an institution, a cultic bureaucracy, a power apparatus? Is the priestly office only the monopolization of sacral privileges? If we do not succeed in overcoming these notions effectively and do not succeed in seeing the Church differently again in our hearts, the liturgy will not be renewed, but the dead will bury the dead and call it reform. There is then, of course, no longer any *Church* music because the subject, the Church, has been lost. Indeed, one cannot even speak properly of the liturgy anymore, for it presupposes the Church. What remains are group rituals that avail themselves of more or less skillful means of musical expression. If liturgy is to be renewed or even to survive, it is fundamental that the Church be rediscovered. I should add: if the alienation of man is to be overcome, if he is to find his identity again, it is indispensable that he find the Church again: a Church which is not an institution inimical to man, but one in which there is the new We in which the I can first win its foundation and its dwelling.

It would be beneficial in this connection to read once again and thoroughly that little book with which Romano Guardini completed his literary work in the last year of the Council.[17] As he himself emphasizes, he wrote the book out of care and love for the Church whose humanity and precariousness he knew very well. But he had learned to discover the scandal of the incarnation of God in its humanity. He had learned to see in it the presence of the Lord who has made the Church his body. Only if that is so is there a simultaneity of Jesus Christ with us. And only if this exists is there real liturgy which is not a mere remembrance of the paschal mystery but its true presence. Once again, only if this is the case is liturgy a participation in the trinitarian dialogue between Father, Son, and Holy Spirit. Only in this way is it not our "doing" but the *opus Dei* — God's action in and with us. For that reason, Romano Guardini stressed emphatically that in the liturgy it is not a question of *doing* something but of *being* something. The idea that general activity is the most central value of the liturgy is the most radical antithesis imaginable to Guardini's conception of the liturgy. In fact, the general activity of all is not only not the basic value of the liturgy, it is as such not a value at all.[18]

I shall forgo dealing with these questions in further detail. We must concentrate on finding a point of departure and a criterion for the correct relation of liturgy and music. The realization that the genu-

17. R. Guardini, *Die Kirche des Herrn: Meditationen* (Würzburg: Werkbund-Verlag, 1965), trans. Stella Lange, *The Church of the Lord: On the Nature and Mission of the Church* (Chicago: H. Regnery, 1967). Guardini takes a stand there on the "opening" that was underway, which he welcomes but to which he also sets an inner limit at the same time: "may the happenings of the present not lead to a trivialization or a softening of the Church, but may it ever stand clearly in our consciousness that the Church is a 'mystery' and a 'rock'" (18). He comments briefly on both concepts and traces the concept of "rock" to that of "truth," from whose claim it follows that the Church must stand "unshakably in the distinction of true and false in spite of all ties to the times": "because only the truth and the demand for truth mean genuine respect, whereas compliancy and letting-things-go is a weakness that does not dare to demand of man the majesty of the self-revealing God; at bottom, it is a contempt of man. . . ." One should also re-read in this connection the *Méditation sur l'Église* by Henri de Lubac, 3rd ed. (Paris: Aubier, 1954), trans. Michael Maron, *The Splendor of the Church* (Glen Park, N.J.: Paulist Press, 1963 [from 2nd ed.]), which has just been republished in French.

18. I have attempted to say something more in detail on Guardini's understanding of the liturgy in my contribution "Von der Liturgie zur Christologie," in J. Ratzinger, ed., *Wege zur Wahrheit: Die bleibende Bedeutung von R. Guardini* (Düsseldorf, 1985), 121-144.

ine subject of the liturgy is the Church, that is, the *communio sanctorum* of all places and all times, is from this point of view really of great importance. For as Guardini showed in detail in his early writing *Liturgische Bildung*, there follows from this realization a removal of the liturgy from the caprice of the group and individual (including clerics and specialists), a removal which he termed the objectivity and positivity of the liturgy.[19] There also follows, and indeed above all, an awareness of the three ontological dimensions in which liturgy lives: cosmos, history, and mystery. The reference to history includes development, i.e., belonging to something living that has a beginning, continues in effect, remains present but is not yet finished, and lives only insofar as it is further developed. Many things die out, many things are forgotten and return later in a new way, but development always means participation in a beginning opened to what lies ahead. With that we have already touched on a second category that gains particular importance through its relation to the cosmos: liturgy, thus conceived, lives in the fundamental form of participation. No one is its one and only creator; for each one it is a participation in something greater; but each one is also an agent precisely because he is a recipient. Finally, the relation to mystery means that the beginning of the liturgical happening never lies in us. It is the response to an initiative from above, to a call and an act of love, which is mystery. Problems are there to be explained; mystery, however, discloses itself not in explanation but only in acceptance, in the "Yes" which today we may still call "obedience" after the Bible.

With that we have arrived at a point of great importance for the beginning of the artistic. For the group, liturgy is not cosmic, it lives from the autonomy of the group. It has no history: it is precisely the emancipation from history and doing things oneself that are characteristic of it, even if one works with historical props. Moreover, it is ignorant of mystery because in it everything is and must be explained. For that reason, development and participation are just as foreign to it as obedience (to which a meaning is disclosed that is greater than the explicable). Instead of all this, we have a creativity in which the autonomy of

---

19. R. Guardini, *Liturgische Bildung*, vol. 1: *Versuche* (Burg Rothenfels: Verlag Deutsches Quickbornhaus, 1923); with a revised edition under the title *Liturgie und liturgische Bildung* (Würzburg: Werkbund-Verlag, 1966).

the emancipated seeks to confirm itself. Such creativity, which would like to be the functioning of autonomy and emancipation, is precisely for that reason strictly opposed to all participation. Its characteristics are caprice, as a necessary form of refusal of every pre-given form or norm; unrepeatability, since a dependency would already lie in the performance of the repetition; and artificiality, since it is necessarily a question of a pure creation of man. It becomes clear, however, that a human creativity that does not will to be reception and participation is of its essence absurd and untrue, because man can only be himself through reception and participation. It is a flight from the *conditio humana* and thus untruth. This is the reason cultural decline sets in where, along with loss of faith in God, there is a protest against the pre-given *ratio* of being.

Let us summarize what we have found thus far in order to draw the consequences for our point of departure and the fundamental form of Church music. It has become clear that the primacy of the group comes from the understanding of the Church as institution which, in turn, is based on an idea of freedom that cannot be united with the idea and reality of the institutional and is unable to perceive the dimension of mystery in the reality of the Church. Freedom is understood in terms of the leading ideas of "autonomy" and "emancipation." It is concretized in the idea of creativity, which against this background becomes a direct antithesis to the objectivity and positivity that belong to the essence of the Church's liturgy. The group always has to fabricate itself anew; only then is it free. At the same time, we saw that any liturgy deserving of the name is radically opposed to this. It is against historical caprice, which knows no development and thus gropes in the dark, and against an unrepeatability, which is also exclusivity and loss of communication over and above individual groupings. It is not against the technical, but it is against the artificial in which man creates a counterworld and loses sight of God's creation in his heart. The oppositions are clear. It is also clear from the beginning that the inner foundation of the group mentality comes from an autonomously conceived idea of freedom. But we must now ask about the anthropological program on which the liturgy as understood by the Church's faith rests.

3. The Anthropological Model of the Church's Liturgy

Two fundamental biblical words offer themselves as a key to answering our question. Paul coined the words *logikē latreia* (Rom 12:1), which are difficult to translate into our modern languages because we lack a genuine equivalent to the concept of the Logos. One could translate it by "Spirit-guided liturgy" and thereby refer to Jesus' words on worship in spirit and truth (Jn 4:23) at the same time. But one could also translate it by "divine worship molded by the Word" and one would then have to add that "Word" in the biblical (and also in the Greek) sense is more than language or speech, namely, creative reality. It is, however, also more than mere thought and mere spirit. It is self-interpreting, self-communicating spirit. At all times, the word-relatedness, the rationality, the intelligibility, and the sobriety of the Christian liturgy have been derived from this and pre-given to liturgical music as its fundamental law. It would be a narrow and false interpretation if by this one wished to understand that all liturgical music must be strictly related to a text and to declare that its general condition lies in serving the understanding of a text. For "Word" in the biblical sense is more than "text." "Understanding" extends further than the banal intelligibility of that which is immediately evident to everyone and can be pressed into the most superficial rationality. It is correct, however, that music, which serves worship in spirit and truth, cannot be rhythmic ecstasy, sensuous suggestion or anesthetization, bliss of feeling, or superficial entertainment, but is subordinated to a message, a comprehensive spiritual and, in this sense, rational declaration. It is also correct, to express it otherwise, that it must correspond to this "word," indeed serve it, in a comprehensive sense.[20]

With that we are automatically led to another truly fundamental text on the question of cult in which we are told more exactly what "Word" means and how it is related to us. I mean the sentence of the Johannine Prologue: "The Word became flesh and made his dwelling among us, and we have seen his glory" (Jn 1:14). The "Word" to which the Christian liturgy is related is not first of all a question of a text but of a living reality, of a God who is self-communicating meaning and

---

20. For the correct understanding of the Pauline *logikē latreia*, see especially Heinrich Schlier, *Der Römerbrief* (Freiburg: Herder, 1977), 350-358, esp. 356ff.

who communicates himself by becoming man. This Incarnation is now the sacred tent, the focal point of all cult that gazes on God's glory and gives him honor. These declarations of the Johannine Prologue are, however, not yet the whole of the matter. One would misunderstand them if one did not read them together with the farewell discourse in which Jesus says to those who are his: "I am going now, but I shall return to you. It is by going that I return. It is good that I go, for only in this way can you receive the Holy Spirit" (Jn 14:2, 14:18, 16:5, and so on). The Incarnation is only the first part of the movement. It first becomes meaningful and definitive in the cross and resurrection: from the cross the Lord sees everything in itself and carries the flesh, i.e., man and the whole created world, into the eternity of God.

The liturgy is ordered to this line of movement, and this line of movement is, so to speak, the fundamental text to which all liturgical music is related. It must be measured by it from within. Liturgical music results from the claim and the dynamics of the Incarnation of the Word. For it means that also among us the Word cannot be mere talk. The sacramental signs are certainly the central way in which the Incarnation continues to work. But they become homeless if they are not immersed in a liturgy that as a whole follows this expansion of the Word into the realm of the bodily and all our senses. From this there comes, in opposition to the Jewish and Islamic types of cult, the right and even the necessity of images.[21] From this there also comes the necessity of summoning up those deeper realms of understanding and response that disclose themselves in music. The "musification" of faith is a part of the process of the Incarnation of the Word. But this musification is at the same time also ordered to that inner turn of the incarnational event which I tried to indicate before: in the cross and resurrection, the Incarnation of the Word becomes the "verbification" of the flesh. Each penetrates the other. The Incarnation is not taken back; it first becomes definitive at the moment in which the movement, so to speak, is reversed. The flesh itself is "logicized," but precisely this verbification of the flesh effects a new unity of all reality, which was obviously so important to God that he let it cost him his Son on the cross. On the one hand, the musification of the Word is

21. See on this point the thorough work of Christian Schörn, *Die Christus-Ikone* (Schaffhausen, 1984).

sensualization, Incarnation, attraction of pre-rational and trans-rational forces, attraction of the hidden sounds of creation, discovery of the song that lies at the bottom of things. But in this way, this musification is now itself also the turning point in the movement: it is not only Incarnation of the Word, but at the same time *"spiritualiza-tion"* of the flesh. Wood and metal become tone, the unconscious and the unreleased become ordered and meaningful sound. A corporealiza-tion takes place which is a spiritualization, and a spiritualization which is a corporealization. The Christian corporealization is always a spiritualization at the same time, and the Christian spiritualization is a corporealization into the body of the incarnate Logos.

4. The Consequences for Liturgical Music

a. Fundamentals

Insofar as this interpenetration of both movements takes place in mu-sic, the latter serves that inner exodus which the liturgy always wishes to be and to become in the highest measure and in an indispensable way. But that means that the appropriateness of liturgical music is measured according to its inner correspondence to this fundamental anthropological and theological form. Such a declaration seems at first to be very far removed from concrete musical reality. It becomes imme-diately concrete, however, when we pay attention to the opposing mod-els of cultic music to which I briefly referred previously.

Let us think first of all, for example, of the Dionysian type of reli-gion and music with which Plato grappled from the standpoint of his religious and philosophical view.[22] In not a few forms of religion, music is ordered to intoxication and ecstasy. The freedom from the limita-tions of being human toward which the hunger for the infinite proper to man is directed is sought through holy madness, through the frenzy of the rhythm and of the instruments. Such music lowers the barriers of individuality and personality. Man frees himself in it from the bur-den of consciousness. Music becomes ecstasy, liberation from the ego,

22. Cf. Ratzinger, *Das Fest des Glaubens*, 86-111; A. Rivaud, "Platon et la musique," *Re-vue d'histoire de la philosophie* (1929): 1-30.

and unification with the universe. We experience the profane return of this type today in rock and pop music, the festivals of which are an anti-culture of the same orientation — the pleasure of destruction, the abolition of everyday barriers, and the illusion of liberation from the ego in the wild ecstasy of noise and masses. It is a question of redemptive practices whose form of redemption is related to drugs and thoroughly opposed to the Christian faith in redemption. The conflict that Plato argued out between Dionysian and Apollonian music is not ours, for Apollo is not Christ. But the question he posed concerns us in a most important way. Music has become today the decisive vehicle of a counter-religion and thus the scene of the discernment of spirits in a form that we could not have suspected a generation ago. Because rock music seeks redemption by way of liberation from the personality and its responsibility, it takes, in one respect, a very precise position in the anarchical ideas of freedom that predominate today in a more unconcealed way in the West than in the East. But precisely for that reason, it is thoroughly opposed to the Christian notion of redemption of freedom as its exact contradiction. Not for aesthetic reasons, not from reactionary obstinacy, not from historical immobility, but because of its very nature music of this type must be excluded from the Church.

We could concretize our question further, if we were to continue analyzing the anthropological ground of different types of music. There is agitation music, which animates man for different collective purposes. There is sensual music, which leads man into the erotic or essentially aims in other ways at sensual feelings of pleasure. There is light music, which does not wish to say anything but only to break up the burden of silence. There is rationalistic music, in which the tones serve only rational constructions but in which no real penetration of spirit and sensibility results. One would have to include many sterile catechism songs and modern hymns constructed under commission here. The music that corresponds to the liturgy of the incarnate Christ raised up on the cross lives from another, greater and broader synthesis of spirit, intuition, and sensuous sound. One can say that Western music, from Gregorian chant through the cathedral music and the great polyphony, through the renaissance and baroque music up until Bruckner and beyond, has come from the inner wealth of this synthesis and developed it in the fullness of its possibilities. This greatness exists only here because it alone was able to grow out of this anthropological ground that joined the spiritual and the profane in an ultimate human unity. This unity is dissolved in the measure that this anthropology disappears. The greatness of this music is, for me, the most immediate and the most evident verification of the Christian image of man and of the Christian faith in redemption that history offers us. He who is touched by it knows somehow in his heart that the faith is true, even if he still has a long way to go to re-enact this insight with reason and will.

That means that the liturgical music of the Church must be ordered to that integration of human being that appears before us in faith in the Incarnation. Such a redemption is more laborious than that of intoxication. But this labor is the exertion of truth itself. In one respect, it must integrate the senses into the spirit; it must correspond to the impulse of the *sursum corda*. However, it does not will a pure spiritualization but an integration of sensibility and spirit so that both become person in one another. It does not debase the spirit when it takes the senses up into itself, but first brings it the whole wealth of creation. And it does not make the senses less real when they are penetrated by the spirit; rather, in this way they first receive a share in its infinity. Every sensual pleasure is strictly circumscribed and is ultimately incapable of intensification because the sense act cannot exceed a certain measure. He who expects redemption from it will be disappointed, "frustrated" — as one would say today. But through integration into the spirit, the senses receive a new depth and reach into the infinity of the spiritual adventure. Only there do they come completely to themselves. But that presupposes that the spirit does not remain closed either. The music of faith seeks the integration of man in the *sursum corda;* man, however, does not find this integration in himself, but only in self-transcendence toward the incarnate Word. Sacred music, which stands in the structure of this movement, thus becomes the purification and the ascent of man. But let us not forget: this music is not the work of a moment but participation in a history. It is not realized by an individual but only in community. Thus, it is precisely in it that the entrance of faith into history and the community of all members of the body of Christ expresses itself. It permits joy again, a higher kind of ecstasy which does not extinguish the person but unites and thus liberates him. It lets us glimpse what a freedom is that does not destroy but gathers and purifies.

b. Remarks on the Present Situation

The question for the musician is, of course: How does one do that? At bottom, great works of Church music can only be bestowed because the transcendence of self, which is not achievable by man alone, is involved, whereas the frenzy of the senses is producible in accordance with the known mechanisms of intoxication. Production ends where the truly great begins. We must first of all see and recognize this limit. To this extent, reverence, receptivity, and the humility that is ready to serve by participating in the great works that have already issued forth necessarily stand at the beginning of great sacred music. Only he who lives from the inner structure of this image of man at least in its essentials can create the music pertaining to it.

The Church has set up two further road markers. In its inner character, liturgical music must correspond to the demands of the great liturgical texts — the *Kyrie, Gloria, Credo, Sanctus, Agnus Dei*. That does not mean, as I have already said, that it may be only text music. But it finds the inner direction of these texts a pointer for its own message. The second road marker is the reference to Gregorian chant and to Palestrina. Again, this reference does not mean that all Church music must be an imitation of this music. On this point, there were in fact many constrictions in the renewal of Church music in the last century and also in the papal documents based on it. Correctly understood, this simply says that norms are given here that provide an orientation. But what may arise through the creative appropriation of such an orientation is not to be established in advance.

The question remains: Humanly speaking, can one hope that new creative possibilities are still open? And how is that to happen? The first question is really quite easy to answer. For if this image of man is inexhaustible, as opposed to the other one, then it also opens up ever new possibilities for the artistic message, and does so all the more, the more vividly it determines the spirit of an age. But here lies the difficulty for the second question. In our times, faith has to a large extent stepped down as a publicly formative force. How is it to become creative? Has it not everywhere been repressed into a subculture? To this one could reply that we are apparently standing before a new blossoming of faith in Africa, Asia, and Latin America, from which new cultural forms may sprout forth. But even in the Western world the word "subculture" should not frighten us. In the cultural crisis we are experiencing, it is only from islands of spiritual composure that new cultural purification and unification can break forth. Where new outbursts of faith take place in living communities, one also sees how a new Christian culture is formed, how the community experience inspires and opens ways we could not see before. Furthermore, F. Doppelbauer has correctly pointed to the fact that liturgical music frequently and not coincidentally bears the character of a late work and presupposes a previously acquired maturity.[23] Here it is important that there be the antechambers of popular piety and its music as well as spiritual music in the wider sense, which should always stand in a fruitful exchange with liturgical music: they are fructified and purified by it on the one hand, but they also prepare new forms of liturgical music. From their freer forms there can then mature what can enter into the common possession of the universal liturgy of the Church. Here then is also the realm in which the group can try its creativity in the hope that something will grow out of it that one day may belong to the whole.[24]

5. Liturgy, Music, and Cosmos

I would like very much to place at the close of my reflections a beautiful saying of Mahatma Gandhi, which I recently found on a calendar. Gandhi refers to the three living spaces of the cosmos and to the way in which each of these living spaces has its own mode of being. Fish live in the sea, and they are silent. Animals on the earth cry. But the birds, whose living space is the heavens, sing. Silence is proper to the sea, crying to the earth, and singing to the heavens. Man, however, has a share in all three. He bears within himself the depths of the sea, the burden of the earth, and the heights of heaven, and for that reason all three properties belong to him: silence, crying, and singing. Today — I should

23. J. F. Doppelbauer, "Die geistliche Musik und die Kirche," *Communio* (German ed.) 5 (1984): 457-466.

24. Important for the theological and musical foundations of Church music, which are only indicated here, is J. Overath, "Kirchenmusik im Dienst des Kultes," *Communio* (German ed.) 4 (1984): 355-368. One finds a broad panorama of ideas in P. W. Scheele, "Die liturgische und apostolische Sendung der Musica sacra," *Musica sacra: Zeitschrift des allgemeinen Cäcilienverbandes für die Länder deutscher Sprache* 105 (1985): 167-207.

like to add — we see how the cry is all that remains for the man without transcendence because he wills to be only earth and also attempts to make heaven and the depths of the sea into his earth. The right liturgy, the liturgy of the communion of saints, restores his totality to him. It teaches him silence and singing again by opening up the depths of the sea to him and by teaching him to fly like the angels. By lifting up his heart, it brings the song buried in him to sound again. Indeed, we can even say the reverse: one recognizes right liturgy in that it frees us from general activity and restores to us again the depths and the heights, quiet and song. One recognizes right liturgy in that it has a cosmic and not a group character. It sings with the angels. It is silent with the waiting depths of the universe. And thus it redeems the earth.

Translated by Stephen Wentworth Arndt

Luther and the Unity of the Churches:
An Interview with Joseph Cardinal Ratzinger

Question: Where does Luther scholarship stand today? Have there been any attempts to research Luther's theology, beyond existing historical investigations?

Cardinal Ratzinger: Nobody can answer this question in a few sentences. Besides, it would require a special kind of knowledge which I do not possess. It might be helpful, however, briefly to mention a few names which represent the various stages and trends of Catholic Luther scholarship. At the beginning of the century we have the decidedly polemical work by the Dominican H. Denifle. He was responsible for placing Luther in the context of the Scholastic tradition, which Denifle knew better than anybody else because of his intimate knowledge of the manuscript materials. He is followed by the much more conciliatory Jesuit, Grisar, who, to be sure, encountered various criticisms because of the psychological patterns in which he sought to explain the problem of Luther. J. Lortz from Luxembourg became the father of modern Catholic Luther scholarship. He is still considered the turning-point in the struggle for a historically truthful and theologically adequate image of Luther. Against the background of the theological movement between the two world wars, Lortz could develop new ways of questioning which, subsequently, would lead to a new as-

This article first appeared as "Luther und die Einheit der Kirchen. Fragen an Joseph Kardinal Ratzinger," in *Internationale katholische Zeitschrift: Communio* 12, no. 6 (November-December 1983): 568-582. English publication in *Communio: International Catholic Review* 11, no. 3 (Fall 1984): 210-226.

sessment of Luther. Meanwhile, the liturgical, biblical, and ecumenical movements on both sides have changed a lot of things. The Protestant side engaged in a renewed search for sacrament and church, that is, for the Catholic Luther (K. A. Meissinger). Catholics strove for a new and more direct relationship with Scripture and, simultaneously, sought a piety which was shaped against the background of traditional liturgy. Much criticism was directed at many a religious form which had developed during the second millennium, especially during the nineteenth century. Such criticism discovered its kinship with Luther. It sought to emphasize the "Evangelical" in the Catholic. It was against this background that Lortz could describe the great religious impulses which stimulated the reformer and which generated theological understanding of Luther's own criticism that had its roots in the late medieval crises of church and theology. With this in mind, Lortz proposed the famous thesis for the period of the great change in the thinking of the reformer: "within himself Luther wrestled and overthrew a Catholicism that was not Catholic."[1] Paradoxically, he could have based his thesis on Denifle, who demonstrated that Luther's revolutionary interpretation of Romans 1:17, which Luther himself later interpreted as the actual turning-point of the Reformation, in reality corresponded to the line of arguments presented by the medieval exegetical tradition. Even concerning the period around 1525 during which, following Luther's excommunication and his polemics which were aimed at the center of Catholic doctrine, the contours of a new evangelical church organization became apparent, Lortz thought he could safely say that Luther was "not yet aware of the fact that he was outside the Church."[2] Though Lortz did not minimize the deep rift which really began to take shape in the controversies of the Reformation, it seemed simple enough, following his work and by simplifying his statements, to develop the thesis that the separation of the churches was, really, the result of a misunderstanding and that it could have been prevented had the Church been more vigilant.

The generation following Lortz stressed various aspects: scholars such as E. Iserloh, P. Manns, and R. Bäumer illustrate how, in departure

1. Joseph Lortz, *The Reformation in Germany,* trans. Ronald Walls (London: Darton, Longman & Todd, 1968), I, 200.
2. Ibid., I, 487.

from Lortz, rather varied directions and positions could be assumed and developed. Younger theologians, such as O. H. Pesch or J. Brosseder, were pupils of H. Fries and remained essentially within the perimeter of J. Lortz. I would also like to mention two outsiders who stand apart from theology as it is taught in the classroom because of the way in which they approach the phenomenon of Luther: first of all the Indologist Paul Hacker, a convert, in his book on Luther entitled *Das Ich im Glauben* (Faith and the Ego),[3] where he perhaps also documents his own spiritual voyage. He concerned himself with the structure of Luther's act of faith. He saw the actual turning point of the Reformation in the change in the basic structure of the act of faith. Subsequently, he vehemently opposed the theory of a misunderstanding as well as all ideas advocating convergence and a complementary nature. Theobald Beer, a pastor in Leipzig, has been tenaciously devoting his life to the reading of Luther as well as the late medieval theology prior to Luther. He has studied not only the changes in theological thought in the difference between Luther and Scholasticism, but also between Luther and St. Augustine. In doing so, he has verified important shifts in the design of a Christology which, postulating the idea of "sacred bargaining," is completely bound up with anthropology and the teachings on grace. This new construct, that is, the changed basic configuration of a sacred bargaining (which Beer insists is found continuously from the early to the late Luther) expresses, in Beer's opinion, the reformer's completely different and new attitude toward faith which permits no harmonization.[4]

Thus it should be clear that there cannot be any Luther scholarship which does not at the same time involve research into his theology. One cannot simply approach Luther with the distant eye of the historian. To be sure, his theology must be analyzed and interpreted from a historical point of view, but, for the Christian historian, it emerges inevitably from the past, affecting him in the present. As far as the directions of this research are concerned, I believe that today one can discern two basic tenets with respect to which Harnack already saw the basic alternatives: with his catechism, his songs, and his liturgical

3. Paul Hacker, *Das Ich im Glauben* (Graz, 1966).

4. Theobald Beer, *Der fröhliche Wechsel und Streit: Grundzüge der Theologie Martin Luthers* (1st ed., Leipzig, 1974; 2nd ed., expanded, Einsiedeln, 1980).

directives Luther created a tradition of ecclesiastical life in the light of which we can both refer to him as the "father" of such an ecclesiastical life and interpret his work with evangelical churchliness in mind. On the other hand, Luther also created a theological and polemical opus of revolutionary radicality which he by no means retracted in his political dealings with the princes and in his stand against the leftists within the Reformation. Thus one can also comprehend Luther on the basis of his revolutionary break with tradition — and one will, on such a reading, then arrive at quite a different overall view. It would be desirable to keep in mind Luther's piety when reading his polemical works and the revolutionary background when dealing with issues concerning the Church.

Question: Would it be realistic for the Catholic Church to lift Luther's excommunication on the basis of the results of more recent scholarship?

Cardinal Ratzinger: In order to do full justice to this question one must differentiate between excommunication as a judicial measure on the part of the legal community of the Church against a certain person, and the factual reasons which led to such a step. Since the Church's jurisdiction naturally only extends to the living, the excommunication of a person ends with his death. Consequently, any questions dealing with the lifting of Luther's excommunication become moot: Luther's excommunication terminated with his death because judgment after death is reserved to God alone. Luther's excommunication does not have to be lifted; it has long since ceased to exist.

However, it is an entirely different matter when we ask if Luther's proposed teachings still separate the churches and thus preclude joint communion. Our ecumenical discussions center on this question. The inter-faith commission instituted following the Pope's visit to Germany will specifically direct its attention to the problem of the exclusions in the sixteenth century and their continued validity, that is, the possibility of moving beyond them. To be sure, one must keep in mind that there exist not only Catholic anathemas against Luther's teachings but also Luther's own definitive rejections of Catholic articles of faith which culminate in Luther's verdict that we will remain eternally separate. It is not necessary to borrow Luther's angry response to the Council of Trent in order to prove the definitiveness of his rejection of anything Catholic: ". . . we should take him — the pope, the cardinals, and whatever riffraff belongs to His Idolatrous and Papal Holiness — and (as blasphemers) tear out their tongues from the back, and nail them on the gallows. . . . Then one could allow them to hold a council, or as many as they wanted, on the gallows, or in hell among all the devils."[5] After his final break with the Church, Luther not only categorically rejected the papacy but he also deemed the Catholic teachings about the Eucharist (Mass) as idolatry because he interpreted the Mass as a relapse into the Law and, thus, a denial of the Gospel. To explain all these contradictions as misunderstandings seems to me like a form of rationalistic arrogance which cannot do any justice to the impassioned struggle of those men as well as the importance of the realities in question. The real issue can only lie in how far we are today able to go beyond the positions of those days and how we can arrive at insights which will overcome the past. To put it differently: unity demands new steps. It cannot be achieved by means of interpretative tricks. If separation occurred as a result of contrary religious insights which could locate no space within the traditional teachings of the Church, it will not be possible to create a unity by means of doctrine and discussion alone, but only with the help of religious strength. Indifference appears only on the surface to be a unifying link.

Question: Can we claim that the present-day pluralism in the theologies of both the Catholic and the Protestant churches will ease the way toward an approximation among the churches, or merely an approximation among Catholic and Protestant theologians?

Cardinal Ratzinger: Here, as always, we will first have to explain the term *pluralism*. Also, we will have to discuss the relationship between theology and Church. It is an indisputable phenomenon that Catholic and Lutheran exegetes have come closer as a result of the advances of the historical-critical method and the more recent methods of literary scholarship, so much so that the church affiliation of the individual exegete is hardly relevant any longer as far as the results are concerned: under certain circumstances, a Lutheran exegete may think

5. *Wider das Papsttum in Rom, vom Teufel gestiftet,* quoted in A. Läpple, *Martin Luther: Leben, Bilder, Dokumente* (Munich/Zurich, 1982), 252f. The above translation is from *Luther's Works,* vol. 41, *Church and Ministry III,* general ed. Helmut T. Lehmann (Philadelphia: Fortress Press, 1966), 308.

more along "Catholic" lines and be more in tune with tradition than his Catholic counterpart. Thus the latest biblical reference works feature both Catholic and Lutheran exegetes, depending on their specialization. The only distinction that remains appears to be their respective area of research. The jointly published Lutheran-Catholic commentary illustrates these points. It is interesting here to note that Lutheran exegetes have a more pronounced tendency to rely more heavily on their "fathers" (Luther, Calvin) and to include them as actual discussants in their endeavors to grasp the meaning of Scripture than their Catholic counterparts, who appear largely to agree that Augustine, Chrysostom, Bonaventure, and Thomas have nothing to contribute to modern exegesis.

Of course, one could ask what kind of a community such an agreement among exegetes would create. While Harnack thought that there was no more solid a foundation than a commonly shared historical method, Karl Barth treated this attempt to establish unity with irony, calling it sheer illusion. Indeed, a common method will create unity; however, it is also capable of continually generating contradictions. Particularly, scholarly agreement on findings designates a different level of unity from, say, an agreement on ultimate convictions and decisions with which we concern ourselves when we deal with questions of church unity. The unity of scholarly results is essentially revisable at any time. Faith is a constant. The history of reformed Christianity very clearly illustrates the limitations of exegetic unity: Luther had largely abandoned the line separating the teachings of the Church from theology. Doctrine which runs counter to exegetic evidence is not a doctrine to him. That is why, throughout his life, his doctorate in theology represented to him a decisive authority in his opposition to the teachings of Rome. The evidence of the interpreter supplants the power of the magisterium. The learned academic (Doctor) now embodies the magisterium, nobody else. The fact that the teachings of the Church became thus tied to the evidence of interpretation has become a constant question mark in church unity itself, ever since the beginnings of the Reformation. For it is this revisable evidence which became an inevitably explosive charge against a unity understood from within. Yet unity without content remains empty and will wither away. The unifying effect of theological pluralism is thus only temporary and sectional. There is inherent in pluralism the inability ultimately to become a basis for unity.

Nevertheless, it is true that agreement among exegetes is capable of surmounting antiquated contradictions and of revealing their secondary character. It can create new avenues of dialogue for all the great themes of intra-Christian controversy: Scripture, tradition, magisterium, the papacy, the Eucharist, and so on. It is in this sense that there is, indeed, hope even for a church which undergoes the aforementioned turmoil. However, the actual solutions which aim for deeper assurance and unity than merely that of scholarly hypotheses cannot proceed from there alone. On the contrary, wherever there develops a total dissociation of Church and exegesis, both become endangered: exegesis turns into mere literary analysis and the Church loses her spiritual underpinnings. That is why the interconnection between church and theology is the issue: wherever this unity comes to an end, any other kind of unity will necessarily lose its roots.

Question: Are there still any serious differences between the Catholic Church and the Reformed Churches and, if so, what are they?

Cardinal Ratzinger: The fact that now, as ever, there are serious differences is illustrated by the existence of papers of agreement which have been published in great numbers in recent years. This is particularly evident in the most progressive dialogues: in the Anglican-Catholic and the Orthodox-Catholic dialogue. To be sure, the Anglican-Catholic documents, made public in 1981, claim to have come up with a basic pattern with which to solve the controversial issues, but they do not claim, by any means, to have arrived at any final solutions. Not only the official reply of the Congregation for the Doctrine of the Faith but also diverse other publications have amply emphasized the grave problems inherent to these documents. Similarly, the Catholic-Lutheran document concerning the Lord's Supper does not conceal the fact that many unsolved issues remain, in spite of the many important convergences in the old questions behind the controversies.[6] The skillful approach leading to unity as suggested by H. Fries and K. Rahner in their theses, remains an artificial exploit of theological acrobatics which, unfortunately, does not live up to real-

---

6. Joint Roman Catholic/Evangelical Lutheran Commission, *The Lord's Supper* (Paderborn and Frankfurt, 1979).

ity.[7] It is impossible to direct denominations toward each other as in a military exercise and then to pronounce that the importance lies in the marching together; that individual thought is of lesser importance. Church unity feeds on the unity of fundamental decisions and convictions. The operative unity of Christians is something different. It does, thank God, already exist in parts and it could be much stronger and more comprehensive, even without solving the actual questions of unity.

To get back to the original question about what separates the Churches, entire libraries have been written on the subject. To answer it succinctly and concisely is rather difficult. Of course, one can readily focus on a number of questions where controversies exist: Scripture and tradition, that is, especially, Scripture and magisterium. Also, in conjunction with this, the question of the spiritual magisterium per se, apostolic succession as a sacramental form of tradition and its epitome in the papal office, the sacrificial character of the Eucharist and the issue of transubstantiation and, thus, of eucharistic adoration and prayer outside the Mass (while there is fundamental agreement on the presence of Christ), the sacrament of penance, varying views in the area of Christian morality whereby, of course, again the magisterium figures very prominently, and so on. Yet such an enumeration of controversial matters of doctrine will trigger the question concerning the fundamental decision: does all this rest on a fundamental difference, and, if so, can it be pinpointed? When, during the festivities surrounding the anniversary of the *Confessio Augustana* in 1980, Cardinal Willebrands noted that the roots had remained despite the separations during the sixteenth century, Cardinal Volk, afterwards, asked both humorously and seriously: Now I would like to know if the contraption of which we speak here is, for instance, a potato or an apple-tree? Or, to put it differently: is everything, with the exception of the roots, merely leaves, or is it the tree which grew from the roots that is important? How deep does the difference really go?

Luther himself was convinced that the separation of the teachings from the customs of the papal Church — to which separation he felt

---

7. H. Fries and K. Rahner, *Einigung der Kirchen — reale Möglichkeit* (Freiburg, 1983). First critical remarks on this are found in the review by H. J. Lauter in *Pastoralblatt* 9 (1983): 286f.

obligated — struck at the very foundation of the act of faith. The act of faith as described by Catholic tradition appeared to Luther as centered and encapsulated in the Law while it should have been an expression of the acceptance of the Gospel. In Luther's opinion, the act of faith was turned into the very opposite of what it was; for faith, to Luther, is tantamount to liberation from the Law, but its Catholic version appeared to him as a subjugation under the Law. Thus Luther was convinced that he now had to carry on St. Paul's fight against the so-called Judaizers in the Epistle to the Galatians and turn it into a fight against Rome and Catholic tradition per se. The identification of the positions of his time with those of St. Paul (we may see in it a certain identification of himself and his mission with St. Paul) are fundamental aspects of his life. It has become fashionable to insist that there are no longer any controversies concerning the teachings on justification. The fact is that Luther's questioning is no longer valid: neither Luther's consciousness of his sinfulness and his fear of hell, nor the terror he felt vis-à-vis the divine Majesty and his cry for mercy. His views on the freedom of the will which had already roused the opposition of Erasmus of Rotterdam are also hard to understand now. Conversely, the justification decree of Trent had already emphasized the pre-eminence of grace so strongly that Harnack believed that, if its text had been available, the Reformation would have had to take a different course. However, after Luther's lifelong insistence on the central differences in the teachings on justification, it seems justifiable to assume that it is here that we will, most likely, discover the fundamental difference. I am unable to elaborate on all this within the context of an interview. Thus, I will try briefly, though in necessarily biased and fragmentary fashion, to comment and, in doing so, attempt at least a perspective on the issues at hand.

It seems to me that the decisive cause of the breach cannot be found solely in changes in the constellation of ideas and in the concomitant shifts in theological theory, no matter how important these elements are. For there is no denying the truth that a new religious movement can be generated only by a new religious experience which is, perhaps, aided by the total configuration of an epoch and which incorporates its resources but is itself not consumed by them. It seems to me that the basic feature is the fear of God by which Luther's very existence was struck down, torn between God's calling and the realization of his own sinfulness, so much so that God appears to him *sub contrario,* as the opposite of Himself, i.e., as the Devil who wants to destroy man. To break free of this fear of God becomes the real issue of redemption. Redemption is realized the moment faith appears as the rescue from the demands of self-justification, that is, as a personal certainty of salvation. This "axis" of the concept of faith is explained very clearly in Luther's *Little Catechism:* "I believe that God created me. . . . I believe that Jesus Christ . . . is *my* Lord who saved *me* . . . in order that *I* may be His . . . and serve Him in justice and innocence forever." Faith assures, above all, the certainty of one's own salvation. The personal certainty of redemption becomes the center of Luther's ideas. Without it, there would be no salvation. Thus, the importance of the three divine virtues, faith, hope, and love, to a Christian formula of existence undergoes a significant change: the certainties of hope and faith, though hitherto essentially different, become identical. To the Catholic, the certainty of faith refers to that which God worked and to which the Church witnesses. The certainty of hope refers to the salvation of individuals and, among them, of oneself. Yet, to Luther, the latter represented the crux without which nothing else really mattered. That is why love, which lies at the center of the Catholic faith, is dropped from the concept of faith, all the way to the polemic formulations of the large commentary on St. Paul's Epistle to the Galatians: *maledicta sit caritas,* down with love! Luther's insistence on "by faith alone" clearly and exactly excludes love from the question of salvation. Love belongs to the realm of "works" and, thus, becomes "profane."

If one wishes, one may call this a radical personalization of the act of faith which consists in an exciting and, in some sense, exclusive "eye for an eye" relationship between God and man. At the same time, man has to depend time and again on the forgiving God against a demanding and judgmental God, that is, Christ, who appears *sub contrario* (as Devil). This dialectic view of God corresponds to a dialectic of existence which Luther himself once formulated as follows: ". . . it is necessary for a Christian to know that these are his own sins, whatever they are, and that they have been borne by Christ, by whom we have been redeemed and saved."[8] This "personalism" and this "dialectic," together to a lesser

8. *Luther's Works,* ed. Helmut T. Lehmann, vol. 17, *Lectures on Isaiah,* Chapters 40-66 (Philadelphia: Fortress Press, 1972), 223.

or greater degree with an anthropology, have also altered the remaining structure of his teachings. For this basic assessment signifies that, according to Luther, faith is no longer, as to the Catholic, essentially the communal belief of the entire Church. In any case, according to Luther, the Church can neither assume the certain guarantee for personal salvation nor decide definitely and compellingly on matters (that is, the content) of faith. On the other hand, to the Catholic, the Church is central to the act of faith itself: only by communal belief do I partake of the certainty on which I can base my life. This corresponds to the Catholic view that Church and Scripture are inseparable while, in Luther, Scripture becomes an independent measure of Church and tradition. This in turn raises the question of the canonicity and the unity of Scripture.

In some respects this incorporates the point of departure for the entire movement; for it was exactly the unity of Scripture — the Old and the New Testament, the gospels, the epistles of St. Paul, and the Catholic letters — on the basis of which Luther felt confronted with a Devil-God whom he felt compelled to resist and whom he resisted with the assistance of the divine God which he discovered in St. Paul. The unity of Scripture which had hitherto been interpreted as a unity of steps toward salvation, as a unity of analogy, is now replaced with the dialectic of law and Gospel. This dialectic is particularly sharpened by the two complementary concepts of the New Testament — that of the "gospels" and that of the epistles of St. Paul — of which only the latter were adopted and even radicalized by the earlier described "by faith alone." I would say that the dialectic of law and Gospel expresses most poignantly Luther's new experience and that it illustrates most concisely the contradiction with the Catholic concepts of faith, salvation, Scripture, and Church.

To sum up, Luther did indeed realize what he meant when he saw the actual point of separation in the teachings on justification which, to him, were identical with the "gospel" in contra-distinction to the "law." To be sure, one has to view justification as radical and as deep as he did, that is, as a reduction of the entire anthropology — and thus also of all other matters of doctrine — to the dialectic of law and Gospel. Since then there have been many revelations based on all his individual pronouncements, so that one should hope to have arrived at the point where the basic decision can be thought over and integrated into a more expansive vision. However, this has, unfortunately, not yet happened. To follow Fries' and Rahner's suggestions, and thus apparently with a few political maneuvers to skip over the quest for truth when it presents itself in terms of clear alternatives would be entirely irresponsible. All the more reason to hope that the commission which was established following the Pope's visit to Germany and the purpose of which is to shed light on the central issues and on the accompanying mutual exclusions will draw us closer to the goal, even though that commission will presumably remain unable to achieve the goal with its own accord.

Question: Considering the relationship of the Catholic Church to the churches of the Reformation, would it be possible to borrow St. Paul's formula and speak of the "Church of Corinth," "the Church of Rome," and "the Church of Wittenberg"?

Cardinal Ratzinger: The answer is a clear "no." This already applies in a church-sociological sense in the case of the "Church of Wittenberg," as there is no such church. Luther had no designs to establish a Lutheran Church. To him, the concept of the church centered in the congregation. Anything that went beyond that was organized and patterned after the existing political structure, i.e., the princes, considering the logic of contemporary thought and development. Thus regional churches were established at the same time that the political structure also replaced the non-existent individual structure of the church. Much has changed since 1918, although the Lutheran Church has retained its regional structures which, in turn, form church associations. It is obvious that the application of the term "church" to churches which took shape as a result of historical accidents will assume a different signification when compared to the intentions of the term "Catholic Church." Regional churches are not the "church" in a theological sense but are, rather, ways in which Christian congregations organize themselves; they are empirically useful, indeed necessary, but they are also interchangeable under different circumstances. Luther was able to transfer the church structure to the principalities only because he did not consider them integral to the concept of the church. On the other hand, to the Catholic, the Catholic Church, i.e., the community of bishops among themselves and together with the Pope, was instituted as such by the Lord. It cannot be interchanged or replaced. It is exactly this visible sacramental nature which is central to the concept of the Catholic Church that at the same time elevates the visible to a symbol of something greater. The transtemporal unity is as much a feature of this function as it is a symbol of the transcendence of the various political and cultural realms in the communion with the Body of Christ — which turns out to be the communion of his body in the very reality of the community of bishops everywhere and at all times. Thus it becomes clear that the plurality of local churches which together form the Catholic Church signifies something quite different from the pluralism of the denominational churches which are not integrated in a concrete single church and behind which are found hidden diverse institutional forms of Christian existence as well as different theological ideas about the spiritual reality of the Church.

Question: Is an ecumenism of the *Basis* (infrastructure) a way toward ecumenism?

Cardinal Ratzinger: In my opinion, the term *Basis* cannot be applied to the concept "church" in this fashion. Sociological and philosophical notions underlie talk about the *Basis* according to which society is characterized by an "above" opposite a "below," whereby "above" signifies the established and exploitative power, while "below," the *Basis,* means the actual sustaining powers, the economic forces, which alone can bring about progress when they are exercised or actuated. Wherever there is talk of *Basis ecumenism,* we can sense the emotions associated with such ideologies. The fact is that it is generally a matter of modifying the idea of community which only considers the congregation as church in the actual sense. The larger, major churches appear as the organizational umbrella which can be fashioned any way one desires. To be sure, the local congregations are naturally the concrete units that make up the life of faith in the Church and, thus, also become sources of inspiration for their way. The Second Vatican Council stated in regard to the development of faith in the Church:

> There is a growth in insight into the realities and words that are being passed on. This comes about . . . through the contemplation and study of believers who ponder these things in their hearts (cf. Luke 2:19 and 51). It comes from the intimate sense of spiritual realities which they experience. And it comes from the preaching of those who have received, along with their right of succession in the episcopate, the sure charism of truth.[9]

9. *Constitution on Revelation* II, 8.

Thus there are three principal factors to be considered in the determination of progress in the Church: reflection on and study of the holy words (Holy Scripture), insight based on experience in spiritual matters, and the teachings by the bishops. Hence the frequently criticized monopoly of the episcopal office in matters of teaching and life does not exist in the tradition of the Church. "Insight resulting from experience in spiritual matters" incorporates the entire contribution of the Christian life and thus also the special contribution by the "base," i.e., the community of believers as a so-called "theological locus." On the other hand, it becomes clear that the three factors belong together: experience without reflection is bound to remain blind, study without experience becomes empty, and proclamations by a bishop lack effectiveness without roots in the former two. All three jointly shape the life of the Church, whereby one or the other element may, at times, manifest itself more strongly, but none must be absent entirely. All in all, even sociologists would dismiss as a fantasy the notion that granting autonomy to the congregations would engender a united church. The opposite is the case: such an autonomy is bound to lead to atomization. Experience has shown that a unification of hitherto separate groups will, at the same time, lead to further separations. Much less will it automatically grow into a united church.

Question: Does St. John's concept of unified Christianity also signify unity among the churches?

Cardinal Ratzinger: First of all, we will have to be careful to avoid simply superimposing our situation and our questions onto St. John. To begin with, it is important to understand the passages in question with their own perspective in mind. Only then can we venture to understand how to extend the lines leading to us. Now it is exactly the proper interpretation of St. John's request for unity which is hotly disputed — though of course there do exist several common basic elements within the variety of the interpretations. First, unity among the faithful is, according to St. John, nothing which could be accomplished by human effort: it remains a request expressed through prayer which itself also implies a commandment directed at Christianity. It is expressed through prayer because the unity of Christianity comes from "above," from the unity of the Father with the Son. It constitutes a participation in the divine unity. I believe that Käsemann is essentially correct when he states that for John, unity is a mark and a quality of the heavenly realm in the same way in which truth, light and life are the quality and mark of the heavenly reality. . . . Unity in our Gospel exists only as a heavenly reality and therefore in antithesis to the earthly, which bears the mark of isolations, differences and antagonisms. If unity exists on earth, then it can only exist as a projection from heaven, that is, as the mark and object of revelation.[10]

However, the completely theological form of unity does not indicate a pressing of the question of unity into the Beyond or a postponement into the future: it is precisely the special characteristic of the Church that heavenly affairs extend into the temporal realm. The Church is the event of incorporation of human history into the realm of the divine. That is why things happen in the world which cannot come from this world: e.g., unity. That is exactly why unity — as a characteristic which is typical only of heavenly affairs — is also the sign of the divine origin of the Church. If we narrow it to the "Word," then one can also come to an agreement with one of Käsemann's formulations:

The accepted Word of God produces an extension of heavenly reality on earth, for the Word participates in the communion of Father and Son. This unity between Father and Son is the quality and mark of the heavenly world. It projects itself to the earth in the Word in order to create the community there which, through rebirth from above, becomes integrated into the unity of Father and Son.[11]

It becomes immediately clear that all this cannot be purely spiritual, but indeed that it envisions a concrete unity of the Church. Otherwise, the significance of the sign which is the object of John 17:20 would be rendered entirely meaningless. Schnackenburg assembled a number of ideas which illustrate the universal orientation ("catholic") of the Church in the fourth gospel: the passages concerning the acceptance of the Samaritans and Greeks into the Christian community, the word about the gathering of the dispersed children of God (11:52), the word about a shepherd and his flock (10:16), and the acceptance of

10. Ernst Käsemann, *The Testament of Jesus: A Study of the Gospel of John in the Light of Chapter 17*, trans. Gerhard Krodel (Philadelphia: Fortress Press, 1968), 68.
11. Ibid., 69-70.

the tradition of St. Peter, the narrative about the 153 large fish (Jn 21).[12] Moreover, Käsemann called attention to certain analogies between the gospel according to St. John and the unitarian vision in the Epistle to the Ephesians which he characterizes as follows:

> In Ephesians 4:5, a formative orthodoxy asserts itself which considers itself to be constitutively bound to heaven and in this respect to be the institution of salvation and not merely the instrument of grace. The unity of this orthodoxy now becomes identical with the truth of the right doctrine which it must administer as the mystery of divine revelation. Earthly reality may show its nature as dispersion and division. The heavenly reality is of necessity one and indivisible.[13]

Even though one cannot help but notice the epigrammatic, almost caricature-like formulation, an important message remains. Käsemann describes the position of the gospel according to St. John vis-à-vis early Catholicism in somewhat ambiguous fashion: on the one hand, he speaks of the "closeness to the rising early Catholicism,"[14] and, on the other, he states that John "is at least spatially 'remote from the beginnings of early Catholicism and theologically he does not share its trends even though he shares a number of its premises.'"[15]

One thing remains clear: St. John wrote his gospel for the universal Church, and the notion of a unity of Christians in separate churches is totally alien to him.

Question: Will there be a unity of all Christians in the future, in the sense implied by your last statement? Also, concerning the churches, will they have to wait until the Day of Judgment?

Cardinal Ratzinger: I should think that the answer is quite clear in view of what was said above: the unity of the Church is the unity of all Christians. The separation or even juxtaposition of both types of unity is a modern fiction whose content is rather vague. Even though St. John appears to show little interest in the individual institutional aspects of the Church, his gospel nevertheless presupposes quite obviously the concrete connection between the story of salvation and the

12. R. Schnackenburg, *Das Johannesevangelium III* (Freiburg, 1975), 241-245.
13. Käsemann, *The Testament of Jesus,* 57.
14. Ibid., 73.
15. Ibid., 66-67.

people of God through which God's act of redemption occurs. For example, the parable of the vine (Jn 15:1-10) reiterates the image of the vine of Israel attested to by Hosea, Jeremiah, and Ezekiel, as well as the psalms. "Vine" is also a traditional way of referring to the "people of God" to whom is given here, in the person of Jesus Christ, a new center. The simultaneous sounding of the reference to the Eucharist in the parable of the vine adds a very realistic ecclesial framework to this seemingly entirely "mystical" way of thinking.[16]

It is quite a different question, however, to ask to which concrete goals the ecumenical movement can aspire. This problem ought to be discussed anew now that it has been twenty years since the Council. It might be profitable to remember on this occasion how the Second Vatican Council formulated it, how it was not determined by the notion that all existing "churchdoms" were only pieces of a true Church that existed nowhere and which one would have to try to create by assembling these pieces: such an idea would render the Church purely a work of man. Also, the Second Vatican Council specifically stated that the only Church of Christ is realized (*subsistit*) "in the Catholic Church which is governed by the successor of Peter and by the bishops in communion with him."[17] As we know, this "realized in" replaces the earlier "is" (the only Church "is" the Catholic Church) because there are also many true Christians and many truly Christian ideas outside the Church. However, the latter insight and recognition which lies at the very foundation of Catholic ecumenism does not mean that, from now on, one would have to view the "true Church" only as a Utopian idea which may ensue at the end of days: the true Church is reality, existing reality, even now, without having to deny others their Christian existence or to dispute the ecclesial character of their communities.

Let us return now to the question of concrete ecumenical goals. The actual goal of all ecumenical endeavors must naturally be to convert the plurality of the separate denominational churches into the plurality of local churches which, in reality, form one Church despite their many and varied characteristics. However, it seems to me that in a given situation it will be necessary to establish realistic intermediate goals; for, otherwise, ecumenical enthusiasm could turn to resignation

16. Schnackenburg, *Das Johannesevangelium III*, 118-123.
17. *Constitution on the Church* I, 8.

or, worse, revert to a new embitterment which would place the blame for the breakdown of the great goal on the others. Thus the final days would be worse than the first. These intermediate goals will be different depending on how far individual dialogues will have progressed. The testimonies of love (charitable, social works) always ought to be given together, or at least in tune with each other whenever separate organizations appear to be more effective for technical reasons. One should equally try to witness together to the great moral questions of our time. And, finally, a joint fundamental testimony of faith ought to be given before a world which is torn by doubts and shaken by fears. The broader the testimony the better. However, if this can only be done on a relatively small scale, one ought to state the possible jointly. All this would have to lead to a point where the common features of Christian living are recognized and loved despite the separations, where separation serves no longer as a reason for contradiction, but rather as a challenge to an inner understanding and an acceptance of the other which will amount to more than mere tolerance: a belonging together in the loyalty and faithfulness we show for Jesus Christ. Perhaps it will be possible for such an attitude to develop which does not lose sight of final things but, meanwhile, does the closest thing by undergoing a deeper maturity toward total unity, rather than making a frantic scramble for unity which will remain superficial and at times rather fictitious.

I am convinced that the question of the final union of all Christians remains, indeed, unanswerable. One must not forget that this question also includes the question of the union between Israel and the Church. At any rate, to me the notion that one could achieve unity through a "really general (ecumenical) council" is a hybrid idea. That would be tantamount to building another tower of Babel which would necessarily result in even greater confusion. Complete union of all Christians will hardly be possible in our time. However, that unity of the Church which already exists indestructibly is a guarantee for us that this greater unity will happen in the future. The more one strives for this unity with all one's might the more Christian one will be.

Translated by Albert K. Wimmer

The Ecclesiology of the Second Vatican Council

Shortly after World War I, Romano Guardini formulated a sentence that soon became a standard quotation in German Catholicism: "An event of incalculable importance has begun: the Church is awakening in people's souls." The Second Vatican Council was the fruit of this awakening. It put into words and dedicated to the entire Church what had matured as the result of a knowledge born of faith in the four decades between 1920 and 1960 — decades that were so full of new openings and hope. In order to understand the Second Vatican Council, we must take a look at this period and try to recognize, at least in broad strokes, the lines and currents that led to the Council. I want to begin in each case with the notions that were held during this period in order to develop from them the basic elements of conciliar doctrine in the Church.

1. The Church as the Body of Christ

a. The Image of the Mystical Body

"The Church is awakening in people's souls" — this sentence of Guardini's was formulated very thoughtfully, for it was especially important to him that the Church be known and experienced as some-

---

This article first appeared as "Die Ekklesiologie des Zweiten Vatikanums," in *Internationale katholische Zeitschrift: Communio* 15, no. 1 (January 1986): 41-52. English publication in *Communio: International Catholic Review* 13, no. 3 (Fall 1986): 239-252.

thing inward, as something that does not stand in opposition to us like some mechanical device, but is alive in us. If the Church had been seen until then as all structure and organization, the insight now arose that we ourselves are the Church. It is more than an organization, it is an organism of the Holy Spirit, something alive encompassing us all from within. This new consciousness of the Church found its linguistic form in the term "the mystical body of Christ." A new and liberating experience of the Church expressed itself in this formula. At the end of his life, in the year in which the Second Vatican Council's Constitution on the Church was adopted, Guardini once again formulated the new view: the Church "is not an institution that was thought out and constructed . . . but a living being. . . . It lives again through time; becoming, just as everything alive becomes; changing . . . and nevertheless always the same in essence, for its innermost core is Christ. . . . As long as we see the Church as only an organization . . . ; as an authority . . . ; as a coalition . . . , we do not yet have a correct understanding of it. [I]t is a living being, and our relation to it must itself be life."

It is difficult to express the enthusiasm and joy which at that time rested in such a realization. In the period of liberal thought which existed up until World War I, the Catholic Church had been considered an ossified apparatus obstinately resisting the achievements of the modern age. In theology, the question of papal primacy had predominated to such an extent that the Church appeared to be essentially a centrally governed institution which one stubbornly defended, but which somehow still confronted one only from the outside. Now it was apparent again that the Church is much more; that all of us carry it together in faith in a living way, just as it carries us. It became apparent that it grows organically, just as it has through the centuries, so too today. It became apparent that the mystery of the Incarnation remains present through it: Christ marches on through the ages. If, then, we ask which elements of this first beginning have remained constant and have entered into the Second Vatican Council, we can say that the first one is the christological determination of the concept of the Church. J. A. Mohler, the great awakener of Catholic theology after the devastation of the Enlightenment, once said that one could caricature a certain false theology with this sentence: "Christ founded the hierarchy at the beginning and that sufficiently provided for the Church until the end of time." But in reply to this one must say that the Church is the mystical body, i.e., that Christ grounds it ever anew, that in it, he is never just past but always and above all present and future. The Church means the presence of Christ, our contemporaneity with him, his contemporaneity with us. It lives from Christ's dwelling in our hearts; from there he forms the Church for himself. For that reason, the Church's first word is Christ and not itself; it is sound in the measure that all attention is directed toward him. The Second Vatican Council placed this insight at the head of its considerations by beginning *Lumen gentium* [hereafter *LG*], 21 November 1964, with the words *"Lumen gentium cum sit Christus."* Because Christ is the light of the world, there is the mirror of his glory, the Church, which transmits his splendor. If one wishes to understand the Second Vatican Council correctly, one must begin with this first sentence again and again.

The aspects of interiority and of the communal character of the Church are to be seen as a second element from this beginning. The Church grows from the inside out, not vice-versa. Above all, it means that the most intimate communion with Christ forms itself in the life of prayer, in the life of the sacraments, and in the basic attitudes of faith, hope, and love. If, then, someone asks, "What must I do for the Church to come about and to progress?" the answer has to be, you must above all seek after faith, hope, and love. Prayer builds the Church, and the community of the sacraments in which the prayers of the Church are heard return to us.

This summer I encountered a pastor who told me that what weighed upon him most when he took over his pastoral responsibilities was that for decades no vocations to the priesthood had emerged from his parish. What was he to do? One cannot make vocations, only the Lord himself can give them. But must we then simply sit with folded hands? With this concern, he decided to make a pilgrimage each year along the arduous path to the Marian shrine in Altötting and to invite all who shared his concern to go along and to pray with him. More and more people went each year, and this year, to the immeasurable joy of the whole village, they were able to celebrate for the very first time a Mass for a newly ordained priest.

The term "body of Christ" tells us that the Church grows from within, but precisely because of this direction it includes another dimension: Christ has built a body for himself, and I must fit into it as a humble member. It is not to be found or had in any other way. But once found and had, it is so entirely, for I have become its member and its organ in this world and thus for all eternity. With this realization, the liberal idea that Jesus is interesting but that the Church is an unsuccessful affair is ruled out quite automatically. Christ exists only in his body but never in a merely spiritual way. That means that Christ exists with the others, with the permanent community that continues through the ages and is his body. The Church is not an idea but a body, and the scandal of the Incarnation on which so many of Jesus' contemporaries foundered continues. But here also the saying holds: blessed is he who is not scandalized by me.

The communal character of the Church necessarily means its "We"-oriented character. It does not exist in some place; rather we ourselves are it. Of course, no one can say, "I am the Church"; but each one can and must say, "*We* are the Church." And "we" is again not a group that isolates itself, but one that holds itself within the entire community of the members of Christ, both living and dead. In this way a group can truly say, "We are the Church." The Church exists in this open We which breaks through social and political boundaries, but also the boundary between heaven and earth. We are the Church — from this there grows co-responsibility and the opportunity for each of us to co-operate; from this there also results the right to criticize, which might nonetheless entail self-criticism. For the Church, I repeat, is not in some place nor is it someone else; we ourselves are the Church. These notions matured in the Council. All that was said about the common responsibility of the laity and the legal forms created for its meaningful realization grew out of this insight.

Finally, the notion of development and thus of the historical dynamics of the Church belong here as well. A body remains identical with itself precisely by continuously becoming new in the process of life. For Cardinal Newman the notion of development was the bridge to his conversion to Catholicism. While I believe that it numbers among the decisive and fundamental concepts of Catholicism, it is far from having been considered adequately, even though the Second Vatican Council has the merit of having formulated it for the first time in a solemn magisterial document. Whoever wishes to cling to the literal text of Scripture or to the forms of the patristic Church banishes Christ into the past. The result is either an entirely sterile faith that has nothing to say to the present, or an arbitrary act that skips over two thousand years of history, throwing them into the waste-bin of failures, and then concocting how Christianity — according to Scripture or according to Jesus — should really look. But what results can only be an artificial product of our own making in which there is no inherent permanence. True identity with the origin exists only where there is a living continuity that develops it and in so doing preserves it at the same time.

b. Eucharistic Ecclesiology

But we must once again return to the developments of the preconciliar period. As already mentioned, the first phase of the rediscovery of the Church centered around the concept of the mystical body of Christ. The concept was developed from Paul and pushed both the notions of the presence of Christ and the dynamics of the living into the foreground. Further research led to new realizations. Above all, Henri de Lubac in a splendid work of extensive scholarship made it clear that the term *corpus mysticum* originally designated the most Holy Eucharist and that for Paul, as well as for the Church Fathers, the notion of the Church as the body of Christ was inseparably bound to the notion of the Eucharist in which the Lord is bodily present and gives us his body to eat. Thus a eucharistic ecclesiology arose which has also been called a *communio*-ecclesiology. This *communio*-ecclesiology became the core of the teaching of the Second Vatican Council on the Church, and at the same time the central element the Council wished to convey.

What then is meant by eucharistic ecclesiology? I shall try to indicate only very briefly a few of its central points. The first is that Jesus' Last Supper is recognized as the true act of the founding of the Church. Jesus bestows the liturgy of his death and Resurrection on those who are his and thus bestows on them the feast of life. He repeats the Sinai Covenant at the Last Supper, or rather what was there only as a beginning in signs now becomes a completed reality — the community of blood and life between God and man. In saying this, it is clear that the Last Supper anticipates the Cross and Resurrection and at the same time necessarily presupposes them, for otherwise it would all remain an empty gesture. For that reason, the Church Fathers could say so beautifully that the Church sprang from the opened side of the

Lord, out of which flowed both blood and water. Seen from another angle, it is the same as saying the Last Supper is the beginning of the Church. For it always means that the Eucharist joins men together, not only with one another but also with Christ, thus making them the Church. At the same time, the fundamental constitution of the Church also says: the Church lives in eucharistic communities. It is liturgical service in its constitution and in its essence, liturgical service and therefore the service of man in the transformation of the world.

That the liturgy is the Church's form means that there is a peculiar and otherwise non-occurring relation between multiplicity and unity. In every eucharistic celebration, the Lord is entirely present. Because he is truly risen and will die no more, one can no longer divide him. He always gives himself whole and undivided. For that reason, the Council says:

> The Church of Christ is truly present in all legitimately organized local groups of the faithful, which, insofar as they are united to their pastors, are quite appropriately called Churches in the New Testament. For these are in fact, in their own localities, the new people called by God in the power of the Holy Spirit and as the result of full conviction (cf. 1 Thess 1:5). . . . In these communities, though they may often be small and poor, or existing in the diaspora, Christ is present through whose power and influence the One, Holy, Catholic, Apostolic Church is constituted.[1]

This means that from the beginnings of a eucharistic ecclesiology there follows an ecclesiology of the local Churches, which is characteristic for the Second Vatican Council and represents the inner, sacramental reason for the doctrine of collegiality.

First, however, we must look more closely at the formulation of the Council in order to appropriate its teaching correctly. For on this point the Second Vatican Council comes into contact with impulses at once from Orthodox and Protestant theology, which it nonetheless integrates into a larger Catholic view. The notion of eucharistic ecclesiology was first of all expressed in the Orthodox theology of Russian theologians in exile, and thereby was opposed to the alleged Roman centralism: every eucharistic community, it was said, is entirely Church already

---

1. *Lumen gentium*, 26.

because it has Christ entirely. External unity with other communities is not constitutive for the Church, and for that reason unity with Rome cannot be constitutive for the Church. Such unity is good because it represents the fullness of Christ toward the outside but it does not really belong to the essence of the Church because one cannot add anything to the totality of Christ.

From another point of view, the Protestant notion of Church pointed in the same direction. Luther was no longer able to recognize the Spirit of Christ in the Church as a whole. Indeed, he practically saw it as the instrument of the antichrist. Nor could he consider the established Protestant churches which arose from the Reformation church in the true sense since they were only sociologically and politically functional devices under the leadership of the political powers, nothing more. For him, the Church withdrew into the community: only the congregation which hears the Word of God on the spot is the Church. For that reason, he replaced the term "Church" with the term "community" and Church became a negative concept.

Turning to the text of the Council, we will notice several interesting nuances. It does not simply say, "The Church exists wholly in every community celebrating the Eucharist." Rather, the formulation runs: "The Church is really present in all legitimately organized local groups of the faithful, which, insofar as they are united to their pastors, are also quite appropriately called Churches." Two elements are important here. First, the community must be "legitimate" in order for it to be Church, and it is legitimate "insofar as it is united to the pastors." What does that mean?

First of all, it means that no one can make himself into the Church. A group cannot simply get together, read the New Testament, and say, "We are now the Church because the Lord is there wherever two or three are gathered in his name." The element of receiving belongs essentially to the Church, just as faith comes from hearing and is not the product of one's own resolutions or reflections. For faith is an encounter with that which I cannot think up or bring about through my own achievements but which simply has to encounter me. We call this structure of receiving and encountering "sacrament." And for this very reason, it is constitutive of the basic form of a sacrament that it is *received* and that no one administers it to himself. No one can baptize himself, no one can confer holy orders on himself, no one can absolve himself from his sins. This structure of encounter is the reason that perfect contrition cannot of its essence remain inward but desires the form of sacramental encounter. For that reason, it is not only an infraction of external canonical directives when one passes the Eucharist around and takes from it oneself but a violation of the innermost structure of the sacrament. The fact that the priest is allowed in the case of this single sacrament to administer the holy gifts to himself points to the *mysterium tremendum* to which he finds himself exposed at the Eucharist. He acts "in the person of Christ" and thus represents Christ and at the same time is a sinful man who lives entirely from the reception of the gift.

One cannot make the Church but only receive it, that is receive it from where it already is and where it really is: from the sacramental community of Christ's body passing through history. But something else is added which helps us to understand the difficult term "legitimate communities." Christ is wholly present everywhere — that is the one and very important thing the Council formulated in common with our Orthodox brethren. But he is only one everywhere, and therefore I can have the one Lord only in the unity that he himself is, in the unity with the others who also are his body and are to become it ever anew in the Eucharist. Therefore the unity with one another of the communities celebrating the Eucharist is not an external addition to eucharistic ecclesiology but its inner condition: the one Christ is found only in unity. To that extent, the Council calls on the self-responsibility of the communities and yet excludes all self-sufficiency. It presents an ecclesiology for which being Catholic, i.e., the community of believers of all places and all times, is not organizational externals but grace coming from within and at the same time a visible sign of the power of the Lord who alone can give unity across so many boundaries.

2. The Collegiality of Bishops

The notion of episcopal collegiality, which likewise numbers among the main pillars of the ecclesiology of the Second Vatican Council, is most intimately connected with eucharistic ecclesiology. The notion grew out of the study of the liturgical structures of the Church. If I am not mistaken, the first one to formulate it clearly and thereby to open the door for the Council on this point was the Belgian liturgical scholar, Bernard Botte. This is important because the connection with the liturgical movement of the time between the World Wars becomes apparent here also. The liturgical movement was the true breeding ground for most of the realizations presented thus far. Beyond the historical dimension, the liturgical movement is important because it illustrates the inner connection of notions without which one cannot understand them correctly. The dispute about collegiality is not a quarrel between Pope and bishops concerning their shares of power in the Church, although it can degenerate into such a quarrel very easily and those concerned must ask themselves ever again whether they are on the wrong track. Nor is it really a quarrel about legal forms and institutional structures. Rather, collegiality is in essence ordered to that service which is the true service of the Church, the liturgical service. Bernard Botte took his concept from the oldest liturgical orders. This was pointed out to the opponents of collegiality who referred during the Council to the fact that collegiality had a meaning in Roman law and in the cooperative law of the early modern period but is not to be harmonized with the Church constitution. A possible conception of the notion of collegiality is touched on here which would distort the sense of ecclesiastical service. For that reason, it is important to return ever again to the core in order to protect it from such distortions.

What, then, does this mean? In his investigations, Botte pointed to two levels of the notion of collegiality. The first level consists in the fact that the bishop is surrounded by a college of presbyters. We have already mentioned what is meant by this, namely, that the primitive Church was not familiar with a self-sufficiency of the individual communities. For the presbyters who serve them belong together; together they are the "council" of the bishop. The communities are held in the greater unity of the Church as a whole through the bishop. Being a priest always includes a relationship among priests themselves, as well as a relationship to the bishop, which, in turn, includes a relationship to the Church as a whole. But that means that the bishops for their part may not work by themselves in isolation. Together they form the *ordo* of the bishops, as was formulated in the language of Roman law which divided society into different *ordines*. Later, the word *ordo* became the formal designation for the sacrament of orders. Entrance into a communal service, into the We of those serving, thus belongs to the essential substance of this sacrament. The word *ordo,* incidentally, alternates with *collegium;* both mean the same thing in a liturgical context. Thus the bishop is not the bishop alone but only in the Catholic community of those who were bishops before him, and will be bishops after him. For the dimension of time is also intended in this word: the Church is not something we make today but something we receive from the history of the faithful and something we pass on as unfinished, which will only be fulfilled at the coming of the Lord.

The Council forged these notions along with the concepts of the sacrament of episcopal consecration and the idea of apostolic succession into an organic synthesis. It reminds us that even the apostles were community. Before they received the name "apostles" they appear under the designation "the Twelve." The calling of twelve men by the Lord has a sign-character which every Israelite understood: it is reminiscent of the twelve sons of Jacob from which the twelve tribes of Israel arose. Twelve is thus the symbolic number of the people of God; if Jesus calls twelve, then his symbolic gesture says that he himself is the new Jacob-Israel and that now, with these men, a new people of God are beginning. Mark expressed this very clearly in his gospel: "He named twelve" (3:14). In this connection, one knew that twelve was also a cosmic number, the number of the signs of the zodiac which divides the year, the time of man. The unity of history and cosmos, the cosmic character of salvation history, was thus underscored. The twelve are to be the new signs of the zodiac of the definitive history of the universe. But let us stay with what immediately occupies us: the apostles are what they are only in the togetherness of the community of the twelve which after the betrayal of Judas is therefore once again made full and complete. One consequently becomes a successor of the apostles by entering into the community of those in whom their office is continued. "Collegiality" belongs to the essence of the episcopal office; it can be lived and enacted only in the togetherness of those who at the same time represent the unity of God's new people.

If we ask ourselves what this means practically, we must answer first of all that the Catholic dimension of the episcopal office (as well as of holy orders and of every community life) is very emphatically underscored. Particularisms thoroughly contradict the idea of collegiality. As formulated by the Council, collegiality is not an immediately legal form but a theological advantage of the first order, both for the law of the Church and for pastoral action. The legal form that represents the immediate expression of the theological "collegiality" is the ecumenical council. For that reason, in the new Code of Canon Law the latter is regulated in the context of the article on the episcopal college in particular (can. 336-341). All other forms of application cannot be directly deduced from it but can only form attempts at a secondary mediation of the great fundamental principle in everyday reality. These attempts must always be measured by the degree to which they correspond to the basic content at issue: transcending the local horizon toward the common element of Catholic unity, to which the dimension of the history of faith has always belonged from the beginning and will continue to do so until the coming of the Lord.

3. The Church as the People of God

In the treatment of the idea of collegiality, the catchword has been mentioned for which the reader has surely been waiting a long time: the Church as the people of God. What does this mean? In order to understand it, we must again return to the developments that preceded the Council. After the first enthusiasm of the discovery of the notion of the body of Christ, the latter was gradually deepened and corrected in a double direction. We have already seen the first correction. It is found above all in the works of Henri de Lubac, who concretized the notion of the body of Christ in the light of the eucharistic ecclesiology and thereby opened it to the concrete questions of the legal order of the Church and the relationship of the local Church to the Church as a whole. The other form of correction began at the end of the 1930s in Germany where various theologians raised the criticism that, with the idea of the mystical body, the relation of the visible to the invisible, of law and grace, of order and life remains ultimately unexplained. They therefore suggested the concept, found above all in the Old Testament, of "the people of God" as the more comprehensive description of the Church. This concept could also be conveyed more easily with sociological and legal categories, whereas the body of Christ remains an image which is important but insufficient for the theological demand for concept formation.

This initially somewhat superficial criticism of the notion of the

72

body of Christ was subsequently deepened from various points of view, from which the positive content developed in terms of which the concept of the people of God entered into the conciliar ecclesiology. A first important point was the dispute about membership in the Church which followed the encyclical on the mystical body of Christ which Pius XII had published on 29 June 1943. He had declared at that time that membership in the Church is tied to three presuppositions: Baptism, right faith, and affiliation with the legal unity of the Church. Non-Catholics, however, were thereby wholly excluded from membership in the Church. In a country where the ecumenical question is so critical, as in Germany, this declaration had to lead to vehement arguments, especially since the Code of Canon Law opened up another perspective. According to the legal tradition of the Church maintained there, Baptism grounds a lasting form of constitutive affiliation with the Church. It thus became apparent that legal thinking can in some cases give more flexibility and openness than a "mystical" conception. One wondered whether the image of the mystical body was not too narrow as a point of departure for defining the manifold forms of affiliation with the Church which have existed in the intricacies of human history. For affiliation, the image of the body provides only the notion of "member"; one is either a member or not, there are no intermediate degrees. But — one asked — isn't the very point of departure of the image too narrow, since there quite obviously are intermediate degrees? In this way, the term "people of God" emerged, which in this respect is more ample and flexible. The Constitution on the Church has taken up precisely this usage when it describes the relation of non-Catholic Christians to the Catholic Church in terms of the concept of "connection," and that of non-Christians with the term "ordainment." It bases itself both times on the notion of the people of God (*LG* 15 and 16).

One can thus say that the concept of the people of God was introduced to the Council above all as an ecumenical bridge. This is true, moreover, in another respect as well. The rediscovery of the Church after World War I was a thoroughly Catholic and Protestant phenomenon; even the liturgical renewal was in no way limited to the Catholic Church. But precisely this commonality also entailed mutual criticism. The notion of the body of Christ was developed in the Catholic Church to the effect that the Church designated as "Christ living on earth" came to mean that the Church was described as the Incarnation of the

Son continuing until the end of time. That elicited protest from Protestants who saw therein an insufferable self-identification of the Church with Christ in which, so to speak, the Church worshipped itself and declared itself infallible. Gradually, however, even Catholic thinkers found — without going so far — that this formula ascribed a definitiveness to the speaking and acting of the Church which made every criticism appear as an attack on Christ himself and which simply overlooked the human — all-too-human — element in the Church. The christological difference, it was said, had to be presented again clearly: the Church is not identical with Christ but stands opposite him. It is the Church of sinners which needs purification and renewal again and again: it must become the Church again and again. The notion of reform thereby became a decisive element of the concept of the people of God, a notion which did not allow itself to be developed from the concept of the body of Christ.

Here we touch on a third aspect that played a role in favoring the notion of the people of God. In 1939, the Lutheran exegete Ernst Käsemann published his monograph on the Letter to the Hebrews with the title "The Pilgrim People of God." This title practically became a catchword within the compass of the conciliar debates, for it let something be heard which was realized more and more clearly in the course of grappling with the Constitution on the Church: the Church is not yet at the goal. It still has its true hope before it. The "eschatological" moment of the concept of the Church became clear. Above all, one was able in this way to enunciate the unity of salvation history, which comprises Israel and the Church together on their pilgrim journey. It was thus possible to express the historicity of the Church, which is still underway and will become itself only when the ways of time have been traveled and end in God's hand. It was also possible to enunciate the inner unity of the people of God itself in which — as in every people — there are different offices and ministries; but above and beyond all such distinctions, all pilgrims are still in the one community of the pilgrim people of God. If, then, we wish to summarize in catchwords the prominent elements of the concept of the people of God which were important to the Council, we could say that here the following become clear: the historical character of the Church, the unity of God's history with men, the inner unity of the people of God beyond the boundaries even of the sacramental states, the eschatological dynamics, the preliminary and broken character of the Church ever in need of renewal, and finally the ecumenical dimension as well, i.e., the different ways in which the connection with and ordainment to the Church are possible and actual beyond the boundaries of the Catholic Church.

But this already also indicates what things we should not seek in the concept of the people of God. I may perhaps be allowed to report here in a somewhat more personal manner because I myself was permitted to take a modest part in the prehistory that led to the Council. At the beginning of the 1940s, when the notion of the people of God was thrown up for debate, my theology teacher, Gottlieb Söhngen, came to the opinion on the basis of many patristic texts and other witnesses of the tradition that "the people of God" could indeed be the fundamental concept of the Church, far more so and far better than "the body of Christ." But because he was a very careful man, he was not satisfied with such approximate certainties but wanted to know more precisely. He thus decided to have a series of doctoral dissertations written on this question, to investigate the matter step by step.

The task fell to me of treating the people of God in Augustine, in whom above all Söhngen thought he detected the notion of the people of God. As I went to work, it soon became apparent that I also had to include the earlier African theologians who had worked in advance of Augustine, especially Tertullian, Cyprian, Optatus of Mileve, and the Donatist, Tyconius. Of course, one also had to keep the more important teachers of the East in view, at least such figures as Origen, Athanasius, and John Chrysostom. And finally, a study of the biblical foundations was likewise indispensable. As I was engaged in this, I came across an unexpected finding: the term "people of God" does indeed appear very often in the New Testament, but only in very few places (probably only in two) does it designate the Church, whereas its normal meaning refers to the people of Israel. Indeed, even where it may indicate the Church, the basic meaning "Israel" survives, but the context makes clear that the Christians have now become Israel. We may thus say that the term "people of God" is not a designation for the Church in the New Testament but only in the christological reinterpretation of the Old Testament; thus it can designate the new Israel through the christological transformation. The normal denomination for the Church in the New Testament is the term *ecclesia,* which in the Old Testament designates the gathering of the people through the beckoning Word of God. The term *ecclesia* (Church) is the New Testament variation and transformation of the Old Testament concept of the people of God. It is employed because it includes the notion that new birth in Christ first makes the non-people to be the people. Paul then consistently summarized this necessary christological transformation process in the concept of the body of Christ.

Before I draw the consequences from this, I must still note that in the meantime the Old Testament scholar Norbert Lohfink has shown that even in the Old Testament the term "people of God" does not simply designate Israel in its empirical factuality. Seen purely empirically, no people is the "people of God." To present God as a sign of descent or as a sociological mark of identification could never be more than an insufferable presumption and ultimately a blasphemy. Israel is designated by the concept of the people of God insofar as it is turned toward the Lord, not simply in itself but in the act of relationship and of self-transcendence which alone makes it what it is not of itself. To that extent, the New Testament continuation is consistent; it concretizes this act of turning to God in the mystery of Jesus Christ who turns to us and takes us in faith and sacrament into his relationship to the Father.

What, then, does all this mean concretely? It means that Christians are not simply the people of God. Empirically considered, they are a non-people, as any sociological analysis can quickly show. And God is no one's property; no one can seize him for himself. The non-people of Christians can only be God's people through inclusion in Christ, the Son of God and the Son of Abraham. Even if one speaks of the people of God, Christology must remain the center of the teaching on the Church and consequently the Church must be thought of essentially in terms of the sacraments of Baptism, the Eucharist, and Orders. We are the people of God only from the crucified and risen body of Christ. We become the Church only in the living ordainment to it, and it is only in this context that the word has meaning. The Council made this connection clear in a very nice way by placing together with the term "people of God" a second basic term for the Church in the foreground: the Church as sacrament. One remains true to the Council only if one always reads and thinks these two central terms of its ecclesiology together, sacrament and people of God. Here it becomes apparent how far ahead of us the Council still is; the notion of the Church as sacrament has still hardly dawned on us.

It would be absurd, therefore, if one wished to deduce a changed conception of the hierarchy and the laity from the fact that the chapter on the people of God comes before the chapter on the hierarchy, as if really all the baptized already bore all the powers of orders in themselves and the hierarchy were only a matter of good order. The second chapter is concerned with the question of laity insofar as the essential inner unity of all the baptized in the order of grace is declared and the ministerial character of the Church is thereby underscored. But this chapter does not ground a theology of the laity for the quite simple reason that all belong to the people of God. The whole of the Church and its essence are treated here. Its individual states are presented afterwards in this succession: hierarchy (chapter 3), laity (chapter 4), religious (chapter 6).

If my presentation of the ecclesiology of the Second Vatican Council were to be complete, I should now have to unfold the contents of these remaining chapters as well as what is said on the common vocation to holiness and on the relation of the earthly to the heavenly Church. But that would far exceed the limits of the present discussion. I have been concerned only to indicate briefly the foundations on which all further applications rest. In conclusion, I should like to refer briefly to one thing. The Council's Constitution on the Church closes with the chapter on the Mother of God. The question of whether one should dedicate a separate text to her was vehemently disputed, as is well known. I think it was nonetheless a fortunate turn of events that the Marian dimension entered directly into the teaching on the Church itself. For in this way our point of departure becomes apparent once again at the end: the Church is not a mechanical device, not merely an institution, nor one of the usual sociological magnitudes — it is person. It is a woman. It is mother. It is alive. The Marian understanding of the Church is the most decisive antithesis to a merely organizational or bureaucratic concept of the Church. We cannot make the Church, we must be the Church. We *are* the Church and the Church is in us only in the measure that beyond our doing, faith also molds our being. Only in being Marian do we become the Church. The Church was not made in its origin but born. It was born when the *fiat* awoke in Mary's soul. The deepest will of the Council is that the Church may awake in our souls. Mary shows us the way.

Translated by Stephen Wentworth Arndt

Church and Economy:
Responsibility for the Future of the World Economy

The economic inequality between the northern and southern hemispheres of the globe is becoming more and more an inner threat to the cohesion of the human family. The danger for our future from such a threat may be no less real than that proceeding from the weapons arsenals with which the East and the West oppose one another. New exertions must be made to overcome this tension, since all methods employed hitherto have proven themselves inadequate. In fact, the misery in the world has increased in shocking measure during the last thirty years. In order to find solutions that will truly lead us forward, new economic ideas will be necessary. But such measures do not seem conceivable or, above all, practicable without new moral impulses. It is at this point that a dialogue between Church and economy becomes both possible and necessary.

Let me clarify somewhat the exact point in question. At first glance, precisely in terms of classical economic theory, it is not obvious what the Church and the economy should actually have to do with one another, aside from the fact that the Church owns businesses and so is a factor in the market. The Church should not enter into dialogue here as a mere component in the economy, but rather in its own right as the Church.

This text was originally presented at a symposium on "Church and Economy in Dialogue," held in Rome (1985). English publication in *Communio: International Catholic Review* 13, no. 3 (Fall 1986): 199-204.

Here, however, we must face the objection raised especially after the Second Vatican Council, that the autonomy of specialized realms is to be respected above all. Such an objection holds that the economy ought to play by its own rules and not according to moral considerations imposed on it from without. Following the tradition inaugurated by Adam Smith, this position holds that the market is incompatible with ethics because voluntary "moral" actions contradict market rules and drive the moralizing entrepreneur out of the game.[1] For a long time, then, "business ethics" rang like hollow metal because the economy was held to work on efficiency and not on morality.[2] The market's inner logic should free us precisely from the necessity of having to depend on the morality of its participants. The true play of market laws best guarantees progress and even distributive justice.

The great successes of this theory concealed its limitations for a long time. But now in a changed situation, its tacit philosophical presuppositions and thus its problems become clearer. Although this position admits the freedom of individual businessmen, and to that extent can be called liberal, it is in fact deterministic in its core. It presupposes that the free play of market forces can operate in *one* direction only, given the constitution of man and the world, namely, toward the self-regulation of supply and demand, and toward economic efficiency and progress.

This determinism, in which man is completely controlled by the binding laws of the market while believing he acts in freedom from them, includes yet another and perhaps even more astounding presupposition, namely, that the natural laws of the market are in essence good (if I may be permitted so to speak) and necessarily work for the good, whatever may be true of the morality of individuals. These two presuppositions are not entirely false, as the successes of the market economy illustrate. But neither are they universally applicable and correct, as is evident in the problems of today's world economy. Without developing the problem in its details here, let me merely underscore a statement from Peter Koslowski that illustrates the point in question:

---

1. Cf. Peter Koslowski, "Über die Notwendigkeit und Möglichkeit einer Wirtschaftsethik," *Scheidewege. Jahresschrift für skeptisches Denken* 15 (1985/86): 204-305, here 301. This fundamental study has given me essential suggestions for my own paper.

2. Ibid., 294.

"The economy is governed not only by economic laws, but is also determined by men. . . ."[3] Even if the market economy does rest on the ordering of the individual within a determinate network of rules, it cannot make man superfluous or exclude his freedom from the world of economics. It is becoming ever more clear that the development of the world economy has also to do with the development of the world community and with the universal family of man, and that the development of the spiritual powers of mankind is essential in the development of the world community. These spiritual powers are themselves a factor in the economy: the market rules function only when a moral consensus exists and sustains them.

If I have attempted so far to point to the tension between a purely liberal model of the economy and ethical considerations, and thereby to circumscribe a first set of questions, I must now point out the opposite tension. The question about market and ethics has long ceased to be merely a theoretical problem. Since the inherent inequality of various individual economic zones endangers the free play of the market, attempts at restoring the balance have been made since the 1950s by means of development projects. It can no longer be overlooked that these attempts have failed and have even intensified the existing inequality. The result is that broad sectors of the Third World, which at first looked forward to development aid with great hopes, now identify the ground of their misery in the market economy which they see as a system of exploitations, as institutionalized sin and injustice. For them, the centralized economy appears to be the moral alternative, toward which one turns with a directly religious fervor, and which becomes the formal content of religion. For while the market economy rests on the beneficial effect of egoism and its automatic limitation through competing egoisms, the thought of just control seems to predominate in a centralized economy, where the goal is equal rights for all and proportionate distribution of goods to all. The examples adduced thus far are certainly not encouraging, but the hope that one could, nonetheless, bring this moral project to fruition is also not thereby refuted. It seems that if the whole were to be attempted on a stronger moral foundation, it should be possible to reconcile morality and efficiency in a society not oriented toward maximum profit, but rather to self-restraint and com-

3. Ibid., 304; cf. 301.

mon service. Thus in this area, the argument between economics and ethics is becoming ever more an attack on the market economy and its spiritual foundations, in favor of a centrally controlled economy, which is believed now to receive its moral grounding.

The full extent of this question becomes even more apparent when we include the third element of economic and theoretical considerations characteristic of today's situation: the Marxist world. In terms of the structure of its economic theory axis, the Marxist system as a centrally administered economy is a radical antithesis to the market economy.[4] Salvation is expected because there is no private control of the means of production, because supply and demand are not brought into harmony through market competition, because there is no place for private profit-seeking, and because all regulations proceed from a central economic administration. Yet, in spite of this radical opposition in the concrete economic mechanisms, there are also points in common in the deeper philosophical presuppositions. The first of these consists in the fact that Marxism, too, is deterministic in nature and that it too promises a perfect liberation as the fruit of this determinism. For this reason, it is a fundamental error to suppose that a centralized economic system is a moral system in contrast to the mechanistic system of the market economy. This becomes clearly visible, for example, in Lenin's acceptance of Sombart's thesis that there is not a particle of ethics in Marxism, but only economic laws.[5] Indeed, determinism is here far more radical and fundamental than in liberalism: for at least the latter recognizes the realm of the subjective and considers it as the place of the ethical. The former, on the other hand, totally reduces becoming and history to economy, and the delimitation of one's own subjective realm appears as resistance to the laws of history, which alone are valid, and as a reaction against progress, which cannot be tolerated. Ethics is reduced to the philosophy of history, and the philosophy of history degenerates into party strategy.

---

4. Cf. Card. J. Höffner, *Wirtschaftsordnung und Wirtschaftsethik. Richtlinien der katholischen Soziallehre,* ed. Sekretariat der Deutschen Bischofskonferenz (Bonn, 1985), 34-44. The English translation of this paper was published by Ordo socialis: *Economic Systems and Economic Ethics — Guidelines in Catholic Social Teaching* (Association for the Advancement of Christian Social Sciences, 1986).

5. Koslowski, "Über die Notwendigkeit und Möglichkeit einer Wirtschaftsethik," 296, with reference to Lenin, *Werke* I (Berlin, 1971), 436.

But let us return once again to the common points in the philosophical foundations of Marxism and capitalism taken strictly. The second point in common — as will already have been clear in passing — consists in the fact that determinism includes the renunciation of ethics as an independent entity relative to the economy. This shows itself in an especially dramatic way in Marxism. Religion is traced back to economics as the reflection of a particular economic system and thus, at the same time, as an obstacle to correct knowledge, to correct action — as an obstacle to progress, at which the natural laws of history aim. It is also presupposed that history, which takes its course from the dialectic of negative and positive, must, of its inner essence and with no further reasons being given, finally end in total positivity. That the Church can contribute nothing positive to the world economy on such a view is clear; its only significance for economics is that it must be overcome. That it can be used temporarily as a means for its own self-destruction and thus as an instrument for the "positive forces of history" is an "insight" that has only recently surfaced. Obviously, it changes nothing in the fundamental thesis.

For the rest, the entire system lives in fact from the apotheosis of the central administration in which the world spirit itself would have to be at work, if this thesis were correct. That this is a myth in the worst sense of the word is simply an empirical statement that is being continually verified. And thus precisely the radical renunciation of a concrete dialogue between Church and economy which is presupposed by this thought becomes a confirmation of its necessity.

In the attempt to describe the constellation of a dialogue between Church and economy, I have discovered yet a fourth aspect. It may be seen in the well-known remark made by Theodore Roosevelt in 1912: "I believe that the assimilation of the Latin-American countries to the United States will be long and difficult as long as these countries remain Catholic." Along the same lines, in a lecture in Rome in 1969, Rockefeller recommended replacing the Catholics there with other Christians[6] — an undertaking which, as is well known, is in full swing. In both these remarks, religion — here a Christian denomination — is presupposed as a socio-political, and hence as an economic-political

---

6. I found these two considerations in the contribution of A. Metalli, "La grande epopea degli evangelici," *Trenta giorni* 3, no. 8 (1984): 8-20, here 9.

factor, which is fundamental for the development of political structures and economic possibilities. This reminds one of Max Weber's thesis about the inner connection between capitalism and Calvinism, between the formation of the economic order and the determining religious idea. Marx's notion seems to be almost inverted: it is not the economy that produces religious notions, but the fundamental religious orientation that decides which economic system can develop. The notion that only Protestantism can bring forth a free economy — whereas Catholicism includes no corresponding education to freedom and to the self-discipline necessary to it, favoring authoritarian systems instead — is doubtless even today still very widespread, and much in recent history seems to speak for it. On the other hand, we can no longer regard the liberal-capitalistic system (even with all the corrections it has since received) so naively as the salvation of the world. We are no longer in the Kennedy era, with its Peace Corps optimism; the Third World's questions about the system may be partial, but they are not groundless. A self-criticism of the Christian confessions with respect to political and economic ethics is the first requirement. But this cannot proceed purely as a dialogue within the Church. It will be fruitful only if it is conducted with those Christians who manage the economy. A long tradition has led them to regard their Christianity as a private concern, while as members of the business community they abide by the laws of the economy.

These realms have come to appear mutually exclusive in the modern context of the separation of the subjective and objective realms. But the whole point is precisely that they *should* meet, preserving their own integrity and yet inseparable. It is becoming an increasingly obvious trend of economic history that the development of economic systems which concentrate on the common good depends on a determinate ethical system, which in turn can be borne and sustained only by strong religious convictions.[7] Conversely, it has also become obvious that the decline of such discipline can actually cause the laws of the market to collapse. An economic policy that is ordered not only to the good of the group — indeed, not only to the common good of a deter-

---

7. For detailed information see P. Koslowski, "Religion, Ökonomie, Ethik. Eine sozialtheoretische und ontologische Analyse ihres Zusammenhangs," *Die religiöse Dimension der Gesellschaft, Religion und ihre Theorien*, ed. P. Koslowski (Tübingen, 1985), 76-96.

minate state — but to the common good of the family of man demands a maximum of ethical discipline and thus a maximum of religious strength. The political formation of a will that employs the inherent economic laws toward this goal appears, in spite of all humanitarian protestations, almost impossible today. It can only be realized if new ethical powers are completely set free. A morality that believes itself able to dispense with the technical knowledge of economic laws is not morality but moralism. As such it is the antithesis of morality. A scientific approach that believes itself capable of managing without an ethos misunderstands the reality of man. Therefore it is not scientific. Today we need a maximum of specialized economic understanding, but also a maximum of ethos so that specialized economic understanding may enter the service of the right goals. Only in this way will its knowledge be both politically practicable and socially tolerable.

Translated by Stephen Wentworth Arndt

Cardinal Frings's Speeches During the Second Vatican Council: Some Reflections Apropos of Muggeridge's The Desolate City

1. Formulating the Question

In her recent book *The Desolate City: Revolution in the Church*, Anne Roche Muggeridge describes the Council as the starting point for a real revolution within the Church.[1] She does not fault the Council itself with the intention of a revolution, but she tries to show with her careful analyses that a revolutionary tendency long in preparation skillfully used the opportunity of the Council and the attitude of the Council Fathers to create the conditions necessary for its revolutionary program. According to this view, Cardinal Frings appears as the head of the liberal group from the Rhineland. Prior to the Council they had already sought out liberal allies in other national episcopacies and thus were in a position to determine decisively the direction of the Council. For the author, Frings is a liberal but not a radical, no revolutionary. On the contrary, she declares that the radicals, who at first carefully kept themselves hidden, became sufficiently confident toward the end of the Council to frighten the most important liberal from the Rhineland, Frings himself, and his *peritus* Joseph Ratzinger, so that

---

1. Anne Roche Muggeridge, *The Desolate City: Revolution in the Church* (San Francisco, 1986).

This article first appeared as "Buchstabe und Geist des Zweiten Vatikanums in den Konzilsreden von Kardinal Frings," in *Internationale katholische Zeitschrift: Communio* 16, no. 3 (May 1987): 251-265. English publication in *Communio: International Catholic Review* 15, no. 1 (Spring 1988): 131-147.

Frings undertook a certain correction in his course and distanced himself from Rahner.[2]

The analyses of Muggeridge's book are careful and the conclusions nuanced. An in-depth discussion would be worthwhile, though that is not my intention in this article. On the centennial of the great Cardinal's birth, I would like merely to present a few thoughts in an attempt to define the areas where his influence on the Council really lay. The reference to Muggeridge's work shows how difficult such an undertaking is: the appraisals that were made during and immediately after the Council were too much the product of the moment's feelings. They lacked distance and perspective. On the other hand, with the growing distance it is becoming ever more difficult to filter the true story from the various sources, not least because the mythmakers — as Muggeridge remarks, very much to the point — were busy at work from the very beginning.[3] Anyone who has had the good fortune of knowing Cardinal Frings personally knows that he was no liberal in the sense of holding a liberal worldview. One could label him a liberal only if the word is used in a very flat sense to mean a certain breadth of conception, openness, nobility. But if the distinction between liberal and radical fails to identify the position which the Archbishop of Cologne took up during the Council, how is one then to categorize him? What did he really want to achieve? That is the question for which I would like in these reflections to provide at least the beginnings of an answer.

It seems to me that the only way to reach our goal is to analyze his speeches during the Council. One can really understand the speeches, however, only when they are read against the background of Cardinal Frings's whole personality and all his work. It is the ignorance of this background that makes the majority of the evaluations of the Archbishop's conciliar initiatives so questionable. The Council is not some anomalous event in his life. It is not a detour from the course he had been following. It is rather its goal. He did not belong to those people who returned home and announced that one could now burn all the books written before, that one had to write completely new ones. He

---

2. Muggeridge, 66, 112. The author obviously does not count Rahner among the revolutionaries either; he is too deep, too original, too complex to be categorized so simply. He remains for her a puzzling and contradictory figure.

3. Muggeridge, 59.

was not the man of book burnings: he was himself too much the burned child for that — because of all that had happened earlier in Germany. On the contrary, if he wanted something, it was precisely to overcome the enthusiastic short-sightedness, the uncritical tendency to conform which forgets the whole in its fascination with what is latest. He wanted to overcome the attitude which, in St. Paul's phrase, allows itself to be tossed here and there by every wind and makes thinking depend on the opinion that comes up with the chance throw of the dice (Eph 4:14). He saw in this attitude — as Paul had seen — not progress but immaturity, and he certainly wanted to help overcome that.

I have gotten ahead of myself. It is time to turn to the Cardinal's conciliar speeches. Whoever reads them will detect in the general avoidance of the specialist's tone a remarkable theological training, and even more, the critical eye of the experienced pastor. While such formal aspects are easily observed, it is much more difficult to recognize a unified intention, a coherent conception in the whole. Anne Roche Muggeridge has without a doubt observed correctly that the positions did become stricter. The joy over the initial breakthrough that inspired the first interventions gave way to a sober realism that wanted to keep the individual forces in proper balance. Still, there was no discontinuity: the search for final results, which I would not want to deny, cannot offer a key adequate for the whole. I would, therefore, like to proceed differently in my analysis and point out four apparently different positions. The seeming or real differences in these positions both propose the question of the Archbishop's driving motive and his actual intention while also leading to an answer. There are, first of all, positions which one has to characterize as progressive in the context of the conciliar debates. There are also the positions which indeed lie close to the main progressive trend but still introduce various nuances. We also find statements which are chiefly of a pragmatic, pastoral nature, and finally, critical statements which clearly oppose the apparently progressive line.

2. The Four Types of Conciliar Speeches by Cardinal Frings

a. Two Formal Principles: Broad Participation and the Whole of Tradition

There are in particular two positions taken up by the Archbishop of Cologne which justify his reputation as a progressive: 1) his motion of seconding on the first day which led to a postponement of the elections for the commissions and thus to a much greater plurality in the composition of these organs than there would have been according to the original membership lists; 2) the speech of 8 November 1963, in which he called for a new procedure in the Holy Office. In both instances, positions were at issue which involved conciliar politics and pastoral concerns of the Church rather than theology. I have previously shown what was involved in the case of the Council elections: the broadest possible participation of the episcopate in the preparation of the texts — that is, the assurance that the Council be accountable in a spirit of catholicity.[4] In the speech on the procedures of the Holy Office, its important, difficult, and thorny service in the protection of the revealed truth is expressly recognized, but at the same time the Cardinal insists on the separation of administrative procedure and juridical process, as well as on the right of the accused to a judicial hearing and the possibility of defending himself. After the Council Cardinal Ottaviani pointed out explicitly that the speech only called attention once again to the legal principles which Benedict XIV had already formulated and that Frings's demand could achieve a revolutionary tone only in the especially emotional atmosphere in which the words were spoken.[5] In the properly theological speeches of

---

4. "Stimme des Vertrauens. Kardinal Frings auf dem Zweiten Vaticanum," N. Trippen and W. Mogge, *Ortskirche im Dienst der Weltkirche* (Cologne, 1976), 183-190, especially 184.

5. The text of the speech can be found in *Acta Synodalia S. Concilii Oecumenici Vaticani Secundi* II/V (Rome, 1973), 616ff. (Cited henceforth as *Acta.*) The interview with Cardinal Ottaviani was originally published on 13 April 1966, in the periodical *Gente;* French translation can be found in *La documentation catholique* 63 (1966): 837-844. The pertinent text in which Cardinal Ottaviani takes up and supports — and even extends — his critique of Cardinal Frings (without mentioning him by name) can be found on 838f. This passage can be found also in a German translation in a piece by L. Kaufmann, "Prophet Ottaviani?" *Orientierung* 39 (1975): 37.

Cardinal Frings, it was especially what he had to say in criticism of the working texts of the preparatory commissions that appeared startling and progressive. Actually, it was a question of breaking out from a particular way of doing theology and of seeking a new one. The Archbishop first of all criticized the texts for their language, which was too much the language of the schools. He was evidently concerned with the difference between the bishop's commission to preach and the special task of scientific theology. The council was not to publish a summa of theology; rather, without being bound to the forms of particular theological systems, it was to illuminate contemporary questions with the vision of faith. A second criticism aims more directly at content: Frings opposed the emphasis on magisterial sources from the nineteenth and twentieth centuries. He expected the perspective of an ecumenical council to be directed toward Scripture itself and the whole of tradition, including especially the Greek Fathers.[6] Here too we see at work his desire for a catholicity without shortcuts. One might even identify this desire as the distinctive theme characterizing all his influence on the Council. We will return again and again to this question of catholicity, in which his life's experience as a bishop can be summed up. Here he did not speak and act in the name of one trend or tendency, but rather as a pastor, as one speaking with the actual voice he had used in lifelong service in the Church. He in fact shunned that positivism based on the magisterium — on the most recent manifestations of which Louis Bouyer has recently made some informative remarks. In connection with the debates with Charles Curran, Bouyer uncovers an absurd positivism in that apparently progressive mentality which wants to adhere only to that in the Church which is expressly defined as infallible. Bouyer also tells of a French Dominican who identifies himself as a specialist in "Christian atheism" and who developed before an American seminar the claim that nothing binds the Christian to believe in God's existence. We believe *in* him, the learned man claimed, which means in the religious and moral values of faith, but an entity existing in itself which is God is a Platonic chimera and has nothing to do with biblical and Christian teaching. A brilliant French Jesuit was of the opinion that the historical existence of

6. His critique of the language of the schools can be found in the speech of 14 December 1962 (*Acta* I/III, 34). Concerning the narrow use of sources from tradition and especially the absence of the Greek Fathers, see the speech of 4 December 1962 (*Acta* I/IV, 219).

Jesus is an issue so full of doubts that it is absolutely useless to discuss something like the *how* of the Resurrection.

A careful thinker does not find it difficult to show that such formulations do not conflict unambiguously with any infallible definition. When Frings took issue with the narrowing of the vision to the more recent decisions of the magisterium, it was precisely his intention to cut short every sort of "shadow boxing" that abuses the thinker's arts of explanation in an effort to press forward to a theological way of thinking which draws from the entire Church's living faith. A progressivism which maintains that nothing preconciliar is any longer of interest today is exactly what Frings wanted to preclude by his criticisms. No, the whole is always of interest. Faith always creates from the whole. Thus, just as after the First Vatican Council and after Pius XII, the Greek Fathers, Augustine, and Thomas Aquinas remained as important as before, so also after the Second Vatican Council, the First Vatican Council remains important and Pius XII remains important. In this sense the progressivism of the Cardinal from Cologne is of the highest relevance: today we also cannot bear that mentality which forgets everything but the last twenty years — or still much more if possible. Today, too, the proclamation of the faith must be catholic — that is, it must live from the whole, draw again and again directly from the Bible, drink again and again from the great, pure sources of all times. Only then does faith remain great and wide; only then does it reach into those depths and grow to that height through which it binds heaven and earth. The dialectician's tricks with which one would free us from the burden of the mystery and seem to bring us right to the pinnacle of our time — such tricks do not survive the moment, on which alone they base themselves. Only the whole will suffice.

b. The Chief Problem with Content: Revelation, Scripture, Tradition

In addition to these more formal principles — freedom from individual theological systematizations and reference to the whole of faith's sources — there came two positions regarding content which must be similarly ranked as progressive in the atmosphere of 1962 and 1963. First, one must mention the controversy over the schema for the document on Revelation, which belonged to the most exciting events of the first session. It would take us too far afield to describe Cardinal Frings's efforts for a new working text, about which only very spotty and inaccurate reports are to be found in the literature.[7] I will restrict myself once again to an analysis of the speeches. At no point did Cardinal Frings espouse the theory of Geiselmann — in my eyes an insufficiently thought through and premature theory — which at the time was thought on all sides to be the cutting edge in theory on tradition and which represented for many the model of what the Council was supposed to say.[8]

Geiselmann himself has summarized his position in the formula "material completeness of Scripture." He thought he had found the reconciliation of the Catholic principle with the Protestant principle of *sola scriptura*. He was mistaken, for the principle of *sola scriptura* is a formal principle and for that reason then also valid materially, that is, with regard to content. This sequence cannot be reversed, as Geiselmann thought. One can reproduce his argument, albeit simplified, in something like the following: in point of fact, Catholic dogma also derives all its content from Scripture; therefore, Scripture as material principle is complete. However, if this were true, then it would ultimately mean the same as if one were to look on the Bible also as the formal principle. A controversy over this issue is no longer worth the trouble. Geiselmann's conclusion, however, is false in two respects. When pushed, one can describe Scripture as the encompassing material principle of Catholic theology in the sense that all dogmas must be linked back to Scripture. But the real question is, what kind of connection is it? The eager ones at that time wanted to deduce from the so-called material completeness of Scripture the notion that in the future every dogma must be proven from the Bible. But then one had logically to apply the requirement also to the past, that is, to all existing dogmas. If in a further step one finally understands "prove" to mean the

---

7. Something on the subject can be found in my article mentioned in note 4 (186f.). Interesting sidelights, which of course refer only to a part of the proceedings, can be found in Yves Congar, "Erinnerungen an eine Episode auf dem II. Vatikanischen Konzil," in *Glaube in Prozess: Christsein nach dem II. Vatikanum — Für Karl Rahner,* ed. E. Klinger and K. Wittstadt (Freiburg, 1984), 22-32; on 33-64, drafts of an alternative schema, the first draft of which was put together in Cardinal Frings's circle, are printed.

8. J. R. Geiselmann has explained his theory in detail in his book *Die Heilige Schrift und die Tradition* (Freiburg, 1962). I have presented my view of the question in K. Rahner and J. Ratzinger, *Offenbarung und Überlieferung* (Freiburg, 1964), 25-69.

consensus of exegetes, then it is clear that from then on there could be no more dogma. To this extent the issue of the material principle is a meaningless tautology in which the real question is obscured — namely, how does one come to a knowledge of what Scripture means; who is the actual subject of Scripture, its current bearer?

These are questions connected with the catchword "formal principle," and if one does not solve the question intended by it — how exegesis proceeds and becomes effective — one has explained absolutely nothing. The fascination with which Geiselmann's thesis was spread at the time shows how dangerous it is to make oneself dependent on theological insights and methods popular at a given moment. I think, however, that due to Cardinal Frings's service the Council did not fall into the trap. But that obviously could not put a halt to the slogan's negative effect as it spread through the channels of Church publicity. A crude version of Geiselmann's position, for which one cannot hold the Tübingen professor responsible, has moreover worked its way into the Church's consciousness. From then on it has largely been held that also in the Catholic Church only what can be proven from Scripture is valid. It seems to me that this thesis has contributed significantly to the post-conciliar crisis of the Catholic consciousness, which has become no longer sure of the Church's continuity with its past and which has felt compelled to question whether everything previous to the Council has ceased to be valid.

Finally, one must still ask: what then did Cardinal Frings actually say? Here also — and to this degree he was a "progressive" — he criticized the neo-scholastic position presented in the working text. But just as before, the criticism hits no less the post-conciliar positions just described. It is directed precisely against the tendency toward such premature conclusions which in the end are in line with a misunderstood neo-scholasticism. Frings criticized, first of all, a formulation in the working text and then went directly from there to the heart of the issue. The schema spoke of the "two sources of revelation," by which it meant Scripture and tradition. This expression can suffice, the Cardinal remarked, if one understands it strictly on the epistemological level: we experience what revelation is from Scripture and tradition. In this sense Frings confirmed the twofold character of the sources.

According to the comments of the Archbishop from Cologne, however, the formula is completely false if one looks at it on a metaphysical level, for there the sequence is reversed: revelation does not flow from Scripture and tradition, but both flow from revelation, which is their common source. Now, on first hearing, one can be inclined to consider this a learned game of semantics, and so it appeared to most of the Council Fathers, who did not know what to do with it and who wanted, insofar as they knew of the controversy, to count Frings on the side of Geiselmann. But in reality a crucial issue is at stake. For if one does not hold clearly that revelation precedes its objectifications in Scripture and tradition, remaining always greater than they, then the concept of revelation is reduced to the dimensions of the historical and simply human. From what is divine and great, which can arise in no human form but exceeds and bursts into something greater, there comes about a collection of texts and customs which are then themselves revelation.

If I equate revelation with the text so that the boundaries of the one perfectly coincide with the boundaries of the other, then it cannot grow and develop; then there is nothing living but rather something dead — having settled down *in illo tempore.* Then revelation is delivered up to historicism; it is subjected to human criteria. If, on the contrary, it is true that Scripture is the objectification of revelation which precedes it, which cannot be fully caught in any human word, then exegesis must look beyond the letter and read the text in connection with what is alive, must understand it in such a connection with life. Exegesis then certainly needs the historical method and its care, but this is not the whole. For if it is further true that what is living, revelation itself, is Christ, that Christ is still alive, and that he did not only live *in illo tempore,* then it is clear that the subject of revelation is precisely this Christ himself and that he is such through his Body with which he binds us irreversibly to that beginning *in illo tempore* and at the same time leads us forward to his "full maturity." Then also other methods must enter into exegesis, and above all the connection with life and experience in which Scripture is Scripture and more than Scripture. Then the speculations about the material completeness are themselves irrelevant because another formal principle rules. The Council's Constitution on Revelation has formulated this view with precision, but its message remains unheard to this day.[9] Because Geiselmann's position,

---

9. See my commentary in *Lexikon für Theologie und Kirche: Das Zweite Vatikanische Konzil, Kommentare Teil II* (Freiburg, 1967), cols. 498-528.

already premature in its conclusions, was so popularized, the notion that only what can be proven exegetically has binding character has been enthusiastically taken up after the Council. After the shipwreck of this position one is now all the less concerned with the literal meaning of the Bible and reads it according to a political or psychological hermeneutics — that is, one reads and confirms only one's own self. Frings's conciliar progressivism is again opposed to such progressivisms which from his viewpoint seem to be additional narrowings bringing to total collapse a point of departure that was already narrowed.

c. The Second Great Problem with Content: Collegiality

Now that I have presented the issue of revelation far beyond its due, I must and can be somewhat briefer with the second question of content which appeared, in the context of the Council, to be progressive. It is the question of collegiality, for the validity of which Cardinal Frings lent his emphatic support. Here also we easily recognize the guiding intention which we have already discovered in his previously analyzed speeches. He again opposed the whole breadth of the faith tradition to a theology whose memory seemed to reach back only to the First Vatican Council. He referred to the theory and the praxis of the Church Fathers not in order to indulge a romanticism for the distant past but in order to measure again and again the new developments against the spirit of the whole and to draw riches from that whole. Here too catholicity is the underlying motive.

Important references to theological epistemology also come into play. Cardinal Frings draws our attention to the principles of development and of analogy. Whoever approaches the Bible or the Fathers with a static concept of primacy or collegiality will have to acknowledge evidence of his error in both cases. Both themes must in this sense be handled in the same way. In both cases it is necessary to allow oneself to be taught by the texts and to follow the inner path by which the concept and the institution took shape. In both cases one can only learn from history by opening up the static concept and searching for its essential content so that one will be able to understand what still plays a role in the living concept. Finally, the speaker links primacy and collegiality together in their common goal: preservation of unity and truth.

One must, moreover, add to the speech on collegiality of 14 December 1963, the general speech on the concept of the Church from 29 September of the same year.[10] Frings establishes four crucial points here. 1) Sacramentality, he emphasizes, is the essence of the concept of the Church *(Ursakrament).* 2) He stresses that the sending of the apostles by Christ is continued in the Church's missionary task, in which the christological dynamic, as the dynamic of the gathering, goes on up to the time of the Lord's coming again. 3) He draws attention to Christ's passion and his poverty in order to point to the suffering aspect of the Church and its particular relation to the poor. 4) He finally makes us aware of the Church's relation to holiness, of the Church as communion of the saints. These are for him the elements which the Council should primarily have in mind when it describes the Church. All this was at that moment "progressive": it was the same progressivity which characterized theologians like de Lubac, Daniélou, Bouyer, and von Balthasar. Whoever grasps their intentions correctly will also understand why precisely these men set themselves most against a postconciliar progressivism which replaces theology's previous foreshortening of memory with a new form of amnesia, and takes it up as modern.

2. Nuanced Progressive and Pastoral Speeches

We have, then, characterized that group of speeches by Frings which one can count as "progressive" in the context of the Council. For the sake of brevity I would like to pass over the second type of speeches which I earlier called "progressive" but nuanced. Above all, the statement on the concept of the Church, which was just characterized and which was delivered in his own name as well as in the name of sixty-six German- and Scandinavian-language bishops on 14 September 1963, would represent this type of speech. We can therefore turn directly to the third type, primarily pastoral statements which belong practically with the second type because of their position in the conciliar debate. We will begin with the reform of the liturgy on which Frings expressed himself not in a fundamentally theological way but, so to speak, from

---

10. For the speech on collegiality, see *Acta* II/II, 493ff.; for that on the concept of Church, see *Acta* II/I, 343-346.

the viewpoint of the shepherd's practical experience. It would be an interesting task, one which has yet hardly been attempted, to investigate which widely disparate conceptions of the Council Fathers linked to which various motives led to liturgical reform. It would be incorrect to say that Frings's position coincided with the formulation which Cardinal Montini expressed in a just recently published letter to the Cardinal Secretary for State Cicognani. Montini complained in that letter that due to the complete absence of an organic program the Council was running the risk of being delivered up to chance. He pointed out — as symptomatic of this condition — that the schema on the liturgy was to be treated first, while such precedence did not reflect any corresponding need.[11] Cardinal Suenens, in his own plan for the Council, which found the support of Cardinals Döpfner, Montini, Siri, and Liénart, also saw the liturgical question as only part of his overall schema *De Ecclesia ad intra,* the discussion and postponement of which he conceived of as the task for the session. According to his proposal, the previously seen text on the liturgy was supposed to be reduced to a few chief questions which should be of equal importance for East and West.[12] Frings's position, as already indicated, was something different, though still not all that far from such formulations. In his memoirs the Cardinal from Cologne says that the schema on the liturgy recommended itself as the beginning of work "because it seemed relatively simple and appropriate to accustom the gathering to the jobs that lay ahead. It was said that everyone indeed could say something on the liturgy, and thus a lively exchange of ideas would come about. . . ."[13] The Cardinal's speeches on this theme during the Council move along this line. Frings expected from the liturgical reforms of the Council not some sort of revolutionary step forward; rather he wanted simply to see the fulfillment promised by popular piety of what Pius XII had begun, following in the footsteps of Pius X.[14] Thus, on the one hand, he wanted to see more room made for the vernacular, but on the other hand he thought that the Latin would not be done away with. At the

11. For the text of the letter, see the appendix (18-21) of Cardinal L.-J. Suenens, "Aux origines du Concile Vatican II," *Nouvelle Revue Théologique* 107 (1985): 3-21.

12. For Suenens's plan for the Council, see "Aux origines," 11-18.

13. J. Cardinal Frings, *Für die Menschen bestellt: Erinnerungen des Alterzbischofs von Köln* (Cologne, 1974), 256f.

14. Speech of 22 October 1962, *Acta* I/I, 309f.

same time he espoused an increased cultivation of Gregorian Chant which could enable believers of all languages to praise God with one voice *(una voce)*.[15] On the whole, Frings's concern was to open up to the Church of the whole world what the liturgical movement had already achieved in Germany. Such a plan did indeed entail an important tendency toward reform. The liturgy lived in some parts of the world in a sort of petrified ritual, overladen with other devotional practices, like a spring that had been sealed off. The reform, in the phrase of Pius XII, worked to purify and deepen the idea of "praying during Mass" to the idea of "praying the Mass." Frings did not want more. If that were to take place, it would mean a new springtime in the Church.

To Cardinal Frings's pastoral statements belong also what he had to say about the episcopal conferences. Here too he did not speak as a theologian but out of practical experience and with the realistic view of a man who had led the episcopal conferences of Fulda for more than a decade and a half. For Frings, a conference was a practical matter of working together and as such was of the greatest help. It should remain such, or it should become such where it was not as yet. But, according to Frings, one should not look for something else in it. In his memoirs the Cardinal points out that there were conferences at Fulda until the Council, but no "Conference" in the singular — that is, the conferences were events, not an institution. Consequently, they also functioned without statutes. Only late in their history did the President realize that there were statutes after all, dating from 1847, which had been preserved informally in the routine.[16] In his speech to the Council Fathers, Frings said, "The statutes were handed down through the praxis and are still valid. Resolutions of the conferences at Fulda [he explicitly uses the plural] had and have no juridical character. Each bishop guides his church according to his conscience and the norms of law. We have no Secretary General: aside from the President there is only one secretary who keeps the minutes. The rest of the work before and after the conference is carried out in the chancery of the President. Quite significant matters have come from our conferences in this free style."[17] Frings warns from his own experiences against putting all too

---

15. Ibid., 309f.
16. Frings, *Erinnerungen,* 238-246.
17. Speech on 13 November 1963, *Acta* II/V, 66-69. The quotation is from 66.

much weight on statutes and paragraphs: the important thing should not be chapter and verse but the "spirit which must be a spirit of freedom, of voluntariness, of brotherly love." He warns above all else against a Secretary General, for then bishops of smaller dioceses could soon become dependent; the diocese would no longer be run by the bishop, but by some far distant secretariat. Legally binding resolutions, if there must be any, must be kept to a minimum. Finally, the Cardinal entreats his confreres, "Esteemed Fathers, preserve in the national conferences the freedom of the individuals and the love of all so that the letter might not kill but the Spirit give life."[18] This was certainly Frings's most personal speech at the Council. Objectively considered, it was just as progressive as the others but imbued with still more of his own experience.

Similarly personal was the speech delivered on 5 November 1964, concerning relief organizations, which the Cardinal wanted to see extended internationally. In weeklong discussions and countless meetings, he had prepared the ground. Here he also spoke from rich experience, from an experience which had become a passion and moved ever more into the center of the bishop's actions and thoughts. At the same time we find ourselves at the source of his concept of catholicity, which was for him not simply an idea but a lived conviction which then translated itself again into thought. Thus far the pastoral speeches of the Council, completely unpretentious in their theology, show Frings's real personality most clearly, but they nonetheless also interpret the theological speeches and allow the inner unity of his personality and desires to become visible. They reveal the point around which the whole of his thought revolves: catholicity as the experience and program of a life becomes the floodlight illuminating also the theological problems and showing where the path lies. Here we can grasp what Cardinal Frings wanted to achieve at the Council, what motivated him.

In 1954 Frings had established the partnership of the Archdioceses of Cologne and Tokyo. Konrad Repgen remarks, "here for the first time a German diocese was linked institutionally in stable, direct missionary work in East Asia, bypassing Rome, which was consulted at the beginning but then always kept informed only after the fact. In its structure it was something fully new, almost revolutionary. None of his predeces-

18. Ibid., 67.

sors since the days of St. Maternus had designated anything even re-
motely comparable as the duty of the Cologne bishopric."[19] Following
the encouragement of his Vicar General Teusch, Frings established in
1959 and 1961 the two relief agencies, Misereor and Adveniat, in which
the same idea then took on new form and assumed new dimensions.
These decisions have their roots far back in the life of Frings. I am convinced that they reach back to the liberating experience of fraternity
with the cardinals from the victorious powers of World War II. In the
midst of that period in which all things German were held in general
contempt, they let their colleagues from the crushed country feel without reserve the sense of being one in the undisturbed Catholic community. One must certainly add as well the impression made by the great
relief efforts which the Germans received above all from their fellow
Christians in the United States. Now that Germany itself lived in abun-
dance, it became an inner responsibility for Frings to show similar solidarity with the other suffering peoples of the world. It seems to me
that these concrete experiences of Frings the shepherd offer the real
key to his desires at the Council.

A brief remark on what the Cardinal said about his conception of
relief. Both what was really revolutionary and what was at the same
time completely traditional in his proposal were given expression – the
links among local churches, which are coordinated by Rome but which
should still at the same time constitute direct links among the local
churches. The other distinctive aspect was that it should not be a matter of charitable help but of actual social work, which Frings – going
beyond everything merely institutional and financial – placed under
the leitmotiv "through their efforts . . . it is human beings who should
be formed."[20] Here a governing principle of The Second Instruction of
the Holy See on Freedom and Liberation is anticipated: that education
of the person to professional competence and to moral self-discovery is
the essence of all real liberation. Hence, with perfect logic, the final
goal of the relief efforts follows, which Frings formulated in the words,
"Let the one motive be to serve Christ in the brothers." It is then more

19. K. Repgen, "Kardinal Josef Frings (1887-1978) im Rückblick: Aktuelle Frage – ein
Jahr nach seinem Tod," *Zeitfragen*, published by the press of the Archdiocese of Cologne,
vol. 3, no. 3 (1980), 11.

20. Speech of 5 November 1964, *Acta* III/IV, 301-303; quotation is on 302, #2.

than a matter of external improvements when the center of every true relief consists in an education which is the liberation of the person to himself and thereby to the One who is closer to us than we ourselves.

3. Critique of Conciliar "Progressivism"

Finally, we must take a look at the interventions of the two last periods of the Council, which led Anne Roche Muggeridge to the diagnosis that the Cardinal had now begun to distance himself from Rahner. It is not clear why Rahner is moved into the foreground here, but we can leave that question aside. One can, however, make the following statement: as the Cardinal during the first period of the Council was critical of the working texts formulated primarily out of the neo-scholastic tradition, so he now showed himself critical of the texts which smacked of a hasty modernity and likewise could not stand up against the criteria formulated in 1962. Without wanting even to outline a comprehensive analysis of the speeches, I would like to name four critical themes that appear here. One can see, first of all, in the discussion of the schema on Religious Freedom as well as in the discussion on the Church in the Modern World, the rejection of every romantic attitude toward modernity which adopts the slogan, "Let's carry out our magnificent work all the way to the very end" and forgets the ambivalence of the new developments, knowing only how to evaluate them as "progress."[21] In opposition to a linear concept of progress, which explains the undeniable advance in mankind's technological capability simply or even as a kind of automatic dynamism in history leading up to the Kingdom of God, the Archbishop emphasizes the different levels of human existence, especially the difference between divine salvation and human progress. Frings did not hesitate to speak in this context of a very dangerous confusion in the prepared schema.[22]

Frings had already provided the theological foundation for this criticism in his speech of 27 October 1964, in which he approved the rejection of a spiritualizing Platonism but at the same time rejected a

21. Speech of 15 September 1965, *Acta* IV/I, 201-203; Speech of 24 September 1965, *Acta* IV/II, 405f.
22. 24 September 1965, *Acta* IV/II, 406, #2.

theology of the Incarnation that did not correspond to the biblical evidence: "Earthly advances do not transfer directly to the Kingdom of God," he said at the time and offered as justification for his statement that the Incarnation only reaches its goal in the cross and resurrection and that all incarnation needs this Easter passage, this mystery of the suffering Passover.[23] The three stages of creation, Incarnation, and Passover must be seen each in their dynamic relation, each with its own weight and each in relation to the others. Only in this way does the whole of the Christian synthesis come into view. Literally, his formulation was, "For the Christian life in the world three revealed truths are creation, which teaches us to love the things of the world as God's work; the Incarnation, which spurs us on to dedicate to God all the things of the world; cross and resurrection, which leads us in the imitation of Christ to sacrifice and continence with regard to the things of the world."[24]

Here a third theme of these speeches is already touched upon. In response to a somewhat loose theological language, Frings, who in 1962 had spoken out for a non-professorial language, now presses hard for a precision of concept — both concerning the concept of "world" and the concept of "freedom" — and thus prevents a misunderstanding of his call for a pastoral language.[25] His distinctions in both concepts have not lost their relevance even for the debates of today. Along the same line lies his criticism of an imprecise concept of the "People of God," which he presented on 24 September 1965.[26]

The fourth group of critical speeches treats the formation of concepts in the realm of ecumenism. Already on 28 November 1963 — that is, just three weeks after the famous speech on the Holy Office — Frings had described the Council as a school of the Holy Spirit, in which we are learning something new and so as learners have spoken a decisive yes to ecumenism. He described the ecumenical movement as the work of the Holy Spirit, which we must necessarily further. But he spoke also

23. *Acta* III/V, 562f.; quotation on 562, #2.

24. Ibid., 563.

25. Concerning the concept of freedom, see *Acta* IV/I, 202, in *Textus scripto traditus* #3a. This is the only time that Frings gave along with his speech detailed criticism of particular points and proposals for improving the schema. Concerning the concept of the world, see *Acta* IV/II, 405, #2.

26. *Acta* IV/II, 496, #3.

of dangers and announced that his speech would consider three sensitive points. I will pick only the first: he required that it be completely clear that the one, holy, catholic Church not be awaited only as some sort of super-denomination formed from the coordination of the churches. Rather, it must be clear that Christ himself has founded her, namely on Peter, that she is always in need of renewal and will be glorious only through the final espousal to the Lord — but that still in her pilgrimage she exists unshakable.[27] We do not create her; Christ has created her, as he alone could and can do. Although Frings had already emphasized what is unchanging in the realm of ecumenism among Christians, he actually felt bound to warn of forgetting the necessary critique of religions in the dialogue with non-Christian religions, that is, of overlooking the errors which are mixed in with the truth of Christ present in these religions.[28] The fact that Frings already in 1963 referred to the sensitive points in ecumenism is only one sign of how very true he remained to himself in his fundamental position during the four sessions. He remained consistent precisely in that he showed himself at the end just as critical and as open as he was at the beginning.

4. The Spirit of Cardinal Frings's Conciliar Speeches

But what then is this basic position really? What did Frings ultimately want at the Council? Again we find ourselves confronting this initial question after having taken the long way around through the conciliar speeches. The fundamental pastoral and at the same time theological motivation which ultimately guided the Cardinal has already become clear: his keen sense for catholicity, which is not only a vertical link with the pope but a horizontal link with the bishops and mutual responsibility for unity and love. If one wants to go further and to characterize an inner desire which stands behind the apparently liberal position of the Archbishop, it seems to me that a reference to Cardinal Newman's attitude can best clarify the question of which battle Frings wanted to fight here. Newman had unreservedly accepted the definitions of the First Vatican Council which in essence fully coincided with the insights which

27. *Acta* II/VI, 194, #1.
28. Speech of 28 September 1964, in *Acta* III/II, 583; in *Textus scripto traditus* 584, #2.

had led him to Catholicism. But nevertheless he still had looked forward at the same time to a new council which would not overturn these definitions but explain and expand them.[29] When he received the cardinal's hat in Rome, he said that for thirty, forty, fifty years he had stood to the best of his ability against the spirit of liberalism in religion. Never before, he declared, did the holy Church need champions against liberalism so painfully as now.[30] That the Church is founded on authority and not on personal preference was the basic insight of his long Christian path. But because this authority on its part rests not on positivistic conclusions but on trust in tradition, trust in the God who reveals himself, it does not for him contradict the conscience, which is God's organ in man. Newman refers to a statement of the Fourth Lateran Council: "Whoever acts against his conscience loses his soul." Conscience in the proper sense — not confused with personal preference — is the basis for papal authority.[31] With this said, the unwavering fighter against liberalism could now say, "It must be borne in mind, that there is much in the liberal theory that is good and true: for example, not to say more, the precepts of justice, truthfulness, sobriety, self-command, benevolence. . . . It is not till we find that this array of principles is intended to supersede, to block out, religion, that we must pronounce it to be evil."[32]

It seems to me that one cannot formulate any more precisely the human and Christian position of Cardinal Frings than it is formulated in these words of Cardinal Newman. Frings was concerned with Catholic generosity, which stands in essential contradiction to ideological liberalism. He wanted to lead the Church beyond all external obedience to authority to a trust which has the source of its strength in the insight of a believing conscience. If he argued for more freedom in theology, he wanted to see it more inclusive of what it hears from the whole tradition and at the same time more critical, more sober — this was the background. Whether he correctly evaluated the historical forces which were colliding at the Council is another question. His guiding intentions are independent of that.

29. See Charles Stephen Dessain, *John Henry Newman* (London: Nelson, 1966), 139-140.

30. Dessain, 165.

31. See Newman's Letter to the Duke of Norfolk, published in 1874, and the comments in Dessain, 140-146, especially 145.

32. Dessain, 165.

In conclusion, we must go one step further. In my contribution for the commemoration of the Cardinal's ninetieth birthday, I already referred to a scene which has left its print indelibly in my memory and which seems even more important as the years pass. Before departing for the Council Frings went with his group into the Cologne cathedral in order to pray. When they were finished he had someone show him the place in the crypt where he would one day be buried and he stood there reflecting. It seems that only from this scene can one grasp what most fundamentally guided the old Archbishop. I would like to put it simply: Cardinal Frings was a God-fearing man. And that is decisive. I have for a long time reflected often on what it really means when the Bible says again and again, "The fear of God is the beginning of wisdom." For a long time I had great difficulty penetrating the meaning of the sentence. But now I am beginning to grasp its meaning in such a real way from its converse that I feel I can almost touch its truth with my hands. For what is played out before our eyes can be put into the words, "The fear of man — that is, the end of the fear of God — is the beginning of all folly." Today, the fear of God has practically disappeared from the list of virtues, for the image of God has been subjected to marketing strategies. In order to be marketable, God must be represented in just the opposite way so that no one would fear him at all. Fear would be the last thing that should come out of our presentation of him. That reversal of values, which was the real sickness of the history of religions before Christ, is thus spreading again and again in our society and in the middle of the Church. For then too the opinion had come to predominate that one need not fear the good God, the real God, because from him as the Good only good could come. Concerning him one can be completely free of worry: one must rather guard against the evil powers. Only they are dangerous, and one must therefore try in every way to be on good terms with them. In this maxim the essence of idolatry is to be seen as the decline of liturgy. We ourselves stand in the middle of this idolatry. The good God obviously does not harm us; one needs to show him nothing more than some kind of primitive trust. But there are only too many of the dangerous powers around us, and one must try to hold out against them. So people both within the Church and outside it, high and low, behave no longer with their eyes on God and his guidelines, which are after all unimportant, but with their eyes on the human powers so that they might get through this world at least partially happily. They no longer act for what exists, for truth, but for appearance — for what one thinks of them and how one imagines them. The tyranny of appearance is the idolatry of our day, and it is also to be found in the Church. The fear of men is the beginning of all foolishness, but the fear of men rules unshakably where the fear of God has retreated.

Cardinal Frings was God-fearing and therefore wise. God was for him a real measuring standard, the standard against which he had to prove himself. It is out of this conviction that he acted. I would not know how to describe his most personal attitude better than with the words which Gregory of Nyssa placed at the end of his *Life of Moses:* "This is true perfection: not to avoid a wicked life because like slaves we servilely fear punishment, nor to do good because we hope for rewards. . . . On the contrary, disregarding all those things for which we hope and which have been reserved by promise, we regard falling from God's friendship as the only thing dreadful and we consider becoming God's friend the only thing worthy of honor and desire."[33] Cardinal Frings looked toward this alone as fearful and this alone as valuable, and that is his enduring message to us.

Translated by Peter Verhalen, O. Cist.

---

33. *De vita Moysis,* PG 44, 429 C-D; English trans. by Abraham J. Malherbe and Everett Ferguson, *The Life of Moses* (New York: Paulist Press, 1978), 137.

Peace and Justice in Crisis:
The Task of Religion

In this paper I have been asked to speak about the present-day crisis of peace and justice and to indicate the contribution which religion can make to the resolution of the problem. Now, there is no such thing as religion in the abstract; it always has a concrete historical form. So my starting point will not be a general concept of religion. Instead I shall direct my questions concretely to my own faith as a Christian and a Catholic. What can our faith, in its true and original character, do to help us resolve these problems? Perhaps also, what can and must it not do if it is to remain true to what it is? To make the first half of the discussion more manageable, I would like to define the issue somewhat more narrowly and precisely. I do not intend to offer an empirical analysis of today's crisis of peace and justice in all its different facets. Given the scale of the thing, it would fill a whole book and is perhaps an impossible undertaking for one person on his own, even supposing he has more specialized knowledge and opportunities for research than I have. My intention is not descriptive but, in the broad sense of the term, normative. In other words, by looking at the actual phenomena, I want to see what peace is, what justice is, and how the two are connected, in order to understand our ethical task. However, such an analysis does not take place "within the limits of reason alone" (to use the words of

---

This article was originally presented as a lecture at the Fifth Christian-Islamic Consultation at the Orthodox Centre at Chambésy, France (12 December 1988). English publication in *Communio: International Catholic Review* 16, no. 1 (Winter 1989): 540-551.

Kant), but in the light of what the Christian faith can tell us about the two themes, that is to say, in an openness of reason to knowledge. Reason does not itself simply produce the knowledge, and yet the knowledge, once given, is real knowledge. In this respect religion has a contribution to make in the analysis of the phenomena as well as in the highlighting of the ethical imperatives.

I.

Our theme links peace and justice. The crisis of the one is the crisis of the other, and vice versa. When justice begins to falter, peace falters too. In fact, one might say that wars always break out when there is no clear or compelling criterion of justice. I think this becomes evident when we consider the four ways in which peace is actually threatened in today's world.

1. The first threat to peace, the one that most preoccupies public awareness, is the danger of world war, the danger that the great power blocks into which the world is divided would unleash against each other those weapons of mass destruction which in all probability would bring about the destruction of the human race.

2. The second way in which peace is endangered and destroyed consists in the so-called "classical" wars. In the last forty years, in different parts of the world, these have taken place in unending succession: wars in the Middle East, in Africa, in Southeast Asia, the war between Argentina and Great Britain, and so on.

3. The third form might be called the state's loss of internal peace. This takes two distinct and yet interrelated forms:

a) The so-called liberation movements struggle for power when they regard the state's legal power as one of injustice. They see rebellion against the order of the state, a rebellion in itself destructive of peace, as a commitment to justice and thus the only way to establish peace, in fact, a duty in the cause of true peace. Interestingly, a large number of those people who consider themselves to be pacifists with regard to the first type of war (world war) look upon this other form of struggle, often very cruel and bloody, as something really sacred, a higher form of the *bellum justum,* an active form of peace. At the same time the heart of the modern crisis becomes clear — the loss of a common criterion of justice.

During the middle ages, after years of multifarious feuding between families and towns, after an era of widespread arbitrary justice, a general peace broke out when the individual legal persons renounced their power. These worked out their relationships with each other within a commonly accepted law of the land *(Landrecht)* and transferred the protection of that law to central authorities — the "judiciary" and its various organs.[1] The result of this was a clear separation of thirty essentially different kinds of power: the state's organs of law have means of implementation which are accepted, within the framework of the peace thus created, as the force of law. They are no longer the "power" which for one person is the means by which he tries to safeguard his rights but for another is an act of injustice to be resisted. Instead they protect the rights of all. They constitute "legal power," something fundamentally different from the law-breaking power of violence. Today a process is under way which may amount to the reversal of the medieval renunciation of power. The reversal could have various causes. Perhaps the state has ceased to defend justice and is palming off arbitrary whim in the guise of justice. On the other hand, it may be that ideological groups are creating their own partial ideas of justice, thereby breaking away from the universality of justice, in order to achieve their own ends. What underlies both is an ethical and religious revolution. On the question of what is right and wrong, consensus has collapsed.

b) We have just said that the reversal of the renunciation of power may be the fault of the state when it passes off injustice as law. Or it may be due to the law-breaking partiality of a group bent on making its own rights the only law, which means that it too legitimizes injustice. Depending on which of the two it is, people will talk of a liberation movement or of terrorism. Of course, every form of terrorism will present itself as a liberation movement, and when there is no clear criterion of justice, it can do that very easily.

It is worth remembering that, in the first phase of German terrorism, when the phenomenon had hardly affected other Western countries, there was a widespread tendency in the West to regard the terrorists as true freedom-fighters, victims of a newly emerging state of

---

1. Cf. H. Maier, *Worauf Frieden beruht* (Freiburg, 1981), 20f.; U. Duchrow, *Christenheit und Weltverantwortung* (Stuttgart, 1970), 533ff.

totalitarianism. Only when the phenomenon became international and people had the chance to see the "freedom struggle" at close quarters did it become indisputably clear that here was a brutal violence, contemptuous of humanity, and that its idealized, anarchic freedom was conceived chiefly as a freedom to be violent and a freedom from law. On the other hand, people in Europe are always enthusiastically ready to celebrate every kind of terrorism in the Third World as a liberation movement. For more than twenty years Helmut Kuhn has been sharpsightedly explaining the reason for this: "As order divorced from justice becomes terrible, so unjust prosperity, obtained by exploitation and the suffering of others, becomes offensive. This is the reason for the bad conscience which spoils the Western world's enjoyment of its post-war prosperity and finds no solace in the thought of giving foreign aid."[2] What is more, though the initial phase of European terrorism may be credited, despite everything, with a certain idealism, at least an idea of something, today the disintegration of justice, and with it the unleashing of violence, is proceeding apace. The worldwide network of drug trafficking, coupled with prostitution, arms trafficking, and the old criminal syndicates, is gradually becoming a threat to humanity. The loss of justice, without a great open war, is destroying peace from the inside and more effectively than the classic wars were ever able to do. It may be that, from an unexpected quarter and in an unusual form, something of the dimensions of a world war is developing.

4. The fourth way in which peace is destroyed has already been hinted at above; in fact, it is closely connected with what we have just said. It can happen that a state falls into the hands of groups which palm off injustice as justice, destroying justice from top to bottom, and thereby, in their own way, creating a peace which in reality is a dictatorship. Such a state, by the methods of modern mass-domination, can produce total subjugation and so give an impression of order and tranquility, while people of uncompromising conscience are thrown into jail, forced into exile, or murdered. As Augustine asserted emphatically, a state without justice is a great band of robbers.[3] Hitler's *Reich* was such a robber state. Outwardly, it may look as if there is peace, but it is

---

2. H. Kuhn, *Der Staat. Eine philosophische Darstellung* (Munich, 1967), 193.

3. *De civitate Dei* IV, 4 (*Corpus Christianorum* XLVII, 101): *Remota itaque iustitia quid sunt regna magna latrocinia? quia et latrocinia quid sunt nisi parua regna?*

the peace of the graveyard. The tragedy is that, under total tyranny, there is no possibility at all of a war of liberation. Dictatorship quietly sets itself up as the triumph of peace. This is what the New Testament means when it predicts that the Antichrist will appear as the harbinger of "peace and security."[4] Here we confront the paradoxical aspect of our subject. What poses as definitive peace may well be the total destruction of peace.

2.

The heart of our contemporary problems can be seen in the third aspect of the crisis. Here again it becomes clear how closely connected religion is with peace and justice. We have shown that today peace is breaking up *within* nations, that agreement about what is right and wrong has collapsed. Now what holds a society together and gives it peace is law. The fact that peace between nations has constantly been wrecked by war is connected with the lack of an effective international law, a law which does not only order a society on the inside, but is also commonly recognized among the nations as their binding norm; they submit to it, whether or not it be to their advantage. Now if law ceases to have a commonly accepted content, it becomes powerless, and the distinction between legal power and wrongful power is blurred. The representatives of legal power become "pigs," and the representatives of wrongful power the champions of liberty. Law without proof of identity looks like arbitrary whim, and all that is left is power: *Homo homini lupus.*

And so the question of peace is in practice identical with the ques-

---

4. 1 Thes 5:3 presents the rule of the slogan "peace and security" as a sign of the imminent end of the world, but it does not link it with the figure of Antichrist. Later reflection does make the connection, absolutely correctly in my opinion. Soloviev does it in a very penetrating way in his story about the Antichrist. Soloviev's Antichrist is the author of a book that has aroused worldwide attention. Its title is "The Open Way to Peace and Prosperity in the World." In the manifesto which he issues after his proclamation as world ruler, he says: "Peoples of the world! The promises have been fulfilled! World peace is ensured forever. . . ." Also important is the penetrating interpretation of the Antichrist traditions in J. Pieper, *Über das Ende der Zeit. Eine geschichtsphilosophische Betrachtung* (Munich, 1980), 113-136.

tion of law, and the real question for the survival of the human race is, therefore, the question of what constitutes the foundations and unalterable content of law. But where and how can an answer be found to the question? Or, rather, let us put it the other way round: why has the distinction between right and wrong ceased to be obvious to us? Why can we not differentiate them? These questions require us to consider the foundation and fashioning of law in the modern world. Of course, once again this cannot take the form of a historical analysis. Instead, I shall try to focus on a few decisive points. As far as I can see, there are three.

1. First, there are the famous words of Thomas Hobbes: *Auctoritas, non veritas facit legem.*[5] The Socratic question about what right and wrong really are, in themselves and according to the inner truth of things, independently of all traditions and enactments of law, is dismissed as impractical.[6] The law is not based on the discernible reality of right and wrong, but on the authority of the person with the power to enact it. It comes about through legislation, and in no other way. Its inner protection is thus the power to push it through, not the truth of being. This thesis enabled various things to happen. First of all, it helped political rule to become independent of the various other powers in medieval society. It was used to support the claims of absolute monarchies. But it also became the axiom of legal positivism, which has been able to establish itself widely since the nineteenth century. The consequences are far-reaching. Now one government can declare to be legal what its neighbor makes illegal. At the same time, in the minds of a large number of politicians today (in other words, the legislative *auctoritas*), this is modified to mean that the law has to mirror, and to translate into norms, the value-judgments actually found in society. When majority opinion becomes in this way the only real source of law and the essential criterion of *auctoritas,* the paradox is not in any way diminished. The man condemned today may see himself as the pioneer of the law of tomorrow and so feel justified to use every means at his

---

5. M. Mettner, "Friede," *Neues Handbuch theologischer Grundbegriffe* I, ed. P. Eicher (Munich, 1981), 404-431, here 421. Cf. on Hobbes, H. Maier, "Hobbes," *Klassiker des politischen Denkens* I, ed. Maier, Rausch and Denzer (Munich, 1969), 351-375.

6. Still important for what it says about the nature and permanent validity of the Socratic question, see R. Guardini, *Der Tod des Sokrates* (Berlin, 1943; recent edition, Mainz-Paderborn, 1987). Cf. also Kuhn, *Der Staat,* 24ff.

disposal to usher in the future, of which he regards himself as the custodian. If truth is as inaccessible as is here supposed, then there is no distinction in reality between right and wrong, no distinction between rightful and wrongful power, but only the pressure of the momentarily stronger group, the supremacy of the majority.

2. This notion of law is matched by an idea of peace, which one might sum up as follows: *Utilitas, non veritas facit pacem*. In similar fashion to Adam Smith, Immanuel Kant developed his doctrine of perpetual peace largely along these lines: "The spirit of commerce sooner or later takes hold of every people, and it cannot exist side by side with war. And of all the powers (or means) at the disposal of the power of the state, financial power can probably be relied on most. Thus states find themselves compelled to promote the noble cause of peace. . . . And wherever in the world there is a threat of war breaking out, they will try to prevent it by mediation, just as if they had entered into a permanent league for this purpose."[7] In other words, it is a question of making egotism, man's strongest and most reliable power and the source of his conflicts, into a real instrument of peace, because it is precisely egotism that makes peace seem more useful than war. Realistic politics will doubtless take account of this view and see it as an element in the peacemaking process. But on its own, as history since Kant adequately proves, it is insufficient for the building of perpetual peace.

3. The two ideas just mentioned (*auctoritas* and *utilitas*) present themselves in our post-metaphysical age. In a situation in which the unknowability of the true and man's incapacity for the good seem to have become absolute certainties, the attempt is made to build justice and peace on the foundation of authority and utility. Opposed to these two post-metaphysical ideas, the political effects of which are obvious, is a more strongly metaphysical current of thought. I am thinking of the three fundamental rights laid down by John Locke in his *Second Treatise of Government* (1690): life, freedom, property. The background to this is *Magna Carta*, the *Bill of Rights*, and ultimately the natural law tra-

---

7. I. Kant, *Zum ewigen Frieden*. The edition I consulted was that of the Wissenschaftliche Buchgesellschaft, vol. 6 (Darmstadt, 1964), 226. For an English translation, see *Kant's Political Writings*, ed. H. Reiss (Cambridge, 1970), 114. Cf. Kuhn, *Der Staat*, 351ff.; Mettner, "Friede," 422.

dition.[8] Here is a quite explicit claim that the rights of the person precede the state's enactments of law. Locke's way of expressing the rights of man doctrine is clearly directed against the state. It is of revolutionary significance. Not surprisingly, long before Marx, the Enlightenment developed a revolutionary tradition of its own. The old doctrine of the just war turned into the doctrine of a struggle for perpetual peace to be conducted in the form of worldwide civil war.[9] This gives an inkling of the ambivalence of the rights of man doctrine. When the concept of freedom is hypertrophied and the state is regarded essentially as an enemy, peace does not have a chance. But there is a sound core to the idea of human rights, and so it continues to be a protective barrier against positivism and a guide to the truth. There is something that is right in itself, and this constitutes the true bond between men, because it stems from our common nature.

Attempting to uncover the roots of the crisis of justice and peace shows us what can heal it. Law can only be the effective power of peace when the yardstick for measuring it is not in our hands. The law is molded, not created, by us. In other words, there can be no foundation for law without transcendence. When God and the basic pattern of human existence laid down by him is ousted from public consciousness and relegated to the private, merely subjective realm, the concept of law dissolves into thin air and with it, the foundation of peace.

3.

This brings us to the third part of our discussion, the contribution which religion can and should make to peace. I have already indicated above why I am taking religion concretely to mean the Church. I think it is necessary to distinguish between what the Church must do for peace and what she must not and cannot do.

The Church's first task in this area is to keep alive, in fidelity to her

---

8. Important on this point and what follows is Kuhn, *Der Staat*, 262-266. Cf. also E. W. Böckenförde and R. Spaemann, eds., *Menschenrechte und Menschenwürde* (Stuttgart, 1987), especially the contribution of G. Stourzh, "Die Begründung der Menschenrechte im englischen und amerikanischen Verfassungsdenken des 17. und 18. Jahrhunderts," 78-90.

9. Cf. Mettner, "Friede," 422f.

holy tradition, the basic criterion of justice and to detach it from the arbitrariness of power. What her great founders have seen and said, what Jesus and his witnesses saw and said, the Church must carry through the years as a great light for the human race. In each generation, she must shine that light on present-day questions and offer the Word given to her as the answer to the problems of the age. She must carry conviction and help men to see with and through Jesus what they cannot see by their own powers. She must ensure that in the conflict between *utilitas* and *veritas*, between *auctoritas* and *veritas*, truth does not founder. Man has been given an organ for apprehending truth as well as an organ for determining utility. There is nothing wrong with utility, but when it is made absolute, it becomes a force for evil. Utility destroys itself when it disregards truth. The same is true of *auctoritas*. The trouble is that the organ of utility and the organ of power are more palpable and more immediate in their effects than the organ of truth. That is why the organ of truth needs assistance, needs support. This is what the Church's task ought to be: to give this otherwise all too easily suppressed faculty the strength it needs.

The task of the Church in this area is, therefore, first and foremost "education," taking that word in the great sense it had for the Greek philosophers. She must break open the prison of positivism and awaken man's receptivity to the truth, to God, and thus to the power of conscience. She must give men the courage to live according to conscience and so keep open the narrow pass between anarchy and tyranny, which is none other than the narrow way of peace. In society she must create the conviction which can support good law. For, though we just now rejected the idea of majority opinion as the source of law, it is also clear that law cannot be permanently effective unless it has some kind of public credibility. In this consideration, it must appear as a highly questionable development that the modern administration of justice has quite publicly ceased to regard moral and religious values as goods deserving of legal protection; it seems to think that only material goods and the libertarian freedom of the individual need defense. In this consideration, it must appear as a highly questionable development that the same holds true in the Church. Hardly anyone looks upon faith as a good deserving of protection, at least not when it is in conflict with individual freedom or public opinion.

Alongside this primary task of creating conviction, forming conscience, and fashioning community as a space for peace, is the mission of the Church's office-bearers, supported by the conviction of the faithful, to speak out publicly on questions of the moment and to be advocates of peace. In our own times, this has been taken up with great passion. In addition to the classical channels of communication in the Church, many kinds of commissions and institutions are developing which dedicate themselves passionately to the question of peace and try to come up with the right words in reply. Not everything that comes to light by this means is enlightened. But the concern itself is, without doubt, a proper part of one of the Church's real tasks. What the Church has to remember is that, though the sources of law have been entrusted to her safekeeping, she does not have any specific answers to concrete political questions. She must not make herself out to be the sole possessor of political reason. She points out paths for reason to follow, and yet reason's own responsibilities remain.

All this comes together in the Church's most interior and yet also most human task: the task of making, not just talking about, peace, in deeds of love. No social service of the state can replace Christian love in both its spontaneous and organized forms. In fact, social service totally disintegrates when it loses the inspiration of the love that comes from faith. The Church's fidelity to her true nature is shown in her ability to support human beings in the vocation to love, to bring the vocation of love to maturity, and to give it concrete form in the life of the community. Through the power of love, the Church must serve the poor, the sick, the lost, the oppressed. She must go into prison, into the suffering of mind and body, as far as the dark way of death. In areas torn by the strife which the human race always has experienced and always will experience, the Church must give men the strength to survive and, with the power of forgiveness, awaken the capacity to make a new start. Only the man who can forgive can build and preserve peace.[10]

All this goes to show the limits of the Church's task and powers. She cannot enforce peace. She could not do it in the past, and she cannot do it in the future. She must not be transformed into a kind of political peace movement, whose only *raison d'être* would be the attaining of perpetual world peace. The planned "peace council" of religions is, there-

10. On the connection of peace and forgiveness, see H. Schlier, "Der Friede nach dem Apostel Paulus," *Der Geist und die Kirche* (Freiburg, 1980), 117-133, especially 133.

fore, because of the nature of the Church, an impossibility. The leaders of the Church have no authority to take direct political action. They have not received a mandate for it from the faithful, certainly not from the Lord himself. In fact, one ought rather to say that the attempt to bring about a worldwide empire of peace through a worldwide union of religions is perilously close to the third temptation of Jesus: "All the kingdoms of the world I will give you, if you fall down and worship me" (cf. Mt 4:9).[11] In this way of thinking, world peace almost inevitably becomes the *Summum bonum,* to which everyone submits, and for whose attainment all other religious acts and values are mere means. But a God who becomes the means to supposedly higher ends is no longer God; in fact, he has given away his divinity to something higher, whose cause he must serve. It is obvious that peace established in this way is, of its very nature, in danger of turning into either the totalitarianism that allows only one way of thinking or worldwide civil war.

Consequently, the Church does less, not more, for peace if she abandons her own sphere of faith, education, witness, counsel, prayer, and serving love, and changes into an organization for direct political action. In so doing, she blocks access to the well-springs from which the powers of peace and reconciliation continually flow. Precisely because the utmost must be done for peace, the Church must remain true to her real nature. Only when she respects her limits is she limitless, and only then can her ministry of love and witness become a call to all men. What the Church ultimately has to contribute to peace has been persuasively summed up, I think, in some words of Metropolitan Damaskinos. I endorse them without qualification and so would like to conclude by quoting them:

> It is my considered opinion that, over and above her social service, the contribution of the Orthodox Church to peace, freedom, justice, and brotherhood among the nations consists in a witness of

---

11. Pieper, *Über das Ende der Zeit,* 123, quotes in a similar context the statement: "A world organization might be what ushers in that most deadly and invincible of all tyrannies, the final reign of Antichrist." "The drawback of a world state embodying the Kantian ideal of there being no more real 'external wars' is that in place of war there would be police operations which would take the form of pest control" (124). Cf. Mettner, "Friede," 355: "It is as martyr that the Church is most truly herself. But as an organization for creating fraternity among men she founders on the earthly supremacy of politics."

love. . . . The Church's role cannot be identified with any kind of political strategy or with the political expediency of the authorities or governments among which her peoples live. In this context the Orthodox Church's scope for initiative and action is restricted. Her witness and presence bring with them dangers which may lead her leaders to martyrdom. . . . But it is precisely this love that is ready for martyrdom which ultimately strengthens the will of the Orthodox Churches. It enables them, in collaboration with their brethren in the other Christian Churches and confessions, to bear witness — the witness of faith and love — in a world which perhaps has more need of it than ever.[12]

Translated by John Saward

---

12. Metropolitan Damaskinos Papandreous, "Contribution de l'Église orthodoxe à la réalisation des idéaux chrétiens de paix, de liberté, de fraternité et d'amour entre les peuples, et la suppression des discriminations raciales," *Weisheit Gottes — Weisheit der Welt. Festschrift für J. Ratzinger,* vol. 2 (St. Ottilien, 1987), 1333-1343, here 1342f.

Communio: A Program

When the first issue of the *International Catholic Review: Communio* appeared at the beginning of 1972, there were two editions, one in German and one in Italian. A Croatian edition was also conceived at the outset. A preface by Franz Greiner served as the introduction to the German edition. Common to the two editions was the fundamental theological contribution of Hans Urs von Balthasar "Communio — A Programme." When we read these pages twenty years later, we are astonished at the relevance of what was then said. Its effect could still be explosive in the contemporary theological landscape. Of course, we could ask to what degree the review retained its guiding principles and what can be done now to do greater justice to them. An examination of conscience of this sort cannot, however, be the topic of my talk. I will only try to refresh our memory and strengthen the resolve which was present at the beginning.

The Origins of the Review *Communio*

To achieve this goal, it may be helpful to reexamine for a moment the formation of the review. In spite of many obstacles, it appears today in

---

This article originally appeared as "Communio — ein Programm," *Internationale katholische Zeitschrift: Communio* 21, no. 5 (September 1992): 454-463. English publication in *Communio: International Catholic Review* 19, no. 3 (Fall 1992): 436-449.

thirteen languages. *Communio* can no longer be removed from the contemporary theological conversation. At the beginning, Hans Urs von Balthasar's initiative was not aimed at founding a journal. The great theologian from Basel had not participated in the event of the Council. Considering the contribution that he could have made, one must admit a great loss. But there was also a good side to his absence. Balthasar was able to view the whole from a distance, and this gave him an independence and clarity of judgment which would have been impossible had he spent four years experiencing the event from within. He understood and accepted without reservation the greatness of the conciliar texts, but also saw the roundabout fashion to which so many small-minded men had become accustomed. They sought to take advantage of the conciliar atmosphere by going on and on about the standard of faith. Their demands corresponded to the taste of their contemporaries and appeared exciting because people had previously assumed that these opinions were irreconcilable with the faith of the Church. Origen once said: "Heretics think more profoundly but not more truly."[1] For the postconciliar period I think that we must modify that statement slightly and say: "Their thinking appears more interesting but at the cost of the truth." What was previously impossible to state was passed off as a continuation of the spirit of the Council. Without having produced anything genuinely new, people could pretend to be interesting at a cheap price. They sold goods from the old liberal flea market as if they were new Catholic theology.

From the very beginning, Balthasar perceived with great acuity the process by which relevance became more important than truth. He opposed it with the inexorability characteristic of his thought and faith. More and more we are recognizing that *The Moment of Christian Witness (Cordula oder der Ernstfall),* which first appeared in 1966, is a classic of impartial polemics. This work worthily joins the great polemical works of the Fathers, which taught us to differentiate gnosis from Christianity. Prior to that, he had written a little book in 1965 called *Who is a Christian?* which made us sit up and take notice of the clarity of his standards. He taught us to distinguish between what is authentically

---

1. Origen, *Commentary on the Psalms,* 36, 23 (PG 17, 133 B), quoted in Hans Urs von Balthasar, *Origenes, Geist und Feuer* (Einsiedeln/Freiburg, 1991), 155. Eng., *Origen: Spirit and Fire,* trans. Robert J. Daley (Washington, D.C., 1984).

Christian and homemade fantasies about Christianity. This book accomplished exactly what Balthasar had described in 1972 as the task of *Communio:* "It is not a matter of bravado, but of Christian courage, to expose oneself to risk."[2] He had made himself vulnerable with the hope that these trumpet blasts would herald a return to the real subject matter of theological thinking. Once theology was no longer being measured according to its content but rather according to the purely formal categories of conservative and progressive, the learned man from Basel must have seen very quickly that his own voice alone was not sufficient. What was classified as conservative in this situation was immediately judged to be irrelevant and no further arguments were required.

So Balthasar went about seeking allies. He planned a common project, "Elucidations" *(Klarstellungen),* a book of no more than one hundred fifty pages. The book was supposed to include brief summaries, by the best specialists of the individual disciplines, of whatever was essential for the foundations of the faith. He worked out a thematic plan and wrote a thirty-five-page preliminary draft, in which he tried to show the prospective authors the inner logic of the work as a whole. He was in conversation with many theologians, but because of the demands placed upon the authors whom he had in mind, the project never really got off the ground. In addition, he realized that rapid changes in theological terminology required another change in the arrangement of question and answer. Sometime in the late sixties, Balthasar discerned that his project could not be realized. It was clear that a single anthology would not suffice but that a continual conversation with different currents was necessary.

Thus the idea for a journal occurred to him, an idea which took shape in conversation with the first session of the International Theological Commission (1969). This setting made him realize that a medium of conversation such as this must be international. Otherwise it would not display the real breadth of Catholicism, and the diversity of Catholicism's cultural expressions would be forgotten. The decisive element in "Elucidations," which was lacking in the earlier, polemical writing, now became fully clear. The undertaking would only achieve permanence and attract loyalty if based upon a Yes and not upon a No.

---

2. Hans Urs von Balthasar, "Communio — A Programme," *International Catholic Review: Communio* 1, no. 1 (Spring 1972): 2-12, here 12.

Only an affirmative foundation would be capable of responding to the questions which had been posed. Balthasar, de Lubac, L. Bouyer, J. Medina, M. J. le Guillou, and I arranged to meet in the fall of 1969 apart from the official consultations of the Commission. There the project took on concrete form. The participants first thought that there should be a German-French collaboration. Le Guillou, who was then completely healthy and capable of getting work done, was supposed to be in charge on the French side. Balthasar made himself father of the joint project with special responsibility for the German branch.

Obviously, it took a long time for the idea to be realized. They had to find a publisher, an editor, financial means, and a relatively solid core of authors. There was also the question of the title. Many different possibilities were tested. For example, I remember a conversation with the founders of the journal *Les quatres fleuves*, which was then being started in Paris with similar objectives. Not only did our French edition never get off the ground, but le Guillou for all practical purposes dropped out because of his illness. Two events were decisive in order for the project to get started. Balthasar contacted the movement *Communione e Liberazione*, which had been conceived in Italy and was just beginning to blossom. The young people who came together in the community founded by Don Giussani displayed the vitality, the willingness to take risks, and the courage of faith which was needed. Thus, the Italian partner was found. In Germany the publishing house Kösel decided to abandon the traditional cultural journal *Hochland* in order to replace it with the short-lived *Neues Hochland*. The word "new" in *Neues Hochland* referred to a decisive change of course. The last editor of *Hochland*, Franz Greiner, was prepared to offer his experience and services to the new journal. He did so with great selflessness and even founded a new publishing house to secure the independence of the project. Consequently, he not only disclaimed any remuneration for himself but also made available his own personal means for the whole project. Without him, starting the journal would not have been possible. Today we need to thank him once again for what he did.

I no longer remember exactly when the name *Communio* first entered into the conversation, but I believe it occurred through contact with *Communione e Liberazione*. The word appeared all of a sudden, like the illumination of a room. It actually expressed everything that we wanted to say. There were some initial difficulties because the name had already been taken. In France there was a small journal with this title and in Rome a book series. For this reason, "International Catholic Review" was chosen as the main title. "Communio" could then be added as a subtitle without violating the rights of others.

Because of the new guiding concept and because of our contact with the Italian partners, we were able to clarify the physiognomy of the journal even further. We also wanted to be structurally different from previous journals. This new structure was supposed to show the creativity and breadth that we were looking for. There were basically two new elements which we wanted to introduce. We were looking for a new kind of internationality. As opposed to the centralized approach of *Concilium,* we thought that the meaning of the word *communio* required a harmonious coexistence of unity and difference. Hans Urs von Balthasar was aware from his experience as a publisher that even today a great deal still separated European cultures from one another. For example, he had founded a series *Theologia Romanica,* in which the best works of French theology were published in German. He must have realized that the reason for their being largely unmarketable in Germany was that the Germans did not understand the culture upon which they were based. The journal was also supposed to open up cultures to one another, to bring them into real conversation with one another, and at the same time to leave one another enough room to develop on their own. The situations in Church and society are so different that what counts as a burning question for one culture remains completely foreign to another. We agreed to publish a primary part with major theological articles designed through common planning. This way, authors from the different countries participating were allowed to have something to say in every edition. The second part was intended to remain in the hands of the editorial staff of the individual countries. Following the *Hochland* tradition, we decided in Germany to dedicate the second part to general cultural issues as much as possible. The combination of theology and culture was also supposed to be a distinguishing feature of the journal. If the journal was to become a forum for conversation between faith and culture, then it was also necessary that the editorial staff consist of priests and laity, as well as theologians and representatives of other disciplines.

The notion of *communio* also suggested another characteristic to us. We did not want simply to throw *Communio* out into the neutral marketplace and wait to see where we would find customers. We thought that the title required that the journal form a community that would always develop on the basis of *communio*. *Communio* circles were supposed to arise with distinct foci. We considered the journal as a kind of intellectual and spiritual foundation for each focus and hoped that it would be discussed as such. Conversely, new ideas as well as criticism of what we were doing could come from each of these circles. In short, we thought that we could have a new kind of dialogue with readers. The journal was not intended to offer intellectual goods for sale but needed a living context to support it. In the same vein, we thought that a new kind of financing might have been possible, one not based upon fixed capital but sustained by the common initiative of every author and every reader who was judged to be a true supporter of the whole project. Unfortunately, after some modest starts in Germany and more decisive attempts in France, we discovered that this plan was not effective. A fragment of what was then attempted has still survived among the contributors to *Communio* in Germany. In any case, we were forced to accept that one cannot found a community with a journal but that the community precedes the journal and must render it necessary, as is the case with *Communione e Liberazione*. *Communio* was never intended to be an instrument of this movement. Rather, *Communio* was founded to attract and bring together Christians simply on the basis of their common faith, independently of their membership in particular communities.

The Name as a Program

When our journal started out twenty years ago, the word *communio* had not yet been discovered by progressive postconciliar theology. At that time everything centered on the "people of God," a concept which was thought to be a genuine innovation of the Second Vatican Council and was quickly contrasted with a hierarchical understanding of the Church. More and more, "people of God" was understood in the sense of popular sovereignty, as a right to a common, democratic determination over everything that the Church is and over everything that she should do. God was taken to be the creator and sovereign of the people because the phrase contained the words "of God," but even with this awareness he was left out. He was amalgamated with the notion of a people who create and form themselves.[3] The word *communio*, which no one used to notice, was now surprisingly fashionable — if only as a foil. According to this interpretation, Vatican II had abandoned the hierarchical ecclesiology of Vatican I and replaced it with an ecclesiology of *communio*. Thereby, *communio* was apparently understood in much the same way the "people of God" had been understood, i.e., as an essentially horizontal notion. On the one hand, this notion supposedly expresses the egalitarian moment of equality under the universal decree of everyone. On the other hand, it also emphasizes as one of its most fundamental ideas an ecclesiology based entirely on the local Church. The Church appears as a network of groups, which as such precede the whole and achieve harmony with one another by building a consensus.[4]

This kind of interpretation of the Second Vatican Council will only be defended by those who refuse to read its texts or who divide them into two parts: an acceptable progressive part and an unacceptable old-fashioned part. In the conciliar documents concerning the Church itself, for example, Vatican I and Vatican II are inextricably bound together. It is simply out of the question to separate an earlier, unsuitable ecclesiology from a new and different one. Ideas like these not only confuse conciliar texts with party platforms and councils with political conventions, but they also reduce the Church to the level of a political party. After a while political parties can throw away an old platform and replace it with one which they regard as better, at least until yet another one appears on the scene.

The Church does not have the right to exchange the faith for something else and at the same time to expect the faithful to stay with her. Councils can therefore neither discover ecclesiologies or other doctrines nor can they repudiate them. In the words of Vatican II, the Church is "not higher than the Word of God but serves it and therefore teaches

3. I have sought to explain the correct, biblical sense of the concept "people of God" in my book *Church, Ecumenism and Politics* (New York, 1988); see also my small book *Zur Gemeinschaft gerufen* (Freiburg, 1991), 27-30. Eng., *Called to Communion* (San Francisco: Ignatius Press, 1996).

4. Cf. also, in this regard, *Zur Gemeinschaft gerufen*, 70-97. Also noteworthy is the document of the Congregation for the Doctrine of the Faith to the bishops of the Catholic Church on "Some Aspects of the Church as Communio" (Vatican City, 1992).

only what is handed on to it."[5] Our understanding of the depth and breadth of the tradition develops because the Holy Spirit broadens and deepens the memory of the Church in order to guide her "into all the truth" (Jn 16:13). According to the Council, growth in the perception *(Wahrnehmung, perceptio)* of what is inherent to the tradition occurs in three ways: through the meditation and study of the faithful, through an interior understanding which stems from the spiritual life, and through the proclamation of those "who have received the sure charism of truth by succeeding to the office of the bishop."[6] The following words basically paraphrase the spiritual position of a council as well as its possibilities and tasks: the council is committed from within to the Word of God and to the tradition. It can only teach what is handed on. As a rule, it must find new language to hand on the tradition in each new context so that — to put it a different way — the tradition remains genuinely the same. If the Second Vatican Council brought the notion of *communio* to the forefront of our attention, it did not do so in order to create a new ecclesiology or even a new Church. Rather, careful study and the spiritual discernment which comes from the experience of the faithful made it possible at this moment to express more completely and more comprehensively what the tradition states.

Even after this excursus we might still ask what *communio* means in the tradition and in the continuation of the tradition which occurs in the Second Vatican Council. First of all, *communio* is not a sociological but a theological notion, one which even extends to the realm of ontology. O. Saier worked this out accurately in his thoroughgoing study of 1973, which details the position of the Second Vatican Council on *communio*. The first chapter, which investigates "the way of speaking of Vatican II," claims that the *communio* between God and man comes first and the *communio* of the faithful among one another follows from this. Even the second chapter, which describes the place of *communio* in theology, repeats this sequence. In the third chapter, Word and sacrament finally appear as the genuine constructive elements of the *Communio ecclesiae.* With his majestic knowledge of the philosophical and theological sources, Hans Urs von Balthasar described the foundations of what the last Council developed on this point. I do not want to repeat what

5. *Dei Verbum,* 10.
6. Ibid., 8.

he said, but I will briefly refer to some of the major elements because they were and still are the basis for what we wanted to accomplish in our journal. In the first place, we must remember that "communion" between men and women is only possible when embraced by a third element. In other words, common human nature creates the very possibility that we can communicate with one another. We are not only nature but also persons, and in such a way that each person represents a unique way of being human different from everyone else. Therefore, nature alone is not sufficient to communicate the inner sensibility of persons. If we want to draw another distinction between individuality and personality, then we could say that individuality divides and being a person opens. Being a person is by nature being related. But why does it open? Because both in its very depths and in its highest aspirations being a person goes beyond its own boundaries toward a greater, universal "something" and even toward a greater, universal "someone." The all-embracing third, to which we return so often, can only bind when it is greater and higher than individuals. On the other hand, the third is itself within each individual because it touches each one from within. Augustine once described this as "higher than my heights, more interior than I am to myself." This third, which in truth is the first, we call God. We touch ourselves in him. Through him and only through him, a *communio* which grasps our own depths comes into being.

We have to proceed one step further. God communicated himself to humanity by himself becoming man. His humanity in Christ is opened up through the Holy Spirit in such a way that it embraces all of us as if we could all be united in a single body, in a single common flesh. Trinitarian faith and faith in the Incarnation guide the idea of communion with God away from the realm of philosophical concepts and locate it in the historical reality of our lives. One can therefore see why the Christian tradition interprets *koinōnia-communio* in 2 Corinthians 13:13 as an outright description of the Holy Spirit.

To put it in the form of a concrete statement: the communion of people with one another is possible because of God, who unites us through Christ in the Holy Spirit so that communion becomes a community, a "church" in the genuine sense of the word. The church discussed in the New Testament is a church "from above," not from a humanly fabricated "above" but from the real "above" about which Jesus says: "You belong to what is below, I belong to what is above" (Jn 8:23).

Jesus clearly gave new meaning to the "below," for "he descended into the lower regions of the earth" (Eph 4:9). The ecclesiology "from below" which is commended to us today presupposes that one regards the Church as a purely sociological quantity and that Christ as an acting subject has no real significance. But in this case, one is no longer speaking about a church at all but about a society which has also set religious goals for itself. According to the logic of this position, such a church will also be "from below" in a theological sense, namely, "of this world," which is how Jesus defines "below" in the gospel of John (Jn 8:23). An ecclesiology based upon *communio* consists of thinking and loving from the real "above." This "above" relativizes every human "above" and "below" because before it the first will be last and the last will be first.

A principal task of the review *Communio* had to be, and therefore must still be, to steer us toward this real "above," the one which disappears from view when understood in merely sociological and psychological terms. The "dreams of the Church" for tomorrow unleash a blind yearning to be committed to forming a church which has disintegrated whatever is essential. Such aspirations can only provoke further disappointments, as Georg Muschalek has shown.[7] Only in the light of the real "above" can one exercise a serious and constructive critique of the hierarchy, the basis of which must not be the philosophy of envy but the Word of God. A journal which goes by the name of *Communio* must therefore keep alive and become engrossed in God's speech before all else, the speech of the trinitarian God, of his revelation in the history of salvation in the Old and New Covenants, in the middle of which stands the Incarnation of the Son, God's being with us. The journal must speak about the Creator, the Redeemer, our likeness to God, and about the sins of humanity as well. It must never lose sight of our eternal destination, and together with theology it must develop an anthropology which gets at the heart of the matter. It must render the Word of God into a response to everyone's questions. This means that it cannot hide behind a group of specialists, of theologians, and of "church-makers," who rush from one meeting to another and manage to strengthen discontent with the Church among themselves and others.

---

7. G. Muschalek, *Kirche — noch heilsnotwendig? Über das Gewissen, die Empörung und das Verlangen* (Tübingen, 1990); this small book offers a thought-provoking analysis and diagnosis of the contemporary crisis in the Church.

A journal whose thought is based upon *communio* is not permitted to hand over its ideology and its recipes to such groups. It must approach those who are questioning and seeking, and in conversation with such people, it must learn to receive anew the light of God's Word itself.

We might also add that they have to be missionary in the proper sense of the word. Europe is about to become pagan again, but among these new pagans there is also a new thirst for God. This situation can often be misleading. The thirst will definitely not be quenched by dreaming about the Church, and not by creating a church which strives to reinvent itself through endless discussions. One is better off escaping in the esoteric, in magic, in places which seem to create an atmosphere of mystery, of something totally other. Faith does not confirm the convictions of those who have time for such things. Faith is the gift of life and must once again become recognizable as such.

We must say a brief word, before we conclude, about two other dimensions of *communio* which we have not yet discussed. Even in pre-Christian literature, the primary meaning of *communio* referred to God and to gods, and the secondary, more concrete meaning referred to the mysteries which mediate communion with God.[8] This scheme prepares the way for the Christian use of language. *Communio* must first be understood theologically. Only then can one draw implications for a sacramental notion of *communio,* and only after that for an ecclesiological notion. *Communio* is a communion of the body and blood of Christ (e.g., 1 Cor 10:16). Now the Whole attains its full concreteness; everyone eats the one bread and thus they themselves become one. "Receive what is yours," says Augustine, presupposing that through the sacraments human existence itself is joined to and transformed into communion with Christ. The Church is entirely herself only in the sacrament, i.e., wherever she hands herself over to him and wherever he hands himself over to her, creating her over and over again. As the one who has descended into the deepest depths of the earth and of human existence, he guides her over and over again back to the heights. Only in this context is it possible to speak about a hierarchical dimension and to renew our understanding of tradition as growth into identity. More than anything else, this clarifies what it means to be Catholic. The Lord is whole

8. The most important reference is found in W. Bauer, *Wörterbuch zum Neuen Testament* (Berlin, 1958, 5th ed.). Keywords: *koinōneō, koinōnia, koinōnos,* cols. 867-870.

wherever he is found, but that also means that together we are but one Church and that the union of humanity is the indispensable definition of the Church. Therefore, "he is our peace." "Through him we both have our access in one Spirit to the Father" (Eph 2:14-18).

For this reason, Hans Urs von Balthasar has dealt a severe blow to the sociology of groups. He reminds us that the ecclesiastical community appears to quite a number of people today as no more than a skeleton of institutions. As a result, "the small group . . . will become more and more the criterion of ecclesiastical vitality. For these people, the Church as Catholic and universal seems to hover like a disconnected roof over the buildings which they inhabit." Balthasar provides an alternative vision:

> Paul's whole endeavor was to rescue the Church communion from the clutches of charismatic "experience" and through the apostolic ministry to carry it beyond itself to what is catholic, universal. Ministry in the Church is certainly service, not domination, but it is service with the authority to demolish all the bulwarks which the charismatics set up against the universal communion, and to bring them "into obedience to Christ" (2 Cor 10:5). Anyone who charismatically (democratically) levels down Church ministry, thereby loses the factor which inexorably and crucifyingly carries every special task beyond itself and raises it to the plane of the Church universal, whose bond of unity is not experience *(gnosis)* but self-sacrificing love *(agape)*.[9]

It goes without saying that this is not a denial of the unique significance of the local Church nor a repudiation of movements and new communities in which the Church and faith can be experienced with new vigor. Every time that the Church has been in a period of crisis and the rusty structures were no longer resisting the maelstrom of universal degeneration, such movements have been the basis for renewal, forces of rebirth.[10] This always presupposes that within these move-

---

9. Balthasar, "Communio — A Programme," 10.

10. This is illustrated very well in the book by B. Hubensteiner, *Vom Geist des Barock* (Munich, 1978, 2nd ed.), esp. 58-158. Cf. also P. J. Cordes, *Mitten in unserer Welt. Kräfte geistlicher Erneuerung* (Freiburg, 1987). Eng., *In the Midst of Our World: Forces of Spiritual Renewal* (San Francisco, 1988).

ments there is an opening up to the whole of Catholicism and that they fit in with the unity of the tradition.

Finally, the word *agape* points to another essential dimension of the notion of *communio*. Communion with God cannot be lived without real care for the human community. The ethical and social dimension found within the idea of God thus belongs to the essence of *communio*. A journal which follows this program also has to take the time to expose itself to the great ethical and social questions of the day. Its role is not to be political, but it must still illuminate the problems of the economy and of politics with the light of God's Word by attending equally to critical and constructive commentary.

Before concluding, we might at least make a preliminary remark about the examination of conscience which I declined to address at the beginning. How successfully has the review carried out its original program in the first twenty years of its existence? The fact that it has taken root in thirteen different editions speaks for its necessity and breadth even if the proper balance between the universal and the particular still causes many difficulties for the individual editions. It has addressed major issues of faith: the Creed, the sacraments, and the Beatitudes, just to name the most important of the ongoing series. It has surely helped many to move closer to the *communio* of the Church or even not to abandon their home in the Church in spite of many hardships. There is still no reason to be self-satisfied. I cannot help but think about a sentence of Hans Urs von Balthasar: "It is not a matter of bravado, but of Christian courage, to expose oneself to risk." Have we been courageous enough? Or have we in fact preferred to hide behind theological learnedness and tried too often to show that we too are up-to-date? Have we really spoken the Word of faith intelligibly and reached the hearts of a hungering world? Or do we mostly try to remain within an inner circle throwing the ball back and forth with technical language? With that I conclude, for along with these questions I also want to express my congratulations and best wishes for the next twenty years of *Communio*.

Translated by Peter Casarella

Christian Universalism:
On Two Collections of Papers
by Hans Urs von Balthasar

The great issue of controversial theology between the Wars was the *analogia entis,* which Erich Przywara had interpreted as the guiding thread of Catholic thought, whereas for Karl Barth it was the only serious reason not to become a Catholic and a true invention of the Antichrist. As his *Church Dogmatics* progressed, Barth rapidly outgrew the formal dispute over *analogia entis* versus *analogia fidei,* over the question whether being itself already contains a likeness to God, or whether Godlikeness derives from faith alone. Christology increasingly assumed the central role in place of the abstract formal principle of the analogy of faith. At the same time, it made possible a rediscovery of creation in the light of Christ and, by this means, a theology of creation which now permitted the whole wealth of reality to pour into Barth's thought. A few years ago, Hans Urs von Balthasar masterfully traced the trajectory of this maturation of Barth's work in his book *The Theology of Karl Barth,* while at the same time demonstrating that the decisive opportunity for an encounter with Catholic theology lay in the latter's christological understanding of creation. However, Balthasar still found it necessary to note the presence of a "christological reduction" in Barth's writings, that is, of a rigorous construction from above which continued to prevent the incorporation of the human basis, of

This article originally appeared as "Christlicher Universalismus: Zum Aufsatzwerk Hans Urs v. Balthasars," *Hochland* 54 (1961): 68-76. English publication in *Communio: International Catholic Review* 22, no. 3 (Fall 1995): 545-557.

the dimensions of history and of man as such, in the christological transformation of Barth's thought. It is here that Balthasar's own thinking has tirelessly moved ahead in the last decade. The question of the unity of everything human with the Christian reality — which in the event of the Cross thwarts, dismisses, and pronounces this entire *humanum* to be foolish and of no account, while nevertheless embracing and renewing it — is one of the fundamental questions which repeatedly recur in Balthasar's collected papers, now out in two volumes, which in the main make available works (including some hitherto unpublished pieces) written in the last few years.[1] If it still seems quite abstract and arcane to begin framing this question in terms of the above-mentioned controversy over the problem of the two analogies, Balthasar's subsequent penetration of the topic nonetheless releases extremely concrete and vital questions of Christian existence from the narrow bonds of specialist concern: Is there such a thing as Christian humanism, and what does it look like? Thus, do the phenomena which typically accompany the reality of man, such as beauty and art, exist in the Christian scheme, and is their existence in it justified, or is the nakedness of the Cross the sheer negation of all of these things? Is there a Christian dialogue with the major world religions, in particular with those of Asia, or is rigid exclusiveness, the same absolute no, perhaps the sole response in this field as well? And if this is the case, what sense are we to make of the fact that a sizeable portion of the history of religion is to be found in the Bible, at least in its early parts?

Starting precisely from this last point, which at least since the Bible-Babylon dispute has been one of the most serious concerns of theology, Balthasar sets about developing his solution and shows how this very circumstance leads in the direction of Catholic thought — thus resolving two problems in one. God speaks as man — this is the reality which we encounter in the Bible, and which reaches its apogee in Jesus Christ. In him God has entered into the "schema" of man (Phil 2:7), thereby embracing human nature within the unity of the God-man. "It certainly fol-

1. [Ratzinger is referring to Balthasar's *Skizzen zur Theologie,* which at the time of this review essay (1961) numbered only two volumes. The English titles of these two works are: *Explorations in Theology I: The Word Made Flesh* (San Francisco: Ignatius Press, 1989); and *Explorations in Theology II: Spouse of the Word* (San Francisco: Ignatius Press, 1991). Throughout this review article, they are referred to as I and II respectively. — Translator.]

lows that the acts of Christ — being acts of his human nature, and therefore insofar as the man Christ manifests his *religio* towards the Father in adoration and obedience during his agony in the garden — are truly acts of natural religion. They are not merely natural religion, but this is no reason for denying that they are *also* natural religion; it does mean that we have both the right and the duty to affirm natural religion as necessarily implied in Christology" (I, 58). God speaks as man — this means that God also assumes the manifold self-transcendence of the human word, which as human is embedded as much in man's history as in his nature. God's word, which is pronounced as a word of man, "passes necessarily beyond itself into a total human word" and thus by definition carries with it the cargo of human history (I, 86). "The word of God takes hold of the people of Israel in its historical place as bound up with a general evolution, not only in its political situation between the great powers to the east of it . . . , but on the deeper level of philosophy of life, wisdom, metaphysics and religion" (I, 87). The religions of Canaan, Babylon, and Egypt, the political and cultural influence of the Near East: all of this is truly present in the human word which God speaks; not merely, let us add, in an external fashion, but as a modality of the word itself, which cannot exist as a human word at all without such implications. Balthasar rightly draws attention to the fact that it is not sufficient to speak in this connection merely of literary genres, "as if . . . God could have used equally well any other appropriate form. One might then say that God could just as well have been incarnated in Paul or Augustine as in Christ. It would be overlooking the essential truth that God does not take man's word out of his mouth and put it into his own, but rather makes the whole man the word of God" (I, 89, n. 11).

However — the word of God which is pronounced as a human word in this way never consists simply in the prolongation of man's own words. This relationship has an analogue in the relation of the human word to natural language: man's spiritual language presupposes the language of nature, yet is something altogether new in comparison which cannot be derived from it. So too God's word presupposes man's word, yet brings about its death and undoing in order to adapt it by this very means into a fit instrument of God's speech. This brief outline necessarily falls far short of the wealth and vitality of what Balthasar, drawing on a masterfully sketched philosophy of language, says *à propos* of the theology of the word. However, it may at least convey some sense of how the debate over the problem of the *analogia entis* all but unexpectedly opens up a path between the extremes of liberalism, which dissolves Christianity into the history of religions, representing it as one, even if especially elevated, form of religion among many, and of a radical dialectic which denies the dimension of natural religion altogether. Such a dialectic can never dispense once and for all with the biblical phenomenon mentioned above; "Such a theology must attempt to relegate it to the forecourts of philology and archeology, *tamen usque redibit*" (I, 67f.). The dogged persistence of this biblical problem proves to be a much needed guidepost for theology, which — weary of the dispute over principles — now unexpectedly stumbles quite concretely on the humanity of God, on man in the Bible, on the *analogia entis* in the *analogia fidei*.

In this way, however, there is a straight path in Balthasar's work from the theology of the word to the theology of silence, that is, to a comparative dialogue with the history of religion, whose supreme "word" is to transcend the word and its positiveness by abandoning all words in the negation of the worldly and earthly. A theology whose initial framework inquiry is dictated by the strictest Biblicism thus enters directly into the broad expanse of a genuine universalism. The history of religions is present in the Bible itself. Since this is so, to what extent is a rapprochement with the major world religions possible for Christianity? — such is the question which we face here. One cannot say that as fully developed and clear a solution emerges on this point as on the preceding one (perhaps such a solution is impossible in this matter). The problem is stated in sharp and unequivocal terms: "There comes a time for the Christian when he wearies of all that is positive and concrete. He finds himself enchained by words and facts, without hope of liberation. In all other religions the finite is seen sooner or later to point beyond itself, to be an intermediary. . . . For the Christian, however, the positive and concrete persist to the end, and isolate him from the rest of mankind" (I, 128). "Missionaries of other religions have their books which they propagate and expound, and it is a source of humiliation for the Christian missionary, not only that he has to begin with a book but that . . . he can never lay it aside as finished with" (I, 129). If my reading is correct, we can discern three directions in which Balthasar approaches dialogue with the Far Eastern religions, which transcend the word in a radical *theologia negativa*.

First of all, Balthasar thinks through what it means for the structure of Christian revelation that it defines the letter as death-dealing and that it aims to lead from the letter to the spirit; what it means, in other words, that Paul binds the Gentiles not to the letter, but to the spirit and "that the Christian mission to the world today is not one of subjecting the nations to the letter but to the spirit" (I, 141). Balthasar points out that "spirit, water, and blood" (1 Jn 5:8) are the world-historical witnesses to the truth of God in Jesus Christ. He recalls that in the books of the Bible the same history is constantly being re-elaborated. And it is clear that "it is not in this instance so much a question of the exact nature of historical events as of the overall 'right' expression for the essential, revelatory event embodied in that history" (I, 138). Above all, however, it also becomes apparent that it is the *one* Word which resounds ever more simply and indubitably through the events which give it form in worldly history, as, for example, when Deuteronomy ultimately focuses everything on the act of the faithful belief in the faithful God, an act which must always be performed here and now. "This singleness of purpose is what Jesus in fulfilling carried over into the eternal covenant. It is what Paul pointed to . . ." (I, 140). This simplification — and this is the second motif which Balthasar develops in this context — attains its fulfillment in the Resurrection: the Risen One, by virtue of his own spiritual existence (2 Cor 3:16), "'took away the veil' which lay over all the words and narratives of the Old . . . Testament" (I, 149; cf. Lk 24:44). "This is why Paul was able to bring out the central doctrines of Christianity, with a truly astonishing freedom, without citing a single word of the gospel. It explains too how it was that he could make himself responsible for dispensing the gentiles from the tradition contained in the word and history, insofar as this tradition was not in its essence the spirit of God who revealed himself in history" (I, 140).

An important corollary follows almost self-evidently in turn, that is, the insight that in regard to the sacred books the question of historical truth must not be posed in the spirit of a narrow historicism, but must be set free from false scruples, as is obvious, for example, in the case of Melchizedek — "And why should it not also apply to Abraham, though admittedly not quite a parallel case?" (I, 139). The Resurrection, in fact, has set a limit to every historical positivism; not, however, in favor of a spirit which man could attain with his own powers using some

THE UNITY OF THE CHURCH

technique of mystical absorption, but in favor of the Spirit whom only that God can give who by grace raises up with Christ those who have been crucified with him. "Thus, God takes false concerns away from us, and at the same time the work of transformation, to the extent that we cooperate in this, can be a work of all who love and not only a work of a small elite, like advanced Oriental contemplation" (II, 358). This is where the immovable boundary separates Christian faith and Asiatic mysticism, and yet it is precisely here that Balthasar picks up the thread of the dialogue with the third theme — the question of to what extent there can be true unity between Christian contemplation and pre- and extra-Christian mysticism. The reader will find it necessary to say, however, that there still remains a certain indecision and lack of clarity on this point. This phenomenon is most likely due to the fact that, while clearly seeing that in Christianity mystical ascent is limited by the descent of the Word and the unmanipulability of the God who freely gives himself, Balthasar brings to the discussion a sympathy for and openness to the full range of mystical concern stemming from a long familiarity with Greek monastic mysticism, as indeed with the entire Christian mystical tradition. Perhaps the unification of the divergent lines is most successful where, commenting on the Letter to the Hebrews (12:2), Balthasar speaks of the faith of Jesus Christ, understood as an attitude of abandonment to God which remains in eternity — in the man Jesus Christ and in all those who believe with and in Christ. In such faith Balthasar likewise sees the "dark night," the culminating point of the mysticism of John of the Cross, for whom it is, in its deepest core, not something provisional, but the superabundance of a self-entrustment to God which is greater than all knowledge.[2]

At the same time, the subject of mysticism forms the link to the third principal group of questions discussed in the present work: the debate over Christian "spirituality" (clergy and laity, secular state and consecrated state, office and charism, the concrete realization of Christian life in today's world). Once again it is altogether impossible, in view of the brevity demanded here, to convey even an approximate idea

---

2. Here, I would like to refer to the outstanding study of R. C. Zaehner, *Zwei Strömungen der muslimschen Mystik* (Kairos, 1959), 92-99, which, in critical dialogue with Asiatic and Muslim mysticism, elaborates the same insight from the heart of that mysticism itself.

of the wealth of insights that Balthasar presents regarding this set of issues, which is the center of so much discussion today. Balthasar begins
by objecting with refreshing frankness to the unfortunately all too
prevalent obsession with specialized spirituality: "Every little association (the more exclusive, the better) tries to incubate its own particular
'spirit,' around which it knocks up some kind of structure, as if engaged in creating a work of art" (I, 221). In opposition to this Balthasar
observes: "After all, we can hardly imagine Francis, for instance, preoc-
cupied with "Franciscanism" instead of with the poverty of Christ, in
the light of which all the graces and gifts of the Holy Spirit were im-
parted to him" (I, 219). Even more to the point: "What is special in
Mary's spirituality is the radical renunciation of any special spirituality
other than the overshadowing of the Most High and the indwelling of
the divine Word. . . . The idea of making out of Marian spirituality one
among others is, therefore, a distortion, as dangerous as attempting to
claim for one's own particular way the status of the 'spirituality of the
Church'" (I, 218f.).

Moreover, these statements already indicate the method with
which Balthasar tackles the general problem of the states of Christian
life and of their correlative spiritual attitudes. This method is far removed from today's fashionable optimism about the retrieval of the
world; it also refuses to think in terms of an opposition between the
secular state and the consecrated state, as if, for instance, temporal existence and its tasks for the kingdom of God were assigned to the secular state, whereas the new aeon and eschatology were the special prov-
ince of the consecrated state. Rather, Balthasar considers that this sort
of thinking in terms of oppositions actually misconceives the problem
and amounts to a split within the Church. There is, in the end, only a
single Christian form, which, as such, is beyond the distinction of laity
and clergy (II, 139). Every Christian is summoned to "eschatological existence," and Christianity as a whole is ordered to the new aeon.
Balthasar rightly calls attention here to the reason that the state of the
counsels is not an eighth sacrament: it is the entrance into the being of
the Church as such, which is the fundamental sacrament prior to all
the individual sacraments. It is, in other words, the center of the
Church's embodiment of itself and thus indicates the form of the
whole (II, 319). The life of the counsels is not a matter for specialists,
but the spirit of the whole: "Whatever there is about it that may be con-

sidered special exists only to serve its availability to the whole. . . . To say it in the shortest possible formula, the life of the counsels is *the particular instance of the general*" (II, 435).

Balthasar therefore does not see sharp boundaries between the single forms of Christian existence — consecrated state-secular state, priesthood-laity — as if it were a question of three altogether diverse possibilities within Christianity. On the contrary, everywhere he discerns fluid transitions and an inner penetration and mutual enfolding which reach far into the properly sacramental sphere. This is true not only in the case of the "sacraments of the laity," baptism and marriage, but also in connection with sacraments as bound up with ministerial office as penance and the Eucharist (esp. II, 311, 322ff., 387-91). Balthasar thus says a resolute no to a certain theology of the laity which to a large extent has already become a catchword of the day, yet threatens to compromise its own intention by the superficiality with which it treats its subject.

We truly ought to listen with the most serious attention when Balthasar points out the absurdity of the increasing clamor for a more extensive juridical status for the laity and of the complaint that the Church's code of canon law has almost nothing to say about the layman: the dignity of the layman in the Church does not, after all, hinge on the number of canons by which he is represented in the code. These canons, in fact, lay down norms for the purely functional aspect of the Church in order to serve the authentic essence of the Church, and this is something which is wholly impossible to formulate in a code: it is to be in the body of Christ and to be immediately related to him in love. The layman who wants to interpret and understand himself in the horizon of Church law therefore fails to appreciate his own dignity, indeed, he diminishes it, "and the laymen who claim 'more rights' in the Church do not know precisely what they want. What they call their 'right' (that which they are permitted to be vis-à-vis Christ) is neither strengthened nor improved by being written down in the code of canon law. Compared with this mighty 'law,' the small participation in the clerical function of ordering (and it cannot be more than a small share, if they wish to remain laymen and not become members of the clergy) would be virtually a microscopic speck" (II, 409). One can only agree. Doubtless Balthasar's ideas concerning this series of issues are not yet fully developed in every point of detail; occasionally the effort to portray the transitions from one individual form of Christian life to another as seamlessly as possible is probably somewhat exaggerated. However, it is safe to affirm that the overall message quite definitely conforms to the data of the New Testament and of the Christian tradition; it is both a summons to awaken, which our confused and secularized generation very much needs to hear, and a testimony to the deep religious seriousness and the true theological stature of Balthasar's work.

There are theologians who are contemporary because they are attuned to "what is in the air," what is in keeping with the *Zeitgeist*. They cease to be contemporary as soon as another *Zeitgeist* comes along, and they deserve no better. But there are also theologians who are contemporary because their inquiry is directed solely toward the truth, from which they refuse to be deterred either by the habit of scholastic tradition or by the wishes of the age. This is the attitude which inspires Balthasar's thinking — otherwise he would not be capable of writing a sentence such as the following, which is so "out of tune with the times," and yet so centrally formulates the task of Christianity in this and in every era: "It is not through Catholic 'action' that the world will be redeemed but through poverty and obedience and an exclusive orientation to God. And it would be in keeping with our advanced age if Catholics were to learn better to understand that responsibility for the world goes well with obedience, disposition over the world goes well with poverty, experience of the world goes well with virginity — indeed, that the ultimate fruitfulness, even in the realm that is most truly that of the laity, can be expected precisely from this source" (II, 331).

Very closely connected with the debate over the spirituality of the Christian states of life is another range of issues having to do with the Church. An extensive piece entitled "Casta meretrix" rehearses the historical attempt to come to grips with the problem of holiness and sin in the Church (II, 193-288); the essay "Who is the Church?" tries to give an objective answer to the questions posed by that history (II, 143-191). In this regard, the formulation "*who* is the Church?," as opposed to the usual statement of the question, "*what* is the Church?," already indicates the particular problem and the particular solution which Balthasar has in view. He begins by noting the fact that the understanding of the Church as Bride of Christ, which portrays it as a subject with its own identity in relation to the Lord, has increasingly receded into the background as compared with the term Body of Christ, which does not express this quality of being a subject. Now, since the eucharistic and mystical bodies of the Lord are reciprocal causes, so that at its core the image of the body is based on the eucharistic event, "the doctrine of the *corpus mysticum* reacts powerfully on the conception of the hierarchical Church, giving it an added strength, and depth of meaning" (II, 154). The main emphasis in the idea of the Church falls on the sacramental-institutional aspect, on the objective dimension, on the structure which precedes the individual. In addition, the living men who are the members of the Church appear more as the bare material in which this structure actively deploys itself, but which is not the "Church" in the proper and primary sense.

In contrast to this tendency toward objectivism inherent in the image of the body, Balthasar discovers in the image of the bride the corrective which allows the other side of the whole to receive its due. If the Church is not only "body" but also "bride," then it is not merely a "what," but also a "who" — the objective spirit embodied in the structures of the Church presupposes a subjective spirit as a receptive vessel: it presupposes faith as the womb in which the seed of the Word of God can first fructify. "It follows that the Church is most fully present where faith, hope, and love, selflessness, and tolerance of others are found in the highest degree" (II, 172). The objective structures of ecclesiastical office do not in themselves create the presence of the Church, which requires the believing womb of the word, that is, the active faith, hope, and love of those who precisely in this way are truly the Church. Both the Fathers and the theologians of the middle ages knew this. According to them, the Church becomes a reality to the extent that "sanctity and love are realized" (II, 176). It was above all the apostles who were regarded as the heart of this true Church "without spot or wrinkle": next were their successors, then the martyrs and doctors of the Church, and finally, since the middle ages, Mary, the pure womb of the Word, in whom the holy Church is prototypically represented and who thus becomes the personal center and full realization of the idea of the Church.

In this manner the question "who is the Church" can at last be answered with precision. Only real subjects can respond satisfactorily to this question, not a mere collective, which ultimately remains a fiction. "Real subjects, then, but only such as participate through divine grace in a normative subject and its consciousness . . . ; the supreme subject demanded by the question posed can only be the Divine itself. Mankind gains participation in it through Christ and the sphere that is his . . . : the Church. Finally insofar as the one grace streams through her, this grace makes all spirits, in all their personal varieties of missions and spiritual ways, converge in a single consciousness, opening in Mary to Christ, and through Christ to the Holy Spirit of the three-personal God" (II, 179f.). The import of such considerations will surely lie not least of all in the fact that they free Mariology from a certain isolation in sentimental devotion and insert it in the larger context of meaning framed by a scriptural theology. Embedded in this context, the Marian idea points the way toward, and is the deepest realization of, an understanding of the Church which, moving beyond a narrow objectivism, restores to its central place the personal realization of the Church's being. This understanding implies a renewed recognition of the seriousness of the Church's call to holiness — inasmuch as the Church, "the more properly she is the Church, the more stainless, the more conformed to Christ she is, the more Marian" (II, 179) — as well as the consolation of this holiness, which is a self-giving, supportive, helping holiness. Hence, the Church of the saints not only represents the Church of the sinners, but also "carries them and is responsible for them before God. With Christ it empties itself, so as, in weakness and shame, to bring in the least member" (II, 169).

Finally, the idea that the Church carries the sinner suggests yet another series of reflections which deserves a brief mention at the conclusion of this survey inasmuch as it promises to reopen to theology a dimension of dialogue which has long been closed to it. In several passages Balthasar expresses the opinion that the tightening vise of the Augustinian doctrine of predestination, which sets a final limit to the Church's ability to aid and bear the sinner, is gradually beginning to open up again today. Not that Balthasar, the great scholar and translator of Origen, intends to argue in favor of Origenism in the sense of a doctrine of *apocatastasis*. He is well aware that such a move jeopardizes every notion of election and he is absolutely resolute in his objection to "a certain exhilaration at being redeemed" (I, 250).

But he teaches us again more plainly to leave to God what is God's and not to take it upon ourselves to fix the decision ahead of time in one direction or another — in Origenian or extreme Augustinian fashion. And above all he reminds us that when God acts historically to reject or to elect, as Holy Scripture records in relating the stories of Isaac and Ishmael, of Jacob and Esau, of Moses and Pharaoh, and finally of the whole of Israel, what is at stake is not the eternal salvation and damnation of these figures, but, quite simply, action belonging to salvation history executed in this world. But this discovery puts the subject of Israel in a new light for Christians. Israel not only is and continues to be the root whose sap gives life to the Church, which is not itself without the Old Testament — that Old Testament whose "inspiration developed and came to completion in the heart of the Israel that fought, prayed, and suffered untold pain" (II, 298) — but, beyond this, it remains true that Israel's rejection in the order of salvation history points to an eschatological salvation which it shares with the Church and in which rejection and election are equalized (II, 295f.). There are, thankfully, many mutual gestures and dialogues between Jews and Christians today, but often enough they bog down in more or less superficial humanistic declarations which lack the power to grasp the true historical burden of the separation. Balthasar ventures here (as he has already done once before in his short book *Einsame Zwiesprache*) a truly theological dialogue. Only such dialogue can penetrate to the true depth of this division, which reaches down inexorably into the theological domain. It follows that only this dialogue can show the way to that "peace" which, according to the Letter to the Ephesians, is the work of the crucified Christ (Eph 2:11-18).

If one had to try to find a title which sums up the character of the many-faceted and far-ranging thought represented in these two volumes, one could probably do no better than resort to the title which Balthasar gave to his paper for the festschrift presented to Karl Barth on the occasion of the latter's seventieth birthday: "Christian Universalism" (cf. I, 241-254). Balthasar's thought is an open thought which grows in dialogue and risks dialogue in all directions: with the severe Protestantism of a Karl Barth, as well as with the contemporary spirit, and its alienation from Christ, with the major world religions, with Israel, with the witnesses of Christian history. But above all, Balthasar is in dialogue with the "Word" itself, the Word of God in Scripture, which — the reader notices it again and again — the author has penetrated by personal contemplation, read and loved even in its most hidden recesses. Everywhere one is conscious of this firm rootedness in the

Word, a rootedness which is unafraid of the hard data of philology and history, which does not seek refuge in a meditative idyll, yet which is not swamped by philology, but is able to hear in the word of man the God who is speaking. And everywhere one also perceives a truly Church-minded attitude, not in the sense of a false servility to traditional opinions which wrongfully label themselves as especially representative of the Church, but much rather in the sense of a life truly lived by the spirit and the faith of the Church; out of a true love for the Church, a love, that is, which is honest, and only by its honesty becomes fully love. That Balthasar's theology for all its breadth and openness is a truly devout theology gives it its special dignity and claim on our attention. Of course, much of what is said in this theology remains a provisional first sketch which requires further debate and inquiry. But can man's mind live at all except by questioning, through which alone he lays hold of new truth, and, even having done so, remains unfinished with his quest and is thus summoned to new questioning? Balthasar's work is a true gift to contemporary theology and, thanks to the uncompromising radicalness with which it totally engages both faith and thought, with which it never fails to accept both the world of faith and the world of today with unreserved honesty, it is an encouraging sign that faith — the whole faith, not merely a watered-down makeshift — can also be thought, lived, and loved in the world of today.

Translated by Adrian J. Walker

Interreligious Dialogue
and Jewish-Christian Relations

In the year 1453, just after the conquest of Constantinople, Cardinal Nicholas of Cusa wrote a remarkable book entitled *De pace fidei*. The crumbling empire was convulsed by religious controversies; the Cardinal himself had taken part in the (ultimately unsuccessful) attempt to reunite the Eastern and Western Churches, and Islam was back on the horizon of Western Christianity. Cusanus learned from the events of his time that religious peace and world peace are intimately connected. His response to this problem was a kind of utopia, which, however, he intended to be a real contribution to the cause of peace. "When Christ, the cosmic Logos, can no longer bear his vexation with the plurality of religions on earth, he summons a heavenly council, assembling all the leaders of the various confessions."[1] At this council "the divine Logos leads seventeen representatives of the various nations and religions to understand how the concerns of all the religions can be fulfilled in the Church represented by Peter."[2] "'You do not find a different faith' in the

---

1. Hans Urs von Balthasar, *Love Alone Is Credible*, trans. D. C. Schindler (San Francisco: Ignatius Press, 2004), 18.
2. R. Haubst, "Nikolaus v. Kues," *Lexikon für Theologie und Kirche*, vol. 2, VII, col. 988-991, citation in col. 990.

This text was originally prepared for a session of the *Académie des sciences morales et politiques* (Paris, 1997). English publication in *Communio: International Catholic Review* 25, no. 1 (Spring 1998): 29-41. Rabbi Sztejnberg, who had suggested the topic, addressed it from the Jewish perspective. This circumstance accounts for the breadth of the issues treated, my specific points of emphases, and the limits of the discussion.

various wisdom teachings, Christ explains, 'but rather one and the same faith lies behind each one.'" "God as Creator is the Threefold and the One; as infinite, he is neither the Threefold nor the One, nor anything that can be uttered in speech. For the names that we attribute to God are drawn from creatures, while he himself, considered in himself, is unutterable and exalted above all things that can be named or expressed."[3]

1. From Christian Ecumenism to Interreligious Dialogue

Since Cusanus's time, this ideal heavenly council has come down to earth, and, because the voice of the Logos can be heard only fragmentarily, has inevitably become much more complicated. The nineteenth century saw the gradual development of the ecumenical movement, whose original impetus came from the experience of the Protestant churches in the missions. Having discovered that their witness to the pagan world was seriously handicapped by their division into various confessions, these churches came to see that ecclesial unity was a condition *sine qua non* of mission. In this sense, ecumenism owes its birth to Protestantism's emergence from the bosom of Christendom onto the world scene.[4] In order to make a case for the universality of their message, Christians could no longer contradict one another or appear as members of splinter groups whose peculiarities and differences were rooted merely in the history of the Western world. Subsequently, the impulse behind the ecumenical movement gradually spread to Christianity as a whole. The Orthodox were the first to associate themselves with the movement, though initially their participation was carefully delimited. The first Catholic overtures came from single groups in countries particularly affected by the division of the churches; this situation lasted until the Second Vatican Council threw open the Church's doors to the quest for unity among all Christians. As we have seen, the encounter with the non-Christian world had at first acted as the catalyst only for the search for Christian unity. It was only a matter of time, however, before Christians

---

3. *De pace fidei,* 7, 11, 16, 20, 62 (Op. Omnia VII. Hamburg, 1959), cited in Balthasar, *Love Alone Is Credible,* 19.

4. Cf. R. Rouse and St. Ch. Neill, *Geschichte der ökumenischen Bewegung 1517-1948,* vol. 2 (Göttingen, 1957), 58; H. J. Urban, H. Wagner, eds., *Handbuch der Ökumenik,* vol. 2 (Paderborn, 1986).

began to appreciate the distinctive values of the world religions. After all, Christians were not preaching the Gospel to an a-religious people who had no knowledge of God. It became increasingly difficult to ignore that the Gospel was being preached to a world deeply imbued with religious beliefs, which influenced even the minutest details of everyday life — so much so, that the religiosity of the non-Christian world was bound to put to shame a Christian faith that here and there already seemed worn out. As time went on, Christians realized the inadequacy of describing the representatives of other religions simply as pagans or else in purely negative terms as non-Christians; it was necessary to become acquainted with the distinctive values of the other religions. Inevitably, Christians began asking whether they had the right simply to destroy the world of the other religions, or whether it was not possible, or even imperative, to understand the other religions from within and to integrate their inheritance into Christianity. In this way, ecumenism eventually expanded into interreligious dialogue.[5]

To be sure, the point of this dialogue was not simply to repeat nineteenth- and early twentieth-century scholarship in comparative religion, which, from the lofty height of a liberal-rationalistic standpoint, had judged the religions with the self-assurance of enlightened reason. Today there is a broad consensus that such a standpoint is an impossibility, and that, in order to understand religion, it is necessary to experience it from within, indeed, that only such experience, which is inevitably particular and tied to a definite historical starting point, can lead the way to mutual understanding and thus to a deepening and purification of religion.

2. Unity in Diversity

This development has made us cautious about definitive judgments. Yet it remains an urgent question whether there is a unity in all this diversity. We discuss interreligious ecumenism today against the backdrop of a world that, while it draws ever closer together, becoming more and more a single theater of human history, is convulsed by wars, torn apart by growing tensions between rich and poor, and radically threatened by

5. Cf. K. Reiser, *Ökumene im Übergang: Paradigmenwechsel in der ökumenischen Bewegung?* (Munich, 1989).

the misuse of man's technological power over the planet. This triple threat has given rise to a new canon of ethical values, which would attempt to sum up humanity's principal moral task at this time in history in three words: peace, justice, and the integrity of creation. Though not identical, religion and morality are inseparably linked. It is therefore obvious that in a time when humanity has acquired the capacity to destroy itself and the planet on which it lives, the religions have a common responsibility for overcoming this temptation. The new canon of values serves as a touchstone, especially of the religions. There is a growing tendency to regard it as defining their common task and thus as the formula for uniting them. Hans Küng spoke for many when he launched the slogan, "there can be no peace in the world without peace among the religions," thereby declaring religious peace, that is, interreligious ecumenism, to be the bound duty of all religious communities.[6]

The question that now arises, however, is: how can this be done? Given the diversity of the religions, given the antagonisms among them that often flare up even in our own day, how can we encounter one another? What sort of unity, if any, can there be? What standard can we use at least to seek this unity? Difficult as it is to discern patterns amidst the bewildering variety of religions, we can make a first distinction between tribal and universal religions. Of course, the tribal religions share certain basic patterns, which in turn converge in various ways with the major tendencies of the universal religions. There is thus a perpetual interchange between the two sorts of religions. Although we cannot explain this interchange in detail now, it does warrant our posing the question of interreligious ecumenism first in terms of the universal religions. If we go by the latest research, we can distinguish two major basic types among the universal religions themselves. J. A. Cuttat has proposed the terms "interiority and transcendence" to describe these two types.[7] Contrasting their concrete center and their cen-

---

6. On the problems with the "planetary ethos" that Küng calls for in this context, see R. Spaemann, "Weltethos als 'Projekt,'" *Merkur. Deutsche Zeitschrift für europäisches Denken* 570/571: 893-904.

7. J. A. Cuttat, "Expérience chrétienne et spiritualité orientale," *La mystique et les mystiques* (Paris, 1965); idem, *Begegnung der Religionen* (Einsiedeln, 1956); cf. on the whole question of interreligious dialogue H. Bürkle, *Der Mensch auf der Suche nach Gott — die Frage der Religionen,* Amateca III (Paderborn, 1996). Also helpful is O. Lacombe, *L'élan spirituel de l'hindouisme* (Paris, 1986).

tral religious act, I would call them — a bit simplistically, to be sure — mystical and theistic religions, respectively. If this diagnosis is correct, then interreligious ecumenism can adopt one of two strategies: it can attempt to assimilate the theistic into the mystical type, which implies regarding the mystical as a more comprehensive category ample enough to accommodate the theistic model, or it can pursue the opposite course. Yet a third alternative, which I would term pragmatic, has appeared on today's scene. It says that the religions should give up their interminable wrangling over truth and realize that their real essence, their real intrinsic goal, is orthopraxy, an option whose context seems rather clear-cut in the light of the challenges of the present day. In the end, orthopraxy could consist only in serving the cause of peace, justice, and the integrity of creation. The religions could retain all their formulas, forms, and rites, but they would be ordered to this right praxis: "By their fruits you shall know them." In this way, they could all keep their customs; every quarrel would become superfluous, and yet all would be one in the way called for by the challenge of the hour.

3. Greatness and Limitations of the Mystical Religions

In what follows, I would like to examine very briefly the three approaches that we have just mentioned. When we come to the theistic approach, I would like to reflect in a particular way, as befits the present occasion, on the relation between Jewish and Christian monotheism. For brevity's sake, however, I must pass over the third of the great monotheistic religions, Islam. In an age when we have learned to doubt the knowability of the transcendent and, even more, when we fear that truth claims about transcendence can lead to intolerance, it seems that the future belongs to mystical religion. It alone seems to take seriously the prohibition of images, whereas Panikkar, for example, thinks that Israel's insistence on a personal God whom it knows by name is ultimately a form of iconolatry, despite the absence of images of God.[8] By contrast, mystical religion, with its rigorously apophatic theology, makes no claim to know the divine; religion is no longer defined in terms of positive content, hence, in terms of sacred institutions. Reli-

8. R. Panikkar, *La Trinidad y la experiencia religiosa* (Barcelona, 1986).

148

gion is reduced entirely to mystical experience, a move which also rules out a priori any clash with scientific reason. New Age is the proclamation, as it were, of the age of mystical religion. The rationality of this kind of religion depends on its suspension of epistemological claims. In other words, such religion is essentially tolerant, even as it affords man the liberation from the limitations of his being that he needs in order to live and to endure his finitude.

If this were the correct approach, ecumenism would have to take the form of a universal agreement consisting in the reduction of positive propositions (that is, propositions that lay claim to substantive truth) and of sacred structures to pure functionality. This reduction would not mean, however, the simple abandonment of hitherto existing forms of theism. Rather, there seems to be a growing consensus that the two ways of viewing the divine can be regarded as compatible, ultimately as synonymous. In this view, it is fundamentally irrelevant whether we conceive of the divine as personal or non-personal. The God who speaks and the silent depths of being are ultimately, it is said, just two different ways of conceiving the ineffable reality lying beyond all concepts. Israel's central imperative, "hear, O Israel, the Lord your God is the only God," whose substance is still constitutive for Christianity and Islam as well, loses its contours. In this view, it is ultimately inconsequential whether you submit to the God who speaks or sink into the silent depths of being. The worship demanded by Israel's God and the emptying of consciousness in self-forgetful acceptance of dissolution in infinity can be regarded basically as variants of one and the same attitude vis-à-vis the infinite.

We seem, then, to have hit upon the most satisfactory solution to our problem. On the one hand, the religions can continue to exist in their present form. On the other hand, they acknowledge the relativity of all outward forms. They realize that they share a common quest for the depth of being as well as the means to attain it: an interiority in which man transcends himself to touch the ineffable, whence he returns to everyday life, consoled and strengthened.

There is no doubt that certain features of this approach can help to deepen the theistic religions. After all, mysticism and even apophatic theology have never been entirely absent from the theistic approach.[9]

9. Cf. L. Bouyer, *Mysterion: Du mystère à la mystique* (Paris, 1986).

The theistic religions have always taught that in the end everything we say about the ineffable is only a distant reflection of it, and that it is always more dissimilar than similar to what we can imagine and conceive.[10] In this respect, adoration is always linked to interiority and interiority to self-transcendence.

Nevertheless, there can be no identification of the two approaches nor can they be finally reduced to the mystical way. For such a reduction means that the world of the senses drops out of our relation to the divine. It therefore becomes impossible to speak of creation. The cosmos, no longer understood as creation, has nothing to do with God. The same is necessarily true of history. God no longer reaches into the world, which becomes in the strict sense god-less, empty of God. Religion loses its power to form a communion of mind and will, becoming instead a matter of individual therapy, as it were. Salvation is outside the world, and we get no guidance for our action in it beyond whatever strength we may acquire from regularly withdrawing into the spiritual dimension. But this dimension as such has no definable message for us. We are therefore left to our own devices when we engage in worldly activity.

Contemporary endeavors to revise ethics in fact readily assume some such conception, and even moral theology has begun to come to terms with this presupposition. The result, however, is that ethics remains something we construct. Ethos loses its binding character and obeys, more or less reluctantly, our interests. Perhaps this point shows most clearly that the theistic model, while indeed having more in common with the mystical than one might initially suppose, is nonetheless irreducible to it. For the acknowledgment of God's will is an essential component of faith in the one God. The worship of God is not simply an absorption, but restores to us our very selves; it lays claim on us in the midst of everyday life, demanding all the powers of our intelligence, our sensibility, and our will. Important as the apophatic element may be, faith in God cannot do without truth, which must have a specifiable content.

10. This is how the fourth Lateran Council (1217) expresses it: "quia inter creatorem et creaturam non potest similitudo notari, quin inter eos maior sit dissimilitudo notanda" [because it is impossible to recognize only likeness between the Creator and the creature without having to recognize an even greater unlikeness between them] (DS 806).

4. The Pragmatic Model

Is it not the case, then, that the pragmatic model, which we mentioned just now, is a solution that measures up equally to the challenges of the modern world and to the realities of the religions? It does not take much to see that this is a false inference. To be sure, commitment to peace, justice, and the integrity of creation is of supreme importance, and there is no doubt that religion ought to offer a major stimulus to this commitment. However, the religions possess no a priori knowledge of what serves peace here and now; of how to build social justice within and among states; of how best to preserve the integrity of creation and to cultivate it responsibly in the name of the Creator. These matters have to be worked out in detail by reason, a process which always includes free debate among diverse opinions and respect for different approaches. Whenever a religiously motivated moralism sidesteps this often irreducible pluralism, declaring *one* way to be the only right one, then religion is perverted into an ideological dictatorship, whose totalitarian passion does not build peace, but destroys it. Man makes God the servant of his own aims, thereby degrading God and himself. J. A. Cuttat had these very wise words to say about this a good forty years ago: "To strive to make humanity better and happier by uniting the religions is one thing. To implore with burning hearts the union of all men in love of the same God is another. And the first is perhaps the subtlest temptation the devil has devised to bring the second to ruin."[11] Needless to say, this refusal to transform religion into a political moralism does not change the fact that education for peace, justice, and the integrity of creation is among the essential tasks of the Christian faith and of every religion — or that the dictum "by their fruits ye shall know them" can rightly be applied to their performance of it.

5. Judaism and Christianity

Let us return to the theistic approach and to its prospects in the "council of religions." As we know, theism appears historically in three major forms: Judaism, Christianity, and Islam. We must therefore explore the

---

11. Cuttat, *Begegnung der Religionen,* 84.

possibility of reconciling the three great monotheisms before we attempt to bring them into dialogue with the mystical approach. As I have already indicated, I will limit myself here to the first split within the monotheistic world, the division between Judaism and Christianity. To deal with this division is also fundamental for the relation of both religions to Islam. Needless to say, I can do no more than attempt a very modest sketch regarding this far-ranging topic. I would like to propose two ideas.

The average observer would probably regard the following statement as obvious: the Hebrew Bible, the "Old Testament," unites Jews and Christians, whereas faith in Jesus Christ as the Son of God and Redeemer divides them. It is not difficult to see, however, that this kind of division between what unites and what divides is superficial. For the primal fact is that through Christ Israel's Bible came to the non-Jews and became their Bible. It is no empty theological rhetoric when the Letter to the Ephesians says that Christ has breached the wall between the Jews and the other religions of the world and made them one. Rather, it is an empirical datum, even though the empirical does not capture all that is contained in the theological statement. For through the encounter with Jesus of Nazareth the God of Israel became the God of the Gentiles. Through him, in fact, the promise that the nations would pray to the God of Israel as the one God, that the "mountain of the Lord" would be exalted above all other mountains, has been fulfilled. Even if Israel cannot join Christians in seeing Jesus as the *Son* of God, it is not altogether impossible for Israel to recognize him as the *servant* of God who brings the light of his God to the nations. The converse is also true: even if Christians wish that Israel might one day recognize Christ as the Son of God and that the fissure that still divides them might thereby be closed, they ought to acknowledge the decree of God, who has obviously entrusted Israel with a distinctive mission in the "time of the Gentiles." The Fathers define this mission in the following way: the Jews must remain as the first proprietors of Holy Scripture with respect to us, in order to establish a testimony to the world.

But what is the tenor of this testimony? This brings us to the second line of reflection that I would like to propose. I think we could say that two things are essential to Israel's faith. The first is the Torah, commitment to God's will, and thus the establishment of his dominion, his kingdom, in this world. The second is the prospect of hope, the expectation of the Messiah — the expectation, indeed, the certainty, that God himself will enter into this history and create justice, which we can only approximate very imperfectly. The three dimensions of time are thus connected: obedience to God's will bears on an already spoken word that now exists in history and at each new moment has to be made present again in obedience. This obedience, which makes present a bit of God's justice in time, is oriented toward a future when God will gather up the fragments of time and usher them as a whole into his justice.

Christianity does not give up this basic configuration. The trinity of faith, hope, and love corresponds in a certain respect to the three dimensions of time: the obedience of faith takes the word that comes from eternity and is spoken in history and transforms it into love, into presence, and in this way opens the door to hope. It is characteristic of the Christian faith that all three dimensions are contained and sustained in the figure of Christ, who also introduces them into eternity. In him, time and eternity exist together, and the infinite gulf between God and man is bridged. For Christ is the one who came to us without therefore ceasing to be with the Father; he is present in the believing community, and yet at the same time is still the one who is coming. The Church too *awaits* the Messiah. She already knows him, yet he has still to reveal his glory. Obedience and promise belong together for the Christian faith, too. For Christians, Christ is the present Sinai, the living Torah that lays its obligations on us, that bindingly commands us, but that in so doing draws us into the broad space of love and its inexhaustible possibilities. In this way, Christ guarantees hope in the God who does not let history sink into a meaningless past, but rather sustains it and brings it to its goal. It likewise follows from this that the figure of Christ simultaneously unites and divides Israel and the Church: it is not in our power to overcome this division, but it keeps us together on the way to what is coming and for this reason must not become an enmity.

6. Christian Faith and the Mystical Religions

We come, then, to the question that we have deferred so far. It is a question that concerns in a very concrete way the place of Christianity in

THE UNITY OF THE CHURCH

THE UNITY OF THE CHURCH

the dialogue of the religions: is theistic, dogmatic, and hierarchically organized religion necessarily intolerant? Does faith in a dogmatically formulated truth make the believer incapable of dialogue? Is renunciation of truth a necessary condition of the capacity for peace?

I would like to try to answer this question in two steps. First of all, we must recall that the Christian faith includes a mystical and apophatic dimension. The new encounter with the Asian religions will be significant for Christians precisely insofar as it reminds them of this aspect of their faith and breaks open any one-sided hardening of the positivity of Christianity. Here we must face an objection: are not the doctrine of the Trinity and faith in the Incarnation so radically positive that they bring God literally within our grasp, indeed, our conceptual grasp? Does not the mystery of God get caught in fixed forms and in a historically datable figure?

At this point it would behoove us to recall the controversy between Gregory of Nyssa and Eunomius. Eunomius, in fact, asserted that, because of revelation, God could be fully grasped in concepts. By contrast, Gregory interprets trinitarian theology and Christology as mystical theology, as an invitation to an infinite path into the always infinitely greater God.[12] As a matter of fact, trinitarian theology is apophatic, for it cancels the simple concept of person derived from human experience and, while affirming the divine Logos, at the same time preserves the greater silence from which the Logos comes and to which the Logos refers us. Analogous things could be shown for the Incarnation. Yes, God becomes altogether concrete, he becomes something we can lay hold of in history. He comes bodily to men. But this very God who has become tangible is wholly mysterious. His self-chosen humiliation, his "kenosis," is a new form, as it were, of the cloud of mystery in which he hides and at the same time shows himself.[13] For what paradox could be greater than the very fact that God is vulnerable and can be killed? The Word that the incarnate and crucified Christ *is* always immeasurably transcends all hu-

---

12. Cf. most recently F. Dünzl, *Braut und Bräutigam: Die Auslegung des Canticum durch Gregor von Nyssa* (Tübingen, 1993); Bouyer, *Mysterion*, 225ff.; still important today is H. U. von Balthasar's *Présence et pensée: Essai sur la Philosophie Religieuse de Grégoire de Nysse* (Paris, 1942). Eng., *Presence and Thought: An Essay on the Religious Philosophy of Gregory of Nyssa* (San Francisco: Ignatius Press, 1995).

13. Cf. B. Stubenrauch, *Dialogisches Dogma: Der christliche Auftrag zur interreligiösen Begegnung* (Freiburg, 1995), especially 84-96.

man words. Consequently, God's kenosis is itself the place where the religions can come into contact without arrogant claims to domination. The Platonic Socrates underscores the connection between truth and defenselessness, truth and poverty, especially in the *Apology* and the *Crito*. Socrates is credible because in taking the part of "the god" he gets neither rank nor possession, but, on the contrary, is thrust into poverty and, finally, into the role of the accused.[14] Poverty is the truly divine form in which truth appears: in its poverty it can demand obedience without alienation.

7. Concluding Theses

A final question remains: what does all of this mean concretely? What can such a conception of Christianity be expected to contribute to interreligious dialogue? Does the theistic, incarnational model get us any further than the mystical and the pragmatic? Now, let me say frankly at the outset that anyone betting that interreligious dialogue will result in the unification of the religions is headed for disappointment. Such unification is hardly possible within our historical time and perhaps it is not even desirable. What can we expect, then? I would like to make three points:

1. The religions can encounter one another only by delving more deeply into the truth, not by giving it up. Skepticism does not unite. Nor does sheer pragmatism. Both are simply an opening for ideologies, which then step in with all the more self-assurance. The renunciation of truth and conviction does not elevate man, but exposes him to the calculus of utility and robs him of his greatness. What is required, however, is reverence for the other's belief, along with the willingness to seek truth in what I find alien — a truth that concerns me and that can correct me and lead me further. What is required is the willingness to look behind what may appear strange in order to find the deeper reality it conceals. I must also be willing to let my narrow understanding of truth be broken open, to learn my own beliefs better by understanding

---

14. Cf., for example, *Apologia* 31 c: "And indeed I believe that I can produce a sufficient witness to the fact that I speak the truth, and that is my poverty"; also see *Crito* 48 c-d.

the other, and in this way to let myself be furthered on the path to God, who is greater — in the certainty that I never wholly possess the truth about God and am always a learner before it, a pilgrim whose way to it is never at an end.

2. Although we must always seek the positive in the other, union means that the other must help me to find the truth; we cannot and must not dispense with criticism. Religion contains, as it were, the precious pearl of truth, but it is also continually hiding it, and is always running the risk of missing its own essence. Religion can grow sick and become a destructive phenomenon. It can and should lead to truth, but it can also cut man off from it. The Old Testament's critique of religion has by no means become superfluous today. It may be relatively easy for us to criticize the religion of others, but we must also be ready to accept criticism of ourselves, of our own religion. Karl Barth distinguished between religion and faith in Christianity. He erred in wanting to separate them entirely, in regarding faith alone as positive and religion as negative. Faith without religion is unreal. Religion is a part of faith, and by its very nature Christianity must live as a religion. But Barth was right in that even the religion of Christians can grow sick and become superstition. He saw correctly, in other words, that the concrete religion in which Christians live their faith must be unceasingly purified by the truth. This is a truth that shows itself in faith and that at the same time newly reveals its mystery and its infinity in dialogue.

3. Does this mean that missionary activity must cease and be replaced by dialogue, in which we do not speak of truth, but help one another be better Christians, Jews, Moslems, Hindus, and Buddhists? My answer is no. For this would be yet another form of the complete lack of belief. Under the pretext of fostering the best in another, we would fail to take both ourselves and the other seriously and would end up renouncing truth. The answer, I think, is that mission and dialogue must no longer be antitheses, but must penetrate each other.[15] Dialogue is not random conversation, but aims at persuasion, at discovering the truth. Otherwise it is worthless. Conversely, future missionaries can no

15. Important on the proper understanding of mission is H. Bürkle, *Missionstheologie* (Stuttgart, 1979); also see P. Beyerhaus, *Er sandte sein Wort. Theologie der christlichen Mission, I: Die Bibel in der Mission* (Wuppertal, 1996). See the important observations in R. Spaemann, "Ist eine nicht-missionarische Praxis universalistischer Religionen möglich?," *Theorie und Praxis. Festschrift N. Lobkowicz zum 65. Geburtstag* (Berlin, 1996), 41-48.

longer presuppose that they are telling someone hitherto devoid of any knowledge of God what he has to believe in. This situation may in fact occur and perhaps will occur with increasing frequency in a world that in many places is becoming atheistic. But among the religions we encounter people who through their religion have heard of God and try to live in relation to him. Preaching must therefore become a dialogical event. We are not saying something completely unknown to the other, but disclosing the hidden depth of what he already touches in his own belief. And, conversely, the preacher is not simply a giver, but also a receiver. In this sense, what Nicholas of Cusa expressed as a wish and a hope in his vision of the heavenly council should take place in interreligious dialogue. It should increasingly become a listening to the Logos, who shows us unity in the midst of our divisions and contradictions.

Translated by Adrian J. Walker

The Theological Locus of Ecclesial Movements

In his great encyclical on mission, *Redemptoris missio,* the Holy Father says:

> Within the church, there are various types of services, functions, ministries and ways of promoting the Christian life. I call to mind, as a new development occurring in many churches in recent times, the rapid growth of "ecclesial movements" filled with missionary dynamism. When these movements humbly seek to become part of the life of local churches and are welcomed by bishops and priests within diocesan and parish structures, they represent a true gift of God both for new evangelization and for missionary activity properly so-called. I therefore recommend that they be spread and that they be used to give fresh energy, especially among young people, to the Christian life and to evangelization, within a pluralistic view of the ways in which Christians can associate and express themselves.[1]

It was a wonderful event for me personally when I came into closer contact with movements such as the Neocatecumenate, Communion and Liberation, and Focolare and experienced the energy and enthusiasm with which they lived the faith and were impelled by their joy in it

---

1. *Redemptoris missio,* 72.

This address was given at the World Congress of Ecclesial Movements, sponsored by the Pontifical Council for the Laity, Rome, 27-29 May 1998. Publication in *Communio: International Catholic Review* 25, no. 3 (Fall 1998).

to share with others the gift they had received. This was in the early 1970s, a time when Karl Rahner and others were speaking of a winter in the Church. And it did seem that, after the great blossoming of the Council, frost was creeping in instead of springtime, and that exhaustion was replacing dynamism. The dynamism now seemed to be somewhere else entirely — where people, relying on their own strength and without resorting to God, were setting about creating a better world of the future. That a world without God could not be good, let alone a better world, was obvious to anyone who had eyes to see. But where was God in all this? Had not the Church in fact become worn out and dispirited after so many debates and so much searching for new structures? What Rahner was saying was perfectly understandable. It put into words an experience that we were all having. But suddenly here was something that no one had planned. Here the Holy Spirit himself had, so to speak, taken the floor. The faith was reawakening precisely among the young, who embraced it without ifs, ands, or buts, without escape hatches and loopholes, and who experienced it in its totality as a precious, life-giving gift. To be sure, many people felt that this interfered with their intellectual discussions or their models for redesigning a completely different Church in their own image — how could it be otherwise? Every irruption of the Holy Spirit always upsets human plans. But there were and are more serious difficulties. For these movements had their share of childhood diseases. One could feel the power of the Spirit in them, but the Spirit works through human beings and does not simply free them from their weaknesses. There were tendencies to exclusivity and one-sidedness that made them unable to insert themselves into the life of the local churches. Buoyed up by their youthful elan, they were convinced that the local church had, as it were, to raise itself to their level, while they had to keep themselves from being dragged into a structure that, to be sure, sometimes really was somewhat crusty. Frictions arose in which both sides were at fault in different ways. It became necessary to reflect on how to properly relate the two realities, the new awakening [*Aufbruch*] in the context of the present situation, on the one hand, and the permanent structures of the Church's life, the parish and the diocese, on the other. To a large extent the issues at stake are very practical ones whose theoretical content should not be unduly inflated. On the other hand, we are dealing with a phenomenon that recurs periodically in various forms throughout the history of the Church. There is the permanent basic structure of the Church's life, which gives continuity to the organization of the Church throughout history, and there are the ever renewed irruptions of the Holy Spirit, which ceaselessly revitalize and renew this structure. But this renewal hardly ever happens entirely without pain and friction. In the end, then, we cannot dismiss the fundamental question about how to determine correctly the theological location of these "movements" within the structural continuity of the Church.

I. Attempts to Clarify the Issue
Through a Dialectic of Principles

A. Institution and Charism

The duality of institution and event, or institution and charism, immediately suggests itself as a fundamental model for resolving the question. But if we try to analyze the two terms more closely in order to arrive at valid rules for defining their relationship, something unexpected happens. The concept of "institution" comes to pieces in our hands when we try to give it a precise theological definition. After all, what are the fundamental institutional factors in the Church, the permanent organization that gives the Church its distinctive shape? The answer is, of course, sacramental office in its different degrees: bishop, priest, deacon. The sacrament that, significantly, bears the name *ordo* is, in the end, the sole permanent and binding structure that forms so to say the fixed organizational pattern of the Church and makes the Church an "institution." But it was not until this century that it became customary, for reasons of ecumenical expediency, to designate the sacrament of *ordo* simply as "office" [*Amt*]. This usage places *ordo* entirely in the light of institution and the institutional. But this "office" is a "sacrament," and this fact signals a break with the ordinary sociological understanding of institutions. That this structural element of the Church, which is the only permanent one, is a sacrament, means that it must be perpetually recreated by God. It is not at the Church's disposal, it is not simply there, and the Church cannot set it up on its own initiative. It comes into being only secondarily through a call on the part of the Church. It is created primarily by God's call to this man, which is to say, only charismatically-pneumatologically. By the same token, the only attitude in which it can be accepted and lived is one unceasingly shaped by the newness of the vocation, by the unmanipulable freedom of the *pneuma*. The reason — ultimately, the only reason — why there can be a priest shortage is this. The Church cannot simply appoint "officials" by itself, but must await the call from God. This is why it has been held from the beginning that this office cannot be made by the institution, but has to be impetrated from God. What Jesus says in the gospels has always been the case: "the harvest is plentiful, but the workers are few; pray the Lord of the harvest to send workers into his harvest" (Mt 9:37). This also explains why the calling of the twelve is the fruit of a night that Jesus had spent in prayer (Lk 6:12ff.).

The Latin Church has expressly underscored this strictly charismatic character of priestly ministry by linking — in accord with ancient Church tradition — priesthood with virginity, which clearly can be understood only as a personal charism, never simply as an official qualification.[2] The demand for their uncoupling ultimately rests on the notion that the priesthood must not be considered charismatically, but must be regarded as an office that the institution itself can fill in order to guarantee its own security and the satisfaction of its needs. When the attempt is made to take control of the priesthood for purposes of institutional security, the sort of charismatic bond implied by the requirement of celibacy is a scandal that has to be removed as quickly as possible. But when that happens, the Church as a whole is also being understood as a purely human organization, and the security that is obtained by these means fails to deliver precisely what it was meant to achieve. That the Church is not *our* institution, but the irruption of something else, that it is by essence "iuris divini," means that we can never simply make the Church ourselves. It means that we may never employ purely institutional criteria, that the Church is wholly itself precisely where it breaks through the criteria and methods of human institutions.

To be sure, alongside the sacrament, which is really the fundamen-

---

2. That priestly celibacy is not a medieval invention, but goes back to the earliest period of the Church, is shown clearly and convincingly by Cardinal A. M. Stickler, *The Case for Clerical Celibacy: Its Historical Development and Theological Foundations* (San Francisco: Ignatius Press, 1995). Cf. also C. Cochini, *Origines apostoliques du célibat sacerdotal* (Paris-Namur, 1981); S. Heid, *Zölibat in der frühen Kirche* (Paderborn, 1997).

tal ordering structure, there are also institutions of purely human right in the Church. These institutions serve various forms of administration, organization, and coordination that can and must develop according to the needs of the times. But it must be said that, while the Church does need such homegrown institutions, when they become too numerous and too powerful, they jeopardize the order and the vitality of the Church's spiritual essence. The Church must constantly check its own institutional structure in order to keep it from taking on too much weight — to prevent it from hardening into an armor that stifles its real, spiritual life. It goes without saying that, when the Church fails to get priestly vocations for a longer period of time, it can fall into the temptation to create for itself what one might call an ersatz clergy of purely human right.[3] The Church must of course try to organize temporary structures in cases of need, and it has successfully done so time and again in the missions or in mission-like situations. We can only heartily thank all those who have served and continue to serve the Church as leaders of prayer and heralds of the Gospel in such emergency situations. If, however, this should become a way of neglecting prayer for vocations to the sacrament, if the Church gradually began to use such situations to gain self-sufficiency and to make itself as it were independent of God's gift, it would be acting like Saul, who, hard pressed by the Philistines, waited long for Samuel, but, when Samuel failed to appear and the people were breaking rank, lost his patience and offered the holocaust himself. He had thought that, given the urgency of the situation, there was no other option and that he could and must take God's business into his own hands. But now he was told that by doing just that he had thrown everything away: I want obedience, not sacrifice (cf. 1 Sam 13:8-14; 15:22).

Let us return to our question: How do we characterize the relationship between the permanent pattern of Church order and ever new charismatic irruptions? The institution-charism model does not answer this question, because the antithesis [of the two terms] does not adequately capture the reality of the Church. Nevertheless, we can infer a few initial rules from what we have said so far:

a) It is important that the spiritual office, the priesthood, itself be understood and lived charismatically. The priest himself should be a

---

3. The 1997 instruction on the ministry of the laity ultimately concerns this question.

"pneumatic," a *homo spiritualis,* a man awakened and driven by the Holy Spirit. It is the Church's task to make sure that this character of the sacrament is seen and accepted. The Church must not put numbers in the foreground and lower spiritual standards out of zeal for the development of its organizational structures. If it did so, the Church would disfigure the meaning of the priesthood itself. A ministry poorly performed does more harm than good. It becomes an obstacle on the way to the priesthood and the faith. The Church must keep faith and must acknowledge the Lord as its creator and sustainer. And it must do everything it can to help those called to remain faithful beyond the initial awakening, to keep from gradual suffocation in routine, and to become more and more truly spiritual men.

b) Where the spiritual office is lived pneumatically and charismatically in this way, there is no institutional hardening. Rather, there is an intrinsic openness to charisms, a sort of "nose" for the Spirit and his action. So too charism can recognize its own origin in the office holder, and ways of fruitful collaboration in the discernment of spirits are found.

c) In situations of scarcity, the Church must create stopgap structures. But these structures must be conceived as intrinsically open to the sacrament; they must tend toward it, not lead away from it. In general the Church must keep the number of self-created administrative structures as small as possible. It must not over-institutionalize itself, but must always remain open to the Lord's unforeseen, unplanned calls.

B. Christology and Pneumatology

Now, what has been said raises a question: if it is only partially correct to see institution and charism as opposites, so that this pair of terms provides only partial answers to our question, are there perhaps other theological viewpoints that can deal with it more adequately? The contrast between christological and pneumatological approaches to the Church is becoming an increasingly prominent theme in contemporary theology. This contrast generates the claim that sacrament belongs on the side of Christology and the Incarnation, which has to be supplemented by the pneumatological-charismatic perspective. It is true, of course, that Christ and the *Pneuma* have to be distinguished. But just as we must not treat the three persons of the Trinity as a *communio* of three gods, we correctly distinguish Christ and the Spirit only when their diversity helps us better understand their unity. The Spirit cannot be correctly understood without Christ, but it is equally impossible to understand Christ without the Holy Spirit. "The Lord is the Spirit" Paul tells us in 2 Cor 3:17. This does not mean that the two are simply the same thing or person. But it does mean that Christ can be among us and for us as the Lord only because the incarnation was not his last word. The Incarnation reaches its apex in the death on the Cross and in the Resurrection. This means that Christ can come only because he has gone before us into the order of life of the Holy Spirit and communicates himself through and in that Spirit. St. Paul's pneumatological Christology and the farewell discourses of the gospel of John have not, I think, been incorporated clearly enough into our vision of Christology and pneumatology. But the new presence of Christ in the Spirit is the essential condition for the existence of sacrament and of a sacramental presence of the Lord.

This sheds light once again on "spiritual" [*geistlich*] office in the Church and on its theological location, which the tradition has defined with the term *successio apostolica*. "Apostolic succession" means precisely the opposite of what it might appear to mean, namely, that through the continuous chain of succession we become as it were independent of the Spirit. Linking to the line of succession in fact means that the sacramental office is never simply at our disposal, but must be given each time by the Spirit, that it is precisely the Spirit-sacrament, which we can neither create nor institute ourselves. Functional competence as such is not by itself sufficient for that; the Lord's gift is necessary. In the sacrament, in the Church's representative, symbolic action, the Lord reserves to himself the permanent institution of the priestly ministry. The totally specific combination of "once" and "always" characteristic of the mystery of Christ appears very beautifully here. The "always" of the sacrament, the presence of the historical origin in every age of the Church, implies a link with the *ephapax*, with the event of the origin that happens once only. This link with the origin, this stake planted in the ground of the once-only and unrepeatable event, is non-negotiable. We can never take refuge in a free-floating pneumatology; we can never leave behind the ground of the Incarnation, of God's action in history. But the converse is also true. This never-to-be-repeated event imparts itself in the gift of the Holy Spirit, who is the Spirit of the risen Lord. It does not vanish, like something dead and gone, into the forever irretrievable past, but has the force of the present, because Christ has passed through the "curtain, that is, through his flesh" (Heb 10:20) and has thereby released what endures forever in what takes place only once. The Incarnation does not stop with the historical Jesus, with his "sarx" (2 Cor 5:16!). The "historical Jesus" has eternal significance precisely because his flesh is transformed in the Resurrection, so that he can make himself present to all places and all times in the power of the Holy Spirit, as the farewell discourses in John wonderfully show (cf. especially Jn 14:28: "I go and I come to you"). Given this christological-pneumatological synthesis, we can expect that a deepening of the concept of "apostolic succession" will be truly helpful for resolving our problem.

C. Hierarchy and Prophecy

Before we pursue further this line of thought, we need to mention briefly a third proposal for explaining the duality [*Gegenüber*] between the permanent order of ecclesial life, on the one hand, and pneumatic movements, on the other. There is a certain tendency today that, building on Luther's interpretation of Scripture in terms of the dialectic of law and gospel, opposes the cultic-sacerdotal aspect and the prophetic aspect of salvation history. On this reading, the movements would be ranged on the side of prophecy. This too, like the other proposals that we have considered so far, is not entirely false. It is, however, extremely inexact and for this reason unhelpful as it now stands. The issue raised in this connection is too big to be dealt with in detail here. The first thing that would have to be said in addressing this point is that the law itself has the character of a promise. It is only because the law has this character that Christ could fulfill it and, at the same time, "suspend" [*aufheben*] it in the act of fulfillment. Second, the writing prophets never meant to annul the Torah, but, on the contrary, to vindicate its true meaning against misuse. Finally, it is also important that the mission of prophecy was always entrusted to single persons and never became a settled class [*Stand*]. Insofar as prophecy claimed to be a "class," it was criticized by the writing prophets just as sharply as the priestly "class" of the Old Testament.[4] There is simply no warrant in Scripture for dividing the Church into a left and a right, into the prophetic class (represented by the orders or the movements) and the hierarchy. On the contrary: this is a construction that is completely foreign to Scripture. The Church is not structured dialectically, but organically. It is correct, then, only that there are various functions in the Church, and that God continually stirs up prophetic men — they can be laypeople or religious, but also bishops and priests — who proclaim to it the right word that is not pronounced with sufficient force in the normal course of the "institution." It is quite obvious, I think, that we cannot interpret the nature and task of the movements from this perspective. It certainly does not capture their own understanding of themselves.

The foregoing reflections thus yield rather meager results for our question. Yet these results are important. The choice of a dialectic of principles as our starting point does not lead to the desired solution. Instead of attempting to resolve the question using such a dialectic of principles, we must, in my opinion, choose a historical approach, as befits the historical nature of the faith and the Church.

II. The Perspectives of History:
Apostolic Succession and Apostolic Movements

A. Universal and Local Offices

Let us ask the question then: what does this origin look like? Anyone who has even a modest acquaintance with the debates surrounding the nascent Church, to whose pattern all Christian churches and communities appeal in order to legitimate themselves, knows how little prospect there seems to be of getting anywhere with this kind of historical question. If, in spite of that, I risk a tentative solution from this angle, I do so on the presupposition of the Catholic view of the Church and its

4. The classical antithesis between prophets sent by God and professional prophets is found in Amos 7:10-17. A similar situation occurs in 1 Kings 22 in the contrast between the 400 prophets and Micah; again in Jeremiah, e.g., 37:19. Cf. also J. Ratzinger, *The Nature and Mission of Theology: Its Role in the Light of Present Controversy* (San Francisco: Ignatius, 1995), 118ff.

origin. This view, while offering a fixed framework, also leaves open areas for further reflection that by no means have been fully explored. There is no doubt that, from Pentecost on, the immediate bearers of Christ's mission are the twelve, who very soon appear also under the name "apostles." It is their task to bring the message of Christ "to the end of the earth" (Acts 1:8), to go out to all nations and to make disciples of all men (Mt 28:19). The territory assigned them for this mission is the world. Without being restricted as to place, they serve the upbuilding of the one body of Christ, the one people of God, the one Church of Christ. The apostles were not bishops of particular local churches, but just that, "apostles," and as such they were responsible for the whole world and for the whole Church that was to be built: the universal Church precedes the local churches, which come into existence as its concrete realizations.[5] To put it even more clearly and unequivocally: Paul was never the bishop of a particular place nor did he ever intend to be. There was only one division of labor at the beginning, and Paul describes it in Gal 2:9: we — Barnabas and I — for the gentiles, they — Peter, James, and John — for the Jews. However, this initial division was soon superseded. Peter and John recognized that they too were sent to the gentiles and at once went beyond the limits of Israel. James, the brother of the Lord, who after the year 42 became a sort of primate of the Jewish Church, was doubtless not an apostle.

Without going into further detail, we can say the following: the apostolic office is a universal one whose scope is the whole of humanity and thus the whole of the one Church. It is the missionary activity of the apostles that gives rise to the local churches, which now need responsible leaders. It is the duty of these men to guarantee unity of faith with the whole Church, to form the life within the local church, and to

---

5. Cf. Congregation for the Doctrine of the Faith, Letter *Communionis notio* (Libreria Editrice Vaticana, 1994), 29, no. 9; cf. there also my introduction, 8ff. I have presented the relations between them in greater detail in my little book: *Called to Communion* (San Francisco: Ignatius Press, 1996), esp. 43f. and 75-103. The fact that the one Church, the one bride of Christ, which carries on the heritage of the people of Israel, of Zion, the "daughter" and "bride," has priority over the empirical concretization of the people of God in the local churches is so evident in Scripture and the Fathers that it is hard for me to understand the oft-repeated contestation of this claim. It is enough to re-read de Lubac's *Catholicisme* (1938) or his *Méditation sur l'Eglise*, 3d ed. (1954), or the marvelous texts that H. Rahner collected in his book *Mater Ecclesiae* (1944).

keep the communities open in order to encourage further growth and to make possible the gift of the Gospel to those fellow citizens who do not yet believe. This local ecclesial [*ortskirchlich*] office, which initially appears under many names, gradually takes on a fixed, uniform figure. Quite clearly, then, two structures existed side by side in the nascent Church. There was of course a certain fluidity between them, but they can be clearly distinguished: on the one side, the local ecclesial ministries, which gradually grew into permanent forms; on the other side, the apostolic ministry, which very soon ceased to be restricted to the twelve. We can clearly distinguish two concepts of apostleship in Paul. On the one hand, he vigorously underscores the uniqueness of his apostolate, which rests upon his encounter with the Risen Lord and thereby places him on a level with the twelve. On the other hand, he understands "apostle" as an office extending far beyond this group, as in 1 Cor 12:28: this broader concept is also in the background when he styles Andronikos and Junias as apostles. We find similar terminology in Eph 2:20, where talk of the apostles and prophets as the foundation of the Church is certainly also meant to include more than just the twelve. In the second century the Didache speaks of prophets, which it very clearly understands in terms of such a missionary, supralocal office. It is all the more interesting that the Didache says of them: "they are your high-priests" (13:3).

We may assume then that the two types of office — the universal and local — continued to coexist far into the second century, that is, into a time when the identity of the bearer of the apostolic succession was quite certainly already becoming a serious question. Various texts suggest that this coexistence of the two structures was not entirely free of conflict. The third Letter of John shows us a very clear example of such a conflict situation. However, the more the then accessible "ends of the earth" were reached, the harder it became to keep open a meaningful place for the "itinerants." Abuses of office on the part of these itinerants may also have contributed to their gradual disappearance. Now it was up to the local communities and their leaders, who had in the meantime acquired a very clear profile as bishop, priest, and deacon, to spread the faith in the respective territory of their local churches. That at the time of the Emperor Constantine Christians made up around 8 percent of the population of the Empire, and that even at the end of the fourth century they remained a minority, shows what an immense task this was. In this situation those who presided over the local churches, the bishops, had to recognize that they were now successors of the apostles and that the apostolic task lay entirely on their shoulders. The realization that the bishops, the responsible leaders of the local churches, are the successors of the apostles, was very clearly articulated in the second half of the second century by Irenaeus of Lyon. This definition of the essence of the episcopal office implies two foundational elements:

a) Apostolic succession entails, first of all, the familiar idea that the bishops guarantee the continuity and unity of faith — in a continuity that we call sacramental.

b) But apostolic succession implies an even more concrete task, which goes beyond the administration of the local churches: the bishops must now ensure the carrying on of Jesus' mission to make all nations his disciples and to bring the Gospel to the ends of the earth. They are responsible — Irenaeus underscores this — for keeping the Church from becoming a sort of federation of local churches that as such are juxtaposed and for ensuring that it retain its universality and unity. The bishops must sustain the universal dynamism of the apostolate.[6]

At the beginning, we spoke of the danger that the priestly office could be understood ultimately in purely institutional and bureaucratic terms, that it might forget its charismatic dimension. Now a second danger appears: the office of the apostolic succession can atrophy to a merely local ecclesial ministry, it can lose sight — and heart — of the universality of Christ's mission. The restlessness that drives us to bring the gift of Christ to others can die out in the stasis of a solidly established Church. Let me put the matter starkly: the concept of apostolic succession projects out beyond the merely local church, in which it can never be exhausted. The universal dimension, the element that transcends the local ecclesial ministries, remains indispensable.

B. Apostolic Movements in the History of the Church

We must now probe more deeply into, and put more concrete historical flesh on, this thesis, which already anticipates my final conclusion, in-

---

6. Cf. on this section once more, Ratzinger, *Called to Communion*, 83ff.

asmuch as it takes us directly to the ecclesial location of the movements. I said before that, for a great variety of reasons, the universal ecclesial ministries gradually disappear in the second century and are absorbed by the episcopal office. In many respects this development was not simply historically inevitable, but also theologically necessary, since it brought to light the unity of the sacrament and the intrinsic unity of the apostolic ministry. But it was also — as was said — a development that was not without its dangers. For this reason it was perfectly logical that as early as the third century a new element should appear in the life of the Church that we may without controversy call a movement: monasticism. Now, one can object that early monasticism had no apostolic and missionary character, that it was, on the contrary, a flight from the world to islands of holiness. To be sure, we can observe the absence of a missionary tendency to spread the faith throughout the world at the beginning of monasticism. With Anthony, who stands as a clearly defined figure at the beginning of monasticism, the dominant impulse was the desire to live the *vita evangelica* — the desire to live the Gospel radically and in its totality.[7] His conversion story is remarkably similar to that of Saint Francis of Assisi. We find in both the same impulsion to take the Gospel literally, to follow Christ in radical poverty, and to let him alone give shape to one's whole life. Anthony's departure into the desert was a removal from the solidly established local ecclesial structure, from a Christianity that had gradually adapted itself to the demands of worldly life, in order to follow Christ without ifs, ands, or buts. But this move generates a new spiritual fatherhood that, while not having a directly missionary character, nonetheless supplements the fatherhood of bishops and priests by the power of a wholly pneumatic life.[8]

In the works of Basil, who gave Eastern monasticism its permanent form, we see the very set of problems that many movements have to face today. Basil had absolutely no intention of creating a separate institution alongside the normal Church. The first and, in the strict

7. See Athanase d'Alexandrie, *Vie d'Antoine*, ed. G. Bartelink, *Sources Chrétiennes* 400 (Paris, 1994); in the introduction especially the section: "L'exemple de la vie évangelique et apostolique," 52f.

8. On the theme of spiritual fatherhood I would like to refer to the insightful little book of G. Bunge, *Geistliche Vaterschaft: Christliche Gnosis bei Evagrios Pontikos* (Regensburg, 1988).

sense, only rule that he composed was not conceived — in Balthasar's words — as the rule of an order, but as an ecclesial rule, as the "manual for the committed Christian."[9] Yet this is true of the origin of almost all movements, not least those of our own century: the point is to seek, not a community apart, but Christianity as a whole, a Church that is obedient to the Gospel and lives by it. Basil, who had first been a monk, accepted the episcopal office and thus powerfully illustrated in his own life the charismatic character of that office and the inner unity of the Church. Basil, like today's movements, was obliged to accept the fact that the movement to follow Christ radically cannot be completely merged with the local church. In the second draft of a rule, which Gribomont calls the small Asketikon, Basil conceives a movement as a "transitional form between a group of committed Christians open to the Church as a whole and a self-organizing and self-institutionalizing monastic order."[10] The same Gribomont sees the monastic community that Basil founded as a "small group for the vitalization of the whole" and does not hesitate "to call [Basil] the patron not only of the teaching and hospital orders, but also of the new communities without vows."[11]

So much is clear: the monastic movement creates a new center of life that does not abolish the local ecclesial structure of the post-apostolic Church, yet does not completely coincide with it, but is active within it as a vitalizing force. This center also functions as a reservoir from which the local church can draw a truly spiritual clergy [*geistliche-Geistliche*] that constantly renews the fusion of institution and charism. An index of this is the fact that the Eastern Church selects bishops from among the monks, thus defining the bishop's office charismatically, perpetually renewing it, as it were, from the apostolic source.

If we now look at the history of the Church as a whole, we see that the local church, as that ecclesial form whose defining mark is the episcopal office, cannot but be the supporting structure that permanently upholds the edifice of the Church through all ages. On the other hand,

---

9. H. U. von Balthasar, *Die Großen Ordensregeln,* 7th ed. (Einsiedeln, 1994), 47.

10. J. Gribomont, "Les Règles Morales de S. Basile et le Nouveau Testament," in Aland-Cross, ed., *Studia Patristica,* vol. 2 (1957), 416-426; Balthasar, *Die Großen Ordensregeln,* 48f.

11. J. Gribomont, "Obéissance et Evangile selon S. Basile le Grand," *Vie Spir. Sppl. Nr. 21* (1952), 192-215, esp. 192; Balthasar, *Die Großen Ordensregeln,* 57.

the Church is also criss-crossed by successive waves of new movements, which reinvigorate the universalistic aspect of its apostolic mission and precisely in so doing also serve the spiritual vitality and truth of the local churches. I would like to mention briefly five such waves that followed early monasticism. In these waves, the spiritual essence of what we may call "movements" emerges more and more clearly, as does the definition of their ecclesiological location.

1) I would call the missionary monasticism that flourished especially between Gregory the Great (590-604) and Gregory II (715-731) and III (731-741) the first of these waves. Pope Gregory the Great recognized monasticism's missionary potential, which he exploited by sending Augustine — who was to become Archbishop of Canterbury — and his companions to the heathen Angles on the British Isles. Even earlier, Patrick, who was likewise spiritually rooted in monasticism, had conducted his mission to Ireland. In this way, monasticism now became the great missionary movement that led the Germanic peoples to the Catholic Church and thereby built up the new Christian Europe. Connecting East and West in the ninth century, the monk brothers Cyril and Methodius brought the Gospel to the Slavic world. Two of the constitutive elements of the reality of "movements" clearly emerge from all this:

a) The papacy did not create the movements, but it did become their principal reference-point in the structure of the Church, their ecclesial support. This brings into view perhaps the deepest meaning and the true essence of the Petrine office as such: the Bishop of Rome is not just the bishop of a local church; his office is always related to the universal Church and therefore has, in a specific sense, an apostolic character. It must keep alive the dynamism of the Church's mission *ad extra* and *ad intra.* In the Eastern Church, the Emperor had at first claimed a sort of office of unity and universality. It was no accident that Constantine was called "bishop" *ad extra* and "equal to the apostles." But that could at best be a temporary, ersatz function, one fraught, moreover, with obvious perils. Nor is it an accident that, from the second century on, when the universal ministries were coming to an end, the papal claim to exercise this aspect of apostolic mission begins to be heard more and more clearly. It is no chance, then, that the movements, which go beyond the scope and structure of the local church, always go hand in hand with the papacy.

b) The motif of evangelical life, which we find already at the beginning of the monastic movement with Anthony of Egypt, remains decisive. But it now becomes apparent that the *vita evangelica* includes the service [*Dienst*] of evangelization. The poverty and freedom of the evangelical life are conditions for a service to the Gospel that goes beyond one's own homeland and its community. At the same time, this service is the goal and the intrinsic reason for the *vita evangelica,* as we shall soon see in greater detail.

2) I want to mention just briefly the reform movement of Cluny, which was of such decisive importance in the tenth century. Likewise supported by the papacy, this movement brought about the emancipation of the *vita religiosa* from the feudal system and from the dominion of episcopal feudal lords. By the association of individual monasteries in a congregation, it became the great movement of piety and renewal in which the idea of Europe took shape.[12] The reforming dynamism of Cluny subsequently gave rise to the eleventh-century Gregorian reform.[13] This latter movement rescued the papacy from the quagmire of strife among the Roman nobility and from its secularization and, in general, took up the battle for the freedom of the Church, for its distinctive spiritual nature, a battle, however, which then degenerated into a power struggle between pope and emperor.

3) The spiritual force of the evangelical movement that exploded in the thirteenth century with Francis of Assisi and Dominic continues to be felt even today. In the case of Francis, it is quite clear that he had no intention of starting a new order, a community apart. He wanted simply to call the Church back to the whole Gospel, to gather the "new people," to renew the Church with the Gospel. The two meanings of the word "evangelical life" are inextricably intertwined: whoever lives the Gospel in poverty, giving up possession and progeny, must at the same time proclaim that Gospel. There was a need for the Gospel in Francis's time, and he saw it precisely as his essential task to proclaim,

---

12. B. Senger points out the connection between the Cluniac reform and the shaping of the idea of Europe in *Lexikon für Theologie und Kirche* (=*LThK*), vol. 2, 2nd ed., 1239. He likewise draws attention to the "juridical independence and help of the popes."

13. Even though P. Engelbert can rightly say that "it is impossible to ascertain a direct influence of the C.R. (= Cluniac reform) on the Gregorian Reform" (*LThK,* vol. 2, 3rd ed., 1236), B. Senger's observation (*LThK,* vol. 2, 2nd ed., 1240) that the C.R. helped to prepare a favorable climate for the Gregorian reform is nonetheless still valid.

along with his brothers, the simple core of Christ's message to men. He and his followers wanted to be evangelists. And the very fact of being evangelists made it necessary to go beyond the borders of Christendom, to bring the Gospel to the ends of the earth.[14]

In the controversy with the secular priests of the University of Paris, who, as representatives of a narrowly closed local ecclesial structure, struggled against the evangelizing movements, Thomas Aquinas summed up the novelty and, at the same time, fidelity to the origin carried in the two movements and in the form of religious life to which they gave shape. The secular priests would accept only the Cluniac type of monasticism in its late, rigid form: monasteries separated from the local church, living in strict enclosure, and serving contemplation alone. Such monasteries could not upset the order of the local church, whereas conflicts inevitably broke out everywhere the new preachers appeared. By contrast, Thomas Aquinas emphasized that Christ himself is the model and, on the basis of this model, defended the superiority of the apostolic life over a purely contemplative form of life. "The active life that brings to others the truths attained through preaching and contemplation is more perfect than the exclusively contemplative life. . . ."[15] Thomas knew that he was heir to the successive renaissances of the monastic life, all of which appealed to the *vita apostolica*.[16] But in his interpretation of the *vita apostolica* — which he drew from the experience of the mendicant orders — he took an important new step, which had indeed been present in practice in the previous monastic tradition, but had as yet been little reflected upon in such an explicit way. The ap-

14. The exemplary edition of the *Fonti Francescane* by the Movimento Francescano (Assisi, 1978), with helpful introductions and bibliographical material, remains normative for the understanding of Saint Francis. Instructive for the self-understanding of the mendicant writers is A. Jotischky, "Some Mendicant Views of the Origins of Monastic Perfection," in *Cristianesimo nella storia* 19, no. 1 (February 1998): 31-49. The author shows that the mendicant authors appealed to the primitive Church, and especially to the desert fathers, in order to give an account of their origin and their significance in the Church.

15. St. Thomas Aquinas, *Summa Theologiae*, 3.40.1.2. Cf. also J. P. Torrell, O.P., *St. Thomas Aquinas: The Person and His Work*, vol. 1, trans. Robert Royal (Washington, D.C.: The Catholic University of America Press, 1996). See there the stimulating and clarifying discussion of the position of Saint Thomas in the controversy surrounding the mendicant orders, esp. 75-95.

16. Thus Torrell, *St. Thomas Aquinas*, 89-90.

peal to the primitive Church as a justification of the *vita apostolica* had been universal. Augustine, for example, designed his whole rule ultimately on the basis of Acts 4:32: they were one heart and one soul.[17] To this essential pattern, however, Thomas Aquinas adds Jesus' missionary discourses to the apostles (Mt 10:5-15): the authentic *vita apostolica* is the life that observes the teachings of Acts 4 *and* Mt 10: "The apostolic life consisted in the fact that the apostles, after they had left everything, went through the world, proclaiming and preaching the Gospel. This becomes clear in Mt 10, where they are given a rule."[18] Matthew 10 now appears as nothing less than a religious rule, or better: the rule of life and mission that the Lord gave to the apostles is itself the permanent rule of the apostolic life, which the Church always needs. It is this rule that justifies the new movement of evangelization.

The Paris controversy between the secular clergy and the representatives of the new movements, in which these texts were written, is of permanent significance. A constricted and impoverished idea of the Church that absolutizes the local ecclesial structure could not tolerate the new class of preachers. For their part, these necessarily looked for their backing in the bearer of an office pertaining to the Church universal, in the pope as guarantor of the mission and the upbuilding of the one Church. It was logical, then, that all this gave a great boost to the development of the doctrine of primacy, which — beyond the coloring of a certain historical period — was now understood anew in the light of its apostolic root.[19]

4) Since the question that concerns us here does not have to do with Church history, but with understanding the forms of the Church's life,

---

17. Cf. A. Zumkeller, in Balthasar, *Die Großen Ordensregeln*, 150-170. On the place of the rule in Augustine's life and work, see C. Vigini, *Agostino d'Ippona: L'avventura della grazia e della carità* (Cinisello Balsamo, 1998), 91-109.

18. St. Thomas Aquinas, *Contra impugnantes Dei cultum et religionem* 4, cited in Torell, *St. Thomas Aquinas*, 90.

19. I first presented the connection between the mendicant controversy and the doctrine of the primacy in a study that appeared in a festschrift for M. Schmaus (*Theologie in Geschichte und Gegenwart*, 1957), which I then included with minor additions in my book *Das neue Volk Gottes* (Düsseldorf, 1969), 49-71. Y. Congar took up my work where it left off, expanding what had been developed chiefly in terms of Bonaventure and his interlocutors to cover the whole field of the relevant sources: "Aspects ecclésiologiques de la querelle entre mendiants et séculiers dans la seconde moitié du XIIIe siècle et le début du XIVe": *Archives d'histoire doctrinale et litteraire du moyen age* 28 (1961): 35-151.

I must limit myself to only a brief mention of the movements of evangelization in the sixteenth century. Preeminent among them are the Jesuits, who now also take up the worldwide mission in the newly discovered America, in Africa, and in Asia, though the Dominicans and Franciscans, powered by the continuing impact of their original impulse, do not lag far behind.

5) Finally, we are all familiar with the new spate of movements that began in the nineteenth century. This period saw the emergence of strictly missionary congregations, that from the very outset aimed not so much at renewal within as mission on those continents that had hardly been touched by Christianity. In this respect, these new congregations largely avoided conflict with the local ecclesial structures. There even arose a fruitful cooperation that lent new strength not least to the historical local churches, inasmuch as the impulse to spread the Gospel and to serve with love animated them from within. An element that, while by no means absent from the movements, can easily be overlooked, now comes powerfully to the fore here: the apostolic movement of the nineteenth century was above all a female movement, in which there was a strong emphasis on *caritas,* on care for the suffering and the poor — we know what the new female communities meant and continue to mean for the hospitals and for the care of the needy — and a central emphasis on schools and education. Thus, the whole gamut of service of the Gospel was present in the combination of teaching, education, and love. When we look back from the nineteenth century, we see that women always played an important role in the apostolic movements. Think of the bold women of the sixteenth century like Mary Ward or, on the other hand, Teresa of Avila, of female figures of the Middle Ages like Hildegard of Bingen and Catherine of Siena, of the women in the circle of Saint Boniface, of the sisters of the Church Fathers and, finally, of the women in the letters of Paul and in the circle around Jesus. The women were never bishops or priests, but they were co-bearers of apostolic life and its universal task.

C. The Breadth of the Concept of Apostolic Succession

After this survey of the great apostolic movements in the history of the Church, we return to our thesis, the statement of which I already anticipated after our brief analysis of the biblical data: the concept of apostolic succession must be given greater breadth and depth if we wish to do justice to all that it claims. What does this mean? First of all, we must keep the sacramental structure of the Church as the permanent core of apostolic succession. It is in this structure that the Church receives ever anew the heritage of the apostles, the heritage of Christ. It is the sacrament, in which Christ acts through the Holy Spirit, that distinguishes the Church from all other institutions. The sacrament means that the Church gets its life as a "creature of the Holy Spirit" from the Lord and is constantly recreated by him. In saying this, we must keep in mind the two inseparable components of the sacraments that we mentioned earlier: first, the incarnational-christological element, that is, the Church's being bound to the "once only" of the Incarnation and of the Easter events, the link to God's action in history; second, and simultaneously, the making present of this event in the power of the Holy Spirit, hence, the christological-pneumatological component, which guarantees at once the novelty and continuity of the living Church.

This account sums up what the Church has always taught about the essence of apostolic succession, the real core of the sacramental concept of the Church. But this core is impoverished, indeed, it atrophies, if we think in this connection only of the system based on the local church. The office of the succession of Peter breaks open the merely local ecclesial model; the successor of Peter is not just the local bishop of Rome, but bishop for the whole Church and in the whole Church. He thus embodies an essential side of the apostolic mission, which must never be absent from the Church. But the Petrine office itself would in turn be understood incorrectly and would become a monstrous exception, if we burdened its bearer alone with the realization of the universal dimension of apostolic succession.[20] There must also always be in the Church ministries and missions that are not tied to the

---

20. The aversion to the primacy and the disappearance of the sense of the universal Church doubtless have to do with the fact that the concept of the universal Church is thought to be tied to the papacy alone. The papacy, isolated and without any living connection with universal ecclesial realities, then appears as a scandalous monolith, that upsets the image of a Church reduced to purely local ecclesial ministries and the coexistence of juxtaposed communities. But this image precisely does not capture the reality of the ancient Church.

local church alone, but serve universal mission and the spreading of the Gospel. The pope has to rely on these ministries, they on him, and the collaboration between the two kinds of ministries completes the symphony of the Church's life. The apostolic age, which is normative for the Church, conspicuously displays these components as indispensable for the Church's life. The sacrament of *ordo,* the sacrament of succession [*Nachfolge*], is necessarily included in this structural form, but it is — even more than in the local churches — surrounded by various ministries, and here the contribution of women to the Church's apostolate cannot be overlooked. We could even say, summing up the whole discussion, that the primacy of the successor of Peter exists in order to guarantee these essential components of the Church's life and to ensure their orderly relation with the local ecclesial structures.

In order to obviate misunderstandings, I must say quite clearly here that the apostolic movements appear in ever new forms throughout history — necessarily, because they are the Holy Spirit's answer to the changing situations in which the Church lives. And just as vocations to the priesthood cannot be produced, cannot be established by administrative protocol, it is all the more true that movements cannot be organized and planned by authority. They must be given, and they are given. We must only be attentive to them — we must only learn, using the gift of discernment, to accept what is right while overcoming what is unhelpful. One looking back at the history of the Church will be able to observe with gratitude that it has managed time and again in spite of all difficulties to make room for the great new awakenings. To be sure, the observer cannot overlook the succession of all those movements that have failed or led to permanent divisions: Montanists, Cathari, Waldensians, Hussites, the Reform movement of the sixteenth century. And we must, I think, say that both sides share the guilt for the permanent division in which these finally resulted.

III. Discernments and Criteria

Thus, the final task of this presentation must be to ask about criteria of discernment. In order to be able to answer this question well, we would first have to define a little more precisely the term "movement," perhaps even essay a typology of movements. Obviously, it is not possible to do all this here. We ought also to be wary of too strict a definition, for the Holy Spirit always has surprises in store, and only in retrospect do we recognize that the movements have a common essence in the midst of their great diversities. However, I would like, as a kind of first try at clarifying terminology, very briefly to distinguish three different types, that can be observed at any rate in recent history. I would call them movement, current, and action. I would not characterize the liturgical movement of the first half of this century, or the Marian movement that had been gaining increasing prominence in the Church since the nineteenth century, as movements, but as currents. These currents might subsequently solidify in concrete movements like the Marian Congregation or groupings of Catholic youth, but they nevertheless extended beyond them. The sorts of petition drives for the proclamation of a dogma or for changes in the Church that are becoming customary today are for their part not movements, but actions. The Franciscan awakening of the thirteenth century probably provides the clearest illustration of what a movement is: movements generally come from a charismatic leader and they take shape in concrete communities that live the whole Gospel anew from this origin and recognize the Church without hesitation as the ground of their life, without which they could not exist.[21]

Although this approach to a sort of definition is doubtless very unsatisfactory, it does already bring us to the criteria that, so to say, take the place of a definition. The essential criterion has just emerged quite by itself: rootedness in the faith of the Church. Whoever does not share the apostolic faith cannot lay claim to apostolic activity. Since there is only one faith for the whole Church; indeed, since this faith is the cause of the Church's unity, it is impossible to have the apostolic faith without the will to be one, to stand in the living communion of the whole Church. And this means, quite concretely, the will to stand by the successors of the apostles and the successor of Peter, who bears responsibility for the harmonious interplay of the local and universal Church as the one people of God. If the "apostolic" dimension is the location of the movements in the Church, then the will to

---

21. Helpful for the definition of the essence of movements is A. Cattaneo, "I movimenti ecclesiali: aspetti ecclesiologici," in *Annales Theologici* 11, no. 2 (1997): 401-427; see esp. 406-409.

the *vita apostolica* must be fundamental for them in all ages. Renunciation of property, of progeny, of the imposition of one's own image of the Church, that is, obedience in the following of Christ, have at all times been considered the essential elements of the apostolic life. To be sure, these cannot be applied in the same way to all the participants of a movement, but they are, in different ways, reference points for each of their lives. The apostolic life is, in turn, not an end unto itself, but creates freedom for service. Apostolic life calls for apostolic activity: pride of place is given — again in different ways — to the proclamation of the Gospel as the missionary element. In the *sequela Christi* evangelization is always primarily "evangelizare pauperibus" — proclamation of the Gospel to the poor. But this proclamation never happens through words alone; love, which is its inner center, at one and the same time the center of its truth and of its action, must be lived and in this way be proclamation. Thus, social service is always connected in one form or another with evangelization. All of this presupposes — and the source is usually the flame of the initial charism — a deep personal encounter with Christ. The formation and upbuilding of community does not exclude the personal element, but calls for it. Only when the person is struck and opened up by Christ in his inmost depth can the other also be inwardly touched, can there be reconciliation in the Holy Spirit, can true community grow. Within this basic christological-pneumatological and existential structure, there can be a great diversity of accents and emphases, in which Christianity is a perpetually new event and the Spirit unceasingly renews the Church "like the youth of the eagle" (Ps 103:5).

This perspective also enables us to see the risks to which the movements are exposed as well as the means to remedy them. There is the risk of one-sidedness resulting from the over-accentuation of the specific task that emerges in one period or through one charism. The fact that the spiritual awakening is not experienced as *one* form of Christian existence, but as a being struck by the totality of the message as such, can lead to the absolutization of the movement, which can understand itself simply as the Church, as *the* way for all, whereas this one way can communicate itself in very different modes. Time and again, then, the freshness and totality of the awakening also leads almost inevitably to conflict with the local community, a conflict in which both sides can be at fault, and which represents a spiritual challenge to both. The local churches may have made peace with the world through a certain conformism — the salt can lose its savor — a situation that Kierkegaard described with mordant acuity in his critique of Christendom. Yet even where the departure from the radical demands of the gospel has not reached the point that provoked Kierkegaard's denunciation, the irruption of the new is experienced as a disruption, especially when it appears with all kinds of childhood diseases and misguided absolutizations, as not infrequently happens.

Both sides must open themselves here to an education by the Holy Spirit and also by the leadership of the Church; both must acquire a selflessness without which there can be no interior consent to the multiformity in which the faith is lived out. Both sides must learn from each other, allow themselves to be purified by each other, put up with each other, and discover how to attain those attitudes of which Paul speaks in his great hymn to love (1 Cor 13:4ff.). Thus, it is necessary to remind the movements that — even though they have found and pass on the whole of the faith in their own way — they are a gift to and in the whole of the Church and must submit themselves to the demands of this totality in order to be true to their own essence.[22] But the local churches, too, even the bishops, must be reminded to avoid making an ideal of uniformity in pastoral organization and planning. They must not make their own pastoral plans the criterion of what the Holy Spirit is allowed to do: an obsession with planning could render the churches impermeable to the Spirit of God, to the power by which they live.[23] It must not be the case that everything has to fit into a single, uniform organization. Better less organization and more spirit! Above all, *communio* must not be conceived as if the avoidance of conflict were the highest pastoral value. Faith is always a sword, too, and it can demand precisely conflict for the sake of truth and love (cf. Mt 10:34). A concept of ecclesial unity in which conflicts are dismissed *a priori* as polarization, and in which domestic peace is bought at the price of sacrificing the integral totality of witness will quickly prove to be illusory. Finally, we must not allow the establishment of a blasé enlightenment that immediately brands the zeal of those seized by the Holy Spirit and their

22. Cf. Cattaneo, "I movimenti ecclesiali," 423-425.

23. See the powerful remarks on this point in Cattaneo, "I movimenti ecclesiali," 413f. and 417.

naive faith in God's Word with the anathema of fundamentalism and allows only a faith for which the ifs, ands, and buts become more important than the very substance of what is believed. All must let themselves be measured by love for the unity of the *one* Church, which is only one in all local churches and appears as such again and again in the apostolic movements. The local churches and the apostolic movements must constantly recognize and accept the simultaneous truth of two propositions: *ubi Petrus, ibi ecclesia — ubi episcopus, ibi ecclesia.* Primacy and episcopacy, the local ecclesial system and apostolic movements, need each other: the primacy can live only with and through a living episcopacy, the episcopacy can preserve its dynamic and apostolic unity only in ordination to the primacy. Where one of the two is weakened, the Church as a whole suffers.

What should remain at the conclusion of all these considerations is above all gratitude and joy. Gratitude that the Holy Spirit is very evidently at work in the Church and gives it new gifts even today, gifts through which it relives the joy of its youth (Ps 42:4, Vulgate). Gratitude for many people, young and old, who accept God's call and joyfully enter into the service of the Gospel without looking back. Gratitude for the bishops who open themselves to the new paths, create room for them in the local churches, and struggle patiently with them in order to overcome their one-sided tendencies and to guide them to the right form. And above all let us thank in this place and at this time Pope John Paul II, who is a leader to Christ for us all — by his capacity for enthusiasm, by his ability for inward rejuvenation in the power of the faith, by his discernment of spirits, by his humble and courageous struggle for the fullness of services for the sake of the Gospel, by his unity with the bishops around the world, a unity in which he both listens and guides. Christ lives, and he sends from the Father the Holy Spirit — that is the joyful and life-giving experience that is ours precisely in the encounter with the ecclesial movements.

Translated by Adrian J. Walker

The Renewal of Moral Theology:
Perspectives of Vatican II and Veritatis Splendor

What is the ultimate intention of the encyclical *Veritatis splendor?* Asking ourselves this question helps us to understand better the train of thought developed in the document. If I have rightly understood the Pope's intention, the original motive that prompted him to write the encyclical was precisely to retrieve and to restate the Second Vatican Council's moral message, which found expression above all in the pastoral constitution *Gaudium et spes.* In order to understand both the core of the council's message and John Paul II's way of restating it, it is perhaps worth our while to refer to the situation of moral theology prior to the council, characterized as it was by the rationalism of the manualist tradition. In reality, that period was not without movements of theological renewal, such as those which led to the constitution on the liturgy, or to the re-thinking of ecclesiology, or again to a new interpretation of revelation.

The text that follows was delivered orally and recorded; it was elaborated in its present written form by Msgr. Livio Melina. It presents a rapid survey of the theme that is intended only to offer brief snapshots, so to speak, which require further exploration. In this sense, the text is an invitation to specialists to render concrete the themes that are presented here only in broad outline. Originally published in *Camminare nella luce: Prospettive della teologia morale a partire da* Veritatis splendor, ed. L. Melina and J. Noriega (Rome: PUL, 2004). Translated and published by permission. English publication in *Communio: International Catholic Review* 32, no. 2 (Summer 2005).

I. Sacred Scripture and Moral Theology

Currents of renewal were also present within moral theology, but they still awaited a full working-out and an authoritative expression. Generally speaking, the manualist tradition really was marked by a decided rationalism; because of this, Sacred Scripture retained only a very marginal function in the elaboration of moral theology. The latter was constructed substantially on the foundation of natural law and therefore in the form of a philosophical reflection based on the ancient Stoic tradition that had in large measure been appropriated by Christianity throughout its history.

At the same time, the development of these manuals was also determined by the practical need to form confessors and to give concrete answers to the questions that might arise in the context of confession. Hence, together with a certain naturalism reflecting a substantially philosophical reflection decorated here and there with biblical citations, the manuals strongly emphasized casuistry so that they could respond to the requirements of practice.

However, the atmosphere of the Scriptures was totally lacking, as was the reference to Christ, in whom man finds the truth and the way in person, and therefore also finds open the door to life, reconciliation with God and communion with him: entering into communion with Christ, who is at one and the same time a man present in my time and the Son of God, we can reconcile the concreteness of the passing moment with the eternal weight of our life. The older type of moral theology no longer allowed people to see the great message of liberation and freedom given to us in the encounter with Christ. Rather, it stressed above all the negative aspect of so many prohibitions, so many "no's." These are no doubt present in Catholic ethics, but they were no longer presented for what they really are: the concretization of a great "yes."

So the need for a profound renewal was felt, and this was certainly the idea of the constitution *Gaudium et spes*: to return to a substantially biblical and christological ethics, inspired by the encounter with Christ, an ethics conceived not as a series of precepts but as the event of an encounter, of a love that then also knows how to create corresponding actions. If this event happens — a living encounter with a living person who is Christ — and this encounter stirs up love, it is from love that everything else flows. To illustrate all this, to show the great biblical vision and thus to develop, from this starting point, the particular contents of ethics as well, was the program the council proposed to theologians.

Then something unexpected happened, perhaps not completely unforeseeable, but in any case unexpected. There were some initial attempts, which were certainly important and valid, to renew a moral theology under biblical inspiration, even if, naturally, not all the concrete contents of this theology could be obtained literally from the Sacred Scriptures, but rather needed to be discovered within the horizon of the great biblical inspiration. These attempts quickly ceased, however, without attaining their goal, without arriving at the new springtime of a profoundly christological and biblical moral theology that had been so hoped for.

It is certainly worthwhile looking into the reasons for this failure, because it was not caused by ill will but rather was the consequence of real problems. A first very real problem was that, in Sacred Scripture, we do not find ready-made answers for the pressing and very grave problems of our era. It also seems difficult to develop from Sacred Scripture adequate responses to the challenges of our time.

Moreover, the awareness began to grow that, in order to be present in today's discussion and to have an impact on contemporary culture, we had to find a language that was adapted to today's world along with forms of argumentation that would be effective in the debate. Clearly, if we think of the discussion regarding cloning, artificial procreation, euthanasia, and so many other questions of bioethics, it is important genuinely to enter into the language and thought of the world community, which finds itself faced with these great problems. It is important to find arguments that can be understood by the modern mind and that are capable of convincing it. From this point of view, too, the Bible seemed too distant from the common way of thinking, unsuitable for public argumentation, and simply too peremptory for a debate that takes place on a human and philosophical level.

Beyond this, there was another issue that emerged from Scripture itself. As we well know, Scripture does not offer us a theological system, and still less a system of moral theology, with a systematic and orderly presentation of the main principles of action. To the contrary, Scripture is a path, a history, the multiple re-readings of which converge on Christ, who, for his part, cannot adequately be understood without retracing the path of all the narratives converging on his person. But how is it possible adequately to understand this path and to find, in the multiple re-readings that advance toward Christ, the permanent substance that can function as the principle of Christian action? Such a reconciliation of history and truth is always a difficult undertaking.

Another question was that the reading of Sacred Scripture played a role in the ecumenical debate, where it found a difficult situation. With regard to this, and without wishing to enter into the differences between the Calvinist and Lutheran visions, I would like to address above all the Lutheran perspective, although even the first is not, in the end, so different from it. According to Luther's conception, Sacred Scripture is to be interpreted in terms of the dialectic between law and Gospel, and even the Christian life must be understood precisely within this dialectic of opposites, of the God who is contrary to himself. Naturally, in this perspective, everything considered law falls onto the negative side of that dialectic, which is supposed to educate us in the Gospel and in reception of the radical forgiveness granted to us without our merits.

But once this dialectic between law and grace, and consequently the interior division of Sacred Scripture itself has been affirmed, a flood of questions emerge: "What is the law?" and "Is ethics a part of the law and thus of a reality that has been overcome by Christ, that no longer has value because it was only a pedagogy and a way of leading us to its opposite?" "Is the Decalogue, too, part of the law and is it perhaps precisely that law which has now been surpassed by the grace of the Gospel?" "And those works that cannot merit salvation for us, are they to be identified with our moral action? If this is the case, what is the point of our moral action? What theological dignity does it have? What link to the figure of Christ, if Christ is the Gospel while moral action is our work?" All this found a very radical expression in Luther, who, at least in a good part of his work, places even love on the level of works. For him, love, too, is our work, so much so that he could not accept the celebrated phrase of the letter to the Galatians (5:6): *fides caritate operans* [faith working in charity]. This seemed to be contrary to the principle of *sola fides,* which was intended to refute precisely the idea of faith that works through charity. But in this way, charity, too, becomes profane or at least problematic. What then is our moral action? What does the Bible say about ethics? In what sense does Christ inspire our moral action? It is true that Luther then adds, "Yes, faith bears fruit, and it is precisely in the fecundity of faith that the truth of faith is demonstrated." But what is the relationship between these "fruits of faith" and the "works" that do not merit? Does ethics have only profane relevance, or, to the contrary, can it be integrated into a christological vision? There is no denying that the problem becomes terribly complicated in the ecumenical debate, and that it therefore becomes difficult to take the Sacred Scriptures as the inspirational source and starting point for the construction of the foundations of moral vision.

The foregoing explains the vicissitudes of post-conciliar moral theology, which has led to a radical heterogeneity of ends: while it was hoped that a renewed moral theology would go beyond the natural law system in order to recover a deeper biblical inspiration, it was precisely moral theology that ended by marginalizing Sacred Scripture even more completely than the pre-conciliar manualist tradition. In the latter, in fact, Sacred Scripture was absent *de facto,* although perhaps in theory it was supposed to inspire, though without success. Now, on the other hand, it is marginalized *de iure:* it is claimed that Sacred Scripture cannot offer moral principles that would suitably guide the construction of our actions. Scripture, according to this position, offers only a horizon of intentions and motivations, but it does not enter into the moral contents of action. These contents are left to properly human rationality. We see here the reflection of the conception that, having instituted a dialectic between law and Gospel, understands moral action to be profane. Such a conception now translates into the claim that ethics is purely rational, so that, in order to open itself to universal communicability and to enter into the common debate of humanity, ethics ought to be constructed solely on the basis of reason. Various justifications are adopted for this new redimensioning of Scripture, which is no longer the starting point, the source of permanent inspiration, the fundamental criterion, but merely a horizon of meaning that does not influence the rigorously rational content of action. The accurate analysis of Sacred Scripture through the so-called historical-critical method is supposed to establish that one cannot identify anything in it that is properly Christian or essentially and uniquely biblical. All the moral contents that appear in Sacred Scripture, according to this view, were taken over from the outside cultural context: they do not derive from Abrahamic faith or from Christian inspiration, but come from outside and were simply incorporated into Scripture. Moreover, one must consider the change of the different cultural contexts in which the biblical text originated.

Such widespread theses are, however, terribly superficial and absolutely untenable. Although it is true that Sacred Scripture does not intend to propose specific moral contents as the only ones and that it is in dialogue with human cultures in search of the most just action, none of this implies that there is nothing original about it. In fact, the originality of Sacred Scripture in the area of ethics does not consist in the exclusivity of the contents it starts from, but rather in the purification, discernment, and maturation of what was proposed by the surrounding culture. If we compare the moral proposals that served as the Bible's material and the contents expressed in the latter, we can observe that the specificity of Sacred Scripture's contribution to human morality lies precisely in this: the critical discernment of what is truly human because it assimilates us to God, and its purification from whatever is dehumanizing; its insertion into a new context of meaning, that of the Covenant, which raises the human and brings it to fulfillment. The true novelty and originality of Scripture is in the path of purification, illumination, and discernment. In this sense, the thesis of the non-originality of biblical ethics is clearly to be rejected. Its novelty, on the other hand, must be properly acknowledged: this consists in assimilating the human contribution, while transfiguring it in the divine light of Revelation, which culminates in Christ, thus offering us the authentic path of life. We must not forget that in its beginnings, Christianity was defined as *hodos,* a road, a way. Not a theory, but the response to the questions, "How do I live?" and "What do I do?"

Another line of argument had to do with the problem of the relation between history and enduring truth, and ultimately between the transcendental and categorical dimensions of ethics. The contribution of Sacred Scripture was held to lie in the transcendental and not in the categorical dimension. Without entering into detail, it seems to me that this distinction is misapplied and its meaning misunderstood. In fact, it cannot be applied to the issue of morality, because the questions "How do I live?" "How can I be a human being?" and "How do I respond to the deepest vocation of our being, that is, to the vocation to be like unto God?" cannot be reduced to a categorical question, which would involve mistakenly distinguishing between levels of knowledge that can function as guiding criteria for our actions.

This is, then, the first element that I wanted to draw out: the marginalization of Sacred Scripture on the part of moral theology, justified *de iure* in post-conciliar moral theology and not simply practiced *de facto*, as in the manualist tradition. Biblical texts may appear in important and rich areas within the treatment of moral theology, but their function, with regard to the constitution of moral action, is marginalized as a matter of principle.

2. The Conception of Reason

Another important point to consider is the profound change in the concept of reason. As has been mentioned above, philosophical rationality in the pre-conciliar era was developed with reference to the fundamental category of natural law. Now, on the other hand, discussion is occurring in a context that is not only post-metaphysical but also a-metaphysical, in which it seems that the natural law is part of a past that is gone without recovery. The concept of nature has undergone radical change. Whereas for the Stoics nature pointed to a divine reality of a pantheistic stripe, so that nature, full of gods and divinities, was saturated with signs of the divine will and of the path to divinization, in Christianity, through the concept of creation, nature became transparent to the intentions of the Creator: it expresses the language of the Creator, who lets himself be perceived through creation.

Today, however, both the Stoic and the Christian conceptions of creation have been obscured and for the most part replaced by a radical evolutionism, in which nature is no longer the expression of a creating reason, but of various causal and necessitating factors that contributed to producing the world in which we live. Consequently, the world no longer has any metaphysical transparency. Human reason has lost the capacity to see, in the world and in itself, the transparency of the divine. This a-metaphysical and post-metaphysical reason thus becomes a reason closed in on itself, in which the divine light does not appear. Alone and left to its own resources, it must find the paths to be taken, the actions to be performed, and the decisions to be made. How could such a post-metaphysical reason construct a moral vision? Certainly no longer by recognizing moral principles inscribed in being, because nothing is inscribed if being is the product of evolution. And yet, reason must nonetheless find reference points for making fitting decisions for the life of the person and of the community and for the future of humanity.

In this way, consequentialist ethics was born, whether we call it teleologism or proportionalism. This view presupposes a post-metaphysical reason, deaf and blind to the divine word in being. It seeks the best way of constructing the world through the calculation of consequences. It identifies what must be done by using this criterion. Thus, it obviously changes the relationship between intention and object. In fact, the object of action is in itself mutable and must be placed in a context in order to mean anything. With the denial of the existence of principles inscribed in being, the possibility of recognizing the *intrinsece bonum aut malum* naturally also disappears. Nothing is *intrinsece bonum* or *intrinsece malum,* because everything depends on context and on the finalities that must be realized.

We have thus arrived at a theory that contradicts the very foundations of the Christian vision; the latter takes its starting point precisely from the language of the Creator, who then makes himself perceptible in a new and definitive way in the person of Christ.

The repercussions of these conceptions became visible above all with the debate following the publication of the encyclical *Humanae vitae.* This debate led to a denial of the authority of the magisterium in concrete questions of morality and to an absolutization of the subjective conscience liberated from the Church as its reference point.

3. The Profound Intention of *Veritatis Splendor*

It was precisely to respond to this inversion of the Catholic vision, with regard both to the use of the Bible and to the definition of reason, that the Holy Father entered the fray with the encyclical *Veritatis splendor.* Considering the panorama we have just described, it seemed necessary to return to the Second Vatican Council. The paradox of the situation was that precisely the newfangled vision that proposed a new way of reading Sacred Scripture, or, to speak more frankly, of marginalizing it, as well as a new concept of reason, claimed to be the authentic heir and the concrete realization of the council. If we consider the texts and the fundamental intentions of Vatican II, however, it becomes clear that this was not at all the will of the council; to the contrary, this vision leads precisely to the position directly opposed to what the council had hoped for. But this means that, precisely within the new context in which we find ourselves, we must carry out the council's mandate, thinking afresh how it can be relevant today and reasonably plausible in our time. The great vision of the council demands to be rethought in its foundations, but also verified and renewed in the face of radical problems.

When I saw the way in which *Veritatis splendor* was received, my disappointment did not come so much from the fact that the encyclical gave rise to many criticisms (since I come from Germany, it is a normal thing to me that even papal documents are objects of criticism), but rather from the fact that people did not enter into this great debate about the principles of ethics, about this magnificent renewed vision that is at once christological and rational, because Christ is the *Logos*. Theologians did not want to enter into a debate about the challenge surrounding the vision of ethics as a whole, but limited themselves to a discussion of details; they defended themselves instead against the charge of consequentialism and accused the encyclical of being simplistic and of drawing caricatures. This kind of debate regarding technical details can also have a certain usefulness, but it is certainly not the right, necessary, and desired response to the challenge that *Veritatis splendor* proposes to moral theologians and that is ultimately a deepening of the council's mandate. My hope would be that, ten years after its publication, the great challenge the encyclical poses to moral theology would finally begin to be confronted. I would like to say a few more words on this subject.

In the first place, as the Holy Father tells us, recognition of the centrality of the figure of Christ implies the true reconciliation between history and reason, between supernatural revelation and reason, because Christ is not just any historical personage who as such would be extraneous to human thought. Rather, Christ is the *Logos* made flesh, that is, the fullness of creative reason itself, who speaks to us and opens our eyes to see anew, even in the darkness of a post-metaphysical era, the presence of a creative truth that lies at the foundation of being and that, with its language, also speaks within being. Thus, the paths of history converge into unity in Christ: he purifies and discerns everything history has expressed, and therefore shows us how history refers to truth, pointing us to the road that leads history precisely along the path that he himself is.

Secondly, I would like briefly to discuss the problem of autonomy, about which moral theologians spoke so much after Vatican Council II. In my opinion, this concept of autonomy, which Kant worked out consistently and systematically as an antithesis to the concept of heteronomy, has not been properly digested in the post-conciliar debates. This concept lost the depth and linearity of Kant's thought, even as it never managed to become integrated with the council's great christological vision.

But what is the correct conception of autonomy that fits with the Christian vision of man? The first certitude we must retain is that man did not create himself: he is a creature. He is not in himself the God who determines alone what the world is and what he must do in it. He is a creature who lives by virtue of a dependence which, thanks to the love of God, becomes participation: it is a union of love in love. If we wish to define love as dependence, we can say that the issue is dependence, but in reality love goes beyond this concept of dependence and reveals to us that it is precisely relationality that is the true form of participation in being itself and in its light. Therefore, living in communion with God and finding one's own path in the divine light, finding there the way, the truth, and the life, is not alienating to man; it is not heteronomy, but rather how he finds himself in his true identity. St. Augustine teaches us that God is *intimior intimo meo,* and that thus, obeying and uniting myself to God and to Christ, I do not leave myself to enter into heteronomy and an unacceptable dependence, a sort of slavery. To the contrary, precisely in this way I find my interiority and my identity, which until this moment remained locked up in sin. Through communion with Christ, I can find myself again and, entering into myself, I can find God and my *theosis,* my true essence, my true autonomy. Precisely in renouncing individualistic self-determination, I enter into the intimacy of my own being, through communion with Christ. This is how we become ourselves and, finding authentic communion with God, attain true freedom. In this sense, the concept of freedom, which is so central for Sacred Scripture and for the debate with modernity, must be read from within the christological vision of man, who is free not when he defends himself against God, but when he accepts the union with God offered to him in Christ. Human freedom is always a shared freedom, and only in the sharing of freedoms can the true freedom of each individual grow. The sharing of freedoms becomes possible in the opening of our freedom to the divine freedom.

Thirdly, we must rediscover the authentic meaning of conscience. In order to do this, we must overcome modern subjectivism. For modernity, the realm of religion and morality has been confined to the subjective sphere, since there is no trace of objective religion or morality in an evolutionistic conception; religion and morality are reduced to a complete subjectivism. Beyond the subject, no roads or further horizons open up. The ultimate competence of the subject, who cannot transcend himself and remains closed within himself, is thus expressed in a certain conception of conscience, according to which man is the measure of himself. As much as he might make use of aids and criteria outside himself, in reality his subjective conscience is what has the last and decisive word. The subject thus becomes really autonomous, but in a dark and terrible way, because he lacks the light that could really give his subjectivity value. This conception of the self-enclosed subject who is the ultimate criterion of judgment is overcome only in the classical concept of conscience, which expresses, on the contrary, the human being's openness to divine light, to the voice of the other, to the language of being, to the eternal *logos,* perceptible in the subject's very interior. It seems to me, then, that it is necessary to return to this vision of the human being as openness to the infinite, in whom the infinite light shines through and speaks.

4. The Theological Horizon of Ethics

I would like to add yet another word: in this way, the christological horizon is truly a theological horizon. In fact, no ethics can be constructed without God. Even the Decalogue, which is without a doubt the moral axis of the Sacred Scriptures, and which is so important in intercultural debate, is not to be interpreted first of all as law, but rather as gift: it is Good News, and it can be understood fully in the perspective that culminates in Christ. Therefore, the Decalogue is not about precepts circumscribed in themselves, but is a dynamic that is open to an ever greater and deeper understanding. Moreover, the second tablet, despite its concreteness and its helpfulness in today's discussions, is not the only one that is important. We cannot prescind from the first tablet, either, for an adequate hermeneutic of the Commandments. In the Sacred Scriptures, in fact, the entire Decalogue is considered to be the self-revelation of God. It always begins with the words, "I am Yahweh, your Lord," and, through the ten words, God reveals his countenance. In the end, the ten words are a concretization, an articulation of the single commandment of love. To this single commandment belongs also love for God and our worship of him, such that without this fundamental reference to God, the second tablet, too, would not work. I believe, then, that for moral theology, the aspect of reason is of the greatest importance. Precisely because Christianity as such, the Gospel and ethics in particular, wants to communicate itself and must be communicable, it demands to enter the common debate of humanity. But the existence of God, too, belongs precisely to this rational dimension. We cannot yield on this point: without God, all the rest would no longer have logical coherence.

Lastly, I would like to draw attention to the importance of the theme of martyrdom, treated in paragraph 90 of the encyclical. It is in martyrdom that the *sequela* of the crucified Christ is realized in the fullest degree. In martyrdom, it becomes clear that a good exists that is worth even dying for. In reality, a life that no longer recognizes a good that gives it value is no longer a true life. Hence, the affirmation of absolute commandments that prescribe what is *intrinsece malum* does not mean submitting oneself to the slavery of prohibitions. Rather, it means opening oneself up to life's great value, which is illuminated by the true good, that is, by the love of God himself. Through the whole of human history, the martyrs represent the true apology of man. They demonstrate that the human creature is not a failure on the part of the Creator, but that, even with all the negative aspects that have occurred throughout history, this creature really stands in the light of the Creator. In testimony unto death, we see the power of life and of divine love. Thus, it is precisely the martyrs who show us, at one and the same time, the path to understanding Christ and to understanding what it means to be human beings.

Translated by Michelle K. Borras

Unity of the Church — Unity of Mankind:
A Congress Report

The Faith and Order Commission of the World Council of Churches in 1971 held the first of its sessions in which Catholic theologians took part as full members.[1] From the constitutional point of view their situation was rather paradoxical, for though members of a church which does not itself belong to the WCC, they were serving in one of the latter's Commissions. The only other German Catholic theologian with me was Walter Kasper; shortly before the beginning of the session he was invited as an adviser, but, in fact, no distinction was made between him and the actual members. The Catholic team of nine was relatively small, corresponding more or less to the delegations of individual Protestant or Orthodox churches. Its representatives, however, worked on all the committees (and P. Lanne, of Chevetogne, and J. Medina, of Santiago, Chile, in particular, performed important functions). Moreover, they were integrated into the work on a footing of equality. Thus, for example, I was called upon in conjunction with the American Methodist J. Deschner and the Indian P. Verghese, of the Syrian-Orthodox Church, to preside at the closing session, when the findings of the five sections detailed to deal with the main topic were summarized and dis-

---

1. Meeting of the Commission of Faith and Order of the World Council of Churches in Louvain, 2-12 August 1971.

This article first appeared as "Einheit der Kirche — Einheit der Menschheit. Ein Tagungsbericht," in *Internationale katholische Zeitschrift: Communio* 2, no. 1 (January-February 1972): 78ff. English publication in *Communio: International Catholic Review* 1, no. 1 (January-February 1972): 53-57.

cussed. Catholic entry to the Commission was given external emphasis by the place chosen for the meeting — the spacious House of Studies of the Flemish Jesuits in Louvain, whose hospitality was even more Benedictine than Jesuit. The main act of worship of the whole congress was a High Mass celebrated by Cardinal Suenens with the Catholic members, at which the Cardinal preached in all the main languages of the congress (English, French, German).

Before I attempt any evaluation, the matters that we worked at together should be indicated. The whole organization ran on dual lines. There were five sections and five committees, meeting alternately; each participant belonged to one section and one committee, but the composition of these was not identical. The sections dealt with the main theme, "The Unity of the Church and the Unity of Mankind," which was subdivided into five topics: the unity of the church and the struggle for justice in society; the unity of the church and the encounter with the religions of our time; the unity of the church and the fight against racialism; the unity of the church and marginal members of society; the unity of the church and cultural differences. The committees, on the other hand, were occupied with specifically theological questions, even matters of controversial theology: the authority of the Bible; catholicity and apostolicity; baptism — confirmation — ordination — intercommunion; common witness and proselytism; the Council of Chalcedon; bilateral discussions between churches.

Almost every one of these themes is so extensive that it could have claimed a full congress to itself, and this created the first difficulty of this gathering. It seemed at first almost impossible to achieve a really serious discussion because complicated questions requiring patient consideration of abundant material had to be brought to some sort of conclusion by a large group in a short time. Furthermore, the backgrounds of those taking part were very different, and not merely in regard to their various denominations; the education, specialist qualifications, and way of approaching questions were as diverse as could possibly be imagined in a motley assembly drawn from every continent and all Christian groups. For a German, the predominance of the Anglo-Saxon (and especially American) mode of thought, linked with the prevalence of the English language, could present itself as an additional difficulty. At first, it was in fact rather discouraging to grope about in ill-defined territory, listening to all kinds of effusions, many with very moderate content. In the course of time, one became increasingly aware of the enrichment involved in having one's own mode of thought reduced to relative proportions. Above all, however, we novices were surprised to see how the discussion on particular questions gradually came to a point; sub-commissions were established and put together reports which, almost unexpectedly, revealed that the discussion had borne fruit after all and was capable of throwing this or that new light on the proposed documents. Fortunately, there were no traces anywhere of that pseudo-democratic attitude recently spreading in Catholic circles, in which mistrust is made the very essence of democracy. Without very generous trust in one another and in the World Council of Churches "Establishment," such as seems to have become simply impossible with us Catholics at the present time, we should in fact have had to go away empty-handed.

Let us return to the content of the debate. The main theme which had been suggested in Bristol in 1967 had become quite inescapable after Uppsala. The point was, by turning in common to the factual situation of the church in the world of the present day, to make visible that profound unity of Christian witness which is often hidden by anachronistic oppositions as long as people notice none but themselves. A shared realistic acceptance of the tasks imposed by the present day can, in fact, supersede disputes, or at least reduce them to merely relative importance when they are rooted not in faith but in past circumstances. This was the positive aspect of the theme, but it also, of course, held concealed dangers. It was easy to get lost in social and economic problems for which the participants had no special qualifications; it was easy to fall in with the trend toward giving the Christian message a political character, for which enormous pressure is, in any case, being exerted on all sides. There was no small temptation to this in Sections I and III. It is, of course, easy to understand the inclination of oppressed groups to interpret the terms "liberation" and "reconciliation" in political terms and to construct a necessary relation between them: without liberation, no reconciliation. But, at bottom, this only mirrors and repeats the same falsification which earlier, in some sections of Anglo-Saxon Protestantism, produced a political and racial interpretation of the concept of election. The concept of the Chosen People, once again given a political and national character, created a special messianic consciousness of mission, giving religious significance to racial distinction, thus making it practically insuperable. The point here was, and is, to rediscover catholicity as a dimension of the church. To this extent, correctly understood, a politico-social conflict at this point can in fact have ecumenical effect, not in the sense of directly unifying the churches, but certainly by leading them to rediscover central ecclesial realities. The way there is undoubtedly difficult. The impending danger was also apparent, to my way of thinking, in the idea of "moral heresy." At a time when orthodoxy has almost become a term of abuse, people are inclined rather to see the limits of the churches in terms of "orthodoxy." Now, of course, it has always been the case that Christian faith includes a moral profession and moral conduct (it was reserved to the latest fashion to deny the existence of any specifically Christian element in morality), but more is at stake here. There is an unmistakable trend to regard faith as indefinable, and therefore to seek the unity of Christians in common programs of action, and this can all too easily lead to transforming the function of the church into that of a party.

The outcome of the discussion as a whole, to my mind, was nevertheless of positive value. At the very beginning of the work, the newly elected Chairman, J. Meyendorff, of the Orthodox Church, spoke out clearly on the basis of Orthodox pneumatology and eschatology, against a politicized church and a politicized theology. Important contributions were made by one of J. Moltmann's assistants, R. Weth, who quite rightly insisted on the urgent need for Christians to have a political ethics, but at the same time expressed his reservations in regard to any political theology that failed to distinguish between faith and politics. The whole matter was unexpectedly clarified by the work of Section IV (on the marginal members of society, "marginal men," as sociologists call them). The points of view that emerged were impressively presented by J. Deschner in the concluding session. Here we came up against the problem of human beings who cannot fight for justice themselves and who cannot be helped by a new economic or social order of any kind. The reality of human suffering reveals the limit of all action, which is only too readily forgotten in our "theologies of liberation." As Deschner put it, "If our unity is most deeply based on God's love present among us, then human suffering is quite precisely as important for the manifestation of the mystery of church unity as human action. And the same principle must certainly be applied in a wider sense to a theology of poverty — or, rather, to a theology of the 'oikonomia,' in which poor and rich can help one another. . . ." With this glimpse of those who suffer, of the incurably handicapped in body or mind, the mystery of the Cross was suddenly present. And it became clear that the real abyss of human reality is not to be understood by a theology of the healthy alone. The importance of those who cannot perform any "function" and who thus bring man face to face with himself, was plain. With them in view, it was impossible not to realize once more the real demand made by the Crucified.

Among the theological themes, I should like briefly to mention the problems dealt with by Sections I and III, since they were concerned primarily with classical themes of denominational controversy. In the committee on the authority of the Bible, I found it exciting to see how far matters have moved from the classical type of controversy, which still tended to dominate Vatican II. It is true that the old problems still persist: Scripture and Tradition, Word of Scripture then and authoritative application of that Word now. But it was in fact the non-Catholic participants who seemed to have difficulty in finding a clear reason for the chronological limit set to the Canon, and for its absolute and inalienable superiority to all later writings. The perpetual operation of the Spirit in the church dominated the outlook so completely that the strict tie with a particular time and its literary expression almost ceased to be intelligible. Similarly, many could not really succeed in discerning any real difference between the Word then and proclamation as an event taking place here and now; the Reformation maxim that the preaching of the Word is the Word of God *(Praedicatio verbi Dei verbum Dei est)* was given its full weight. Consequently, the old kind of Biblicism was not under discussion; our common question was, rather, how we are to conceive the mediation between the necessarily present actuality of Christian reality and its original formation. In a lengthier inquiry, the significance of the church and its ministry would inevitably have come up for consideration; as it was, the question was really no more than outlined. One result of this committee must certainly be mentioned. A sub-commission was appointed to consider whether a common formulation of belief is possible today. It gave me cause for thought to see that there was none of that strained talk of pluralism which has become such an item for us these days. I spontaneously formed the idea, which I have since seen thoroughly confirmed by

W. Siebel,[2] that the pluralism thesis as one finds it in recent writings of Karl Rahner, for example, is not theological in origin, but has its roots in the sociology of knowledge; it is a way in which a theology declares itself unimpeachable. Here, there was unanimity that though perhaps no verbal formularies common to all can be had, there must nevertheless be standards by which the objective identity of what is formulated differently can be recognized, so that exchange in unity is possible.

The document on the ordained ministry produced conflicting impressions on me. It incontestably attempted to do justice to all traditions (Orthodox, Roman Catholic, and the various forms of Protestant Christianity) and to find a way common to all without infidelity to what each regards as essential. The respect with which church tradition (including Trent) is spoken of, forms an agreeable contrast with the kind of tone which has become habitual in some quarters among us. The ministry is seen as a spiritual reality and is thought of as such. It is expressly stated that "Ordination confers an authority *(exousia)* which is not that of the minister himself, but an expression of the authority of God with which the community is endowed." It is declared as the "almost unanimous" view "that (a) ordination is established by God and (b) the prayer of the church at the ordination effectively calls down the power of the Holy Spirit on the ordinands." Consequently it is also declared that the episcopal office "is to be striven for where it is lacking, as a special sign of apostolic succession. . . ." On the other hand, however, the Orthodox and Catholic position is declared to be compatible with conceptions for which the only succession is that of the Word. This practically reduces the form of ministry that existed in the ancient church to a mere matter of fact; as a logical consequence, a charismatic recognition of all ministries between the churches is regarded as possible and is requested. What is said about future possibilities and goals also contains much that is worthy of consideration and even practicable, but the jump from the "Catholic" to the "charismatic" structure (using these misleading labels for convenience to denote the opposed positions) is made all too easily, and fails to recognize the gravity of the question involved. We have to ask Protestant Christians to understand that this problem is relatively easy for them, but that all "Catholic" churches see it as vitally concerning their whole existence. This ex-

2. W. Siebel, *Freiheit und Herrschaftsstruktur in der Kirche* (Berlin, 1971).

plains the sharp reaction of even so open-minded an Orthodox theologian as J. Meyendorff, who is also thoroughly familiar with the WCC. He declared during the course of the discussion that the document almost sounded like an invitation to Orthodox and Catholics to become Protestant. The attitude of the Orthodox here, as in the directly connected question of intercommunion, was therefore hard and clear. It was probably significant that in the plenary session debate on intercommunion, no Catholic spoke, apart from one rather marginal observation contributed by the young Jesuit Rayan.

It may be asked why this was so. In the first place it was certainly due to lack of time and to the frequently dilettante character of the plenary session discussions (in marked contrast to those in some of the sections), which did not exactly encourage speech. Some also probably felt themselves sufficiently represented by the Orthodox, while others hesitated to express a definitely divergent view. On the whole, the impression emerged that the Catholic group to some extent occupied a middle position between Orthodox and Protestants, sharing the dogma of the ancient church with the former and all the modern distress of the latter. That is precisely where its special opportunities, as well as its special difficulties, lie. It would lose its own identity and import if it abandoned this character of being extended between two poles, which in fact is bound up with the very essence of Catholicism. Apart from this, however, its particular features did not emerge very clearly. The questions were exactly the same with Catholics and Protestants; the answers, which necessarily still differ in many cases, were seldom very clearly formulated. In the present state of the Catholic Church, to some extent the courage and also the necessary support seem to be lacking.

It would be impossible to overlook the weaknesses of a congress which was far too fragmented and consequently often merely marked time, but the general impression remains favorable. On no occasion did I meet with that pretentious wordy dogmatism which with us seems in many quarters to have become an obligatory exercise. Efforts were really made to come to grips with the real issues. Prayer had its assured place in the whole proceedings quite as a matter of course, not only in the services but also at the beginning and end of the sessions. What was most enriching were the human contacts. The seriousness with which Christians of all denominations and continents are seeking the one Lord remains unforgettable. It was most impressive, too, to meet Christians from the communist world, whose faith, amidst the stress of often very difficult situations, is clearer-sighted in many ways than we are given to have. And although I do not believe in easy solutions, for example in regard to the ministry or intercommunion, and although the whole distress of Christendom, the terrible threat to its faith, was present, a great hope nevertheless permeated the whole. Again and again one was surprised to encounter the identical Christian reality despite frontiers; a "catholicity" was evident which cannot be comprised in denominational terms, yet represents a reality on which one can count.

Translated by W. J. O'Hara